Global Airlines

*To my wife Janet
and my daughter Helen*

Global Airlines

Competition in a transnational industry

Second Edition

Pat Hanlon
University of Birmingham

OXFORD   AUCKLAND   BOSTON   JOHANNESBURGH   MELBOURNE   NEW DELHI

Butterworth-Heinemann
Linacre House, Jordan Hill, Oxford OX2 8DP
225 Wildwood Avenue, Woburn, MA 01801-2041
A division of Reed Educational and Professional Publishing Ltd

 A member of the Reed Elsevier plc group

First published 1996
Reprinted 1996, 1997
Second edition 1999
Reprinted 2000, 2002

British Library Cataloguing in Publication Data
Hanlon, J. P. (James Patrick), *1942–*
  Global Airlines: competition in a transnational
  industry – 2nd edn.
  I. Title
  387.7′1

ISBN 0 7506 4350 1

For more information on all Butterworth-Heinemann
publications please visit our website at www.bh.com

Composition by Scribe Design, Gillingham, Kent
Printed and bound in Great Britain by Biddles Ltd
www.biddles.co.uk

Contents

Figures

Tables

Preface to the Second Edition

In the years that have passed since the first edition of this book appeared much has happened in the airline industry. Perhaps the single most important development has been the clear emergence of Oneworld, Star, Wings and Atlantic Excellence as four major alliance groupings with firm intentions to set up and operate global networks. More and more airlines are aligning themselves with one or other of these groupings and there is currently an intensive focus on the pro- and anti-competitive effects to which these global alliances may lead. The development has been attended by a great deal of publicity in the trade and national presses, with issues like the British Airways/American alliance, the shortage of airport slots, the advent of specialist low-cost airlines, the marketing of customer loyalty schemes, etc. all receiving extensive coverage. All these things are reflected in the revision, updating and expansion of this book, which nonetheless retains its original theme of charting the progress of the industry as it moves from one dominated by national firms in public ownership to one in which the major players are global entities all in private ownership.

Once again it behoves me to thank various people who have helped in the preparation of this book. My wife Janet (with some assistance from Christy Ringrose) has somehow found the time to re-type whole chapters and many other portions of the text. David Allen skilfully updated most of the drawings while adding a number of completely new ones. And at Butterworth-Heinemann, Catherine Clarke and Kathryn Grant have, as always, been extremely efficient in dealing with all my correspondence whilst at the same time giving me a lot of encouragement. Finally, I would also like to record my appreciation of the many comments made by Professor Kidani (of the University of Hiroshima) who supervised the translation of the first edition into Japanese. I am most grateful to all these people. Their help is much appreciated.

Pat Hanlon, 1999

Preface to the First Edition

Stephen Wheatcroft, a well known authority in the field of air transport, explained at the beginning of his book *Air Transport Policy* (Wheatcroft, 1964) the problem he encountered in keeping up with a constant flow of new material. If that was a problem then, it is certainly no less of one now. Hardly a day goes by without the announcement of some new development in the airline industry. At the time Wheatcroft was writing the main concerns were with the reasons why governments needed to control entry to routes, the capacities supplied by each airline and the fares and rates airlines charged; with the national interests governments were pursuing in regulating an industry very largely in public owner-ship; and with the economic impact of larger and faster aircraft. Today the focus of attention has shifted to deregulation and privatization; to the emergence of global carriers in a transnational industry; and to the problems posed by an increase in industrial concentration and by capac-ity constraints at major airports. But many of the issues Wheatcroft addressed still find their parallels in current debates. So, following Wheatcroft's good example, the present volume lays rather less empha-sis on reporting the details of the very latest developments and rather more on the underlying trends and policy issues.

The book is addressed to policymakers and managers, not just in airlines, but also in government departments, regulatory authorities, inter-national organizations and other bodies concerned with civil aviation. There are many important questions to be resolved, as the industry moves from one dominated by flag carriers owned or supported by national governments to one in which privatized airlines pursue more purely commercial objectives. For policymakers, the issues involve trade-offs between pro- and anti-competitive effects, weighing positive, efficiency enhancing effects, against any adverse effects flowing from increases in market power. For managers, fundamental changes in the industry are throwing up some crucial strategic decisions on network configurations, sales distribution systems, relationships with other carriers and so on. The book is also written for students. Those who may find it useful are likely to be following courses in business, economics, management or tourism, or preparing for professional examinations of bodies like the Chartered Institute of Transport. The transition taking place in the airline industry has attracted some attention in the microeconomics and strategic manage-ment literature, recent texts in these fields often containing a number of vignettes on the experience of airlines in the process of profound and continuous change. In many ways the airline industry provides a kind of

'test bed' for theories on deregulation, contestable markets, alliance formation, etc. This book goes into these matters in far greater depth than is
possible in more general texts, and as such it is hoped it will be useful for
essays, projects, dissertations and theses as well as supplying a reference
to support lecture courses and classes.

In one way or another a great many people have helped me prepare
this book, none of whom can in any way be held responsible for any
errors that may appear in it. At the University of Birmingham I have
received much encouragement from my Head of School, Colin
Rickwood, and from my Head of Department, Noel Kavanagh; and I
have benefited from some useful discussions with other colleagues,
especially John Burton, John Driver, Stephen Littlechild and Roger
Sugden. Two people who, at one time or another, used to be at
Birmingham University have also been helpful: Rigas Doganis, Head of
the Department of Air Transport at Cranfield University and recently
appointed Chairman of Olympic Airways, the Greek national flag
carrier; and Nigel Dennis, of the University of Westminster, who was
one of my PhD research students. I also wish to acknowledge the stimu-
lation provided by BCom undergraduates, in particular those who chose
to write their final year dissertations in this field. Their intelligent and
searching questions forced me to clarify quite a few points.

From the airline industry itself a lot of people helped to shape my
thoughts, by supplying comments, data and ideas. The individuals
involved are too numerous to mention, but I am especially indebted to
managers in British Airways who have always been very helpful to me.
Managers in other airlines have been helpful too, including in particular those in Aerolineas Argentinas, Air India, American, Delta, KLM,
Lufthansa, Swissair and United. Some enormous benefits have been
derived from discussions and correspondence with officials in various
regulatory bodies, especially the UK Civil Aviation Authority and the
US Department of Transportation. In search of source material, librari-
ans at the CAA, Royal Aeronautical Society and Chartered Institute of
Transport were helpfulness itself when, on frequent occasions, they
assisted me in tracking down references.

In the production of the manuscript I received a great deal of assistance from my wife Janet, who, despite the fact that she never trained
as a secretary, was able to wordprocess the book from start to finish. Her
skill in doing so was remarkable, especially since she was looking after
me generally at the same time! I was fortunate to secure the services of
Rachel Southall, of the Public Affairs Department at the University of
Birmingham, for the drawing of the majority of the diagrams, which she
accomplished with consummate skill and my 12-year-old daughter,
Helen, was also able to contribute something to the drawings, using her
graphics package. Finally, the staff at Butterworth-Heinemann gave
much helpful advice. I am extremely grateful to all these people.

Pat Hanlon, 1996

1 Introduction

Air transport is now a big industry. Its origins can be traced back so far as 1919 just after the First World War, but it was not until peace was restored after the Second World War that the era of major expansion really began. Half a century on and the industry now caters for around 1.5 billion passengers a year, generating some $300 billion in revenue and employing about 1.7 million people. It is the key element in the 'world's largest industry', travel and tourism, which accounts for approximately 10 per cent of world GDP, takes almost 11 per cent of consumer spending, and employs roughly one in every nine people in the global labour force. Over the last 50 years the airline industry has consistently grown at a very fast rate, well above the growth in world GDP. Only once in that time has world air traffic fallen, in 1991, when the economic recession, the Gulf War and threats of international terrorism directed at commercial aviation all combined to cause a 3 per cent drop. This was a relatively small fall in relation to the overall level of traffic, but it was sufficient to set off considerable alarm throughout the industry. But once the Gulf War ended there was a quick recovery in traffic which once again is growing strongly and is forecast to increase by between 5 and 7 per cent per annum over the next five to ten years.

The industry may have achieved high rates of growth, but this has not been accompanied by high rates of profitability, quite the opposite. Airline profit margins have been well below average compared with firms in other industries, and in some years there have been some very heavy losses indeed. There has often been a lot of excess capacity in the industry, following some overly optimistic forecasts.

It is against this background that the industry is undergoing some radical restructuring. For most of the post-war period the industry was dominated by state owned airlines, called 'flag carriers', and the governments which owned them often subsidized and used them as instruments to further their mercantilist interests or to promote their countries' status, power and prestige. Where airlines were in private ownership (e.g. in the United States) governments still exercised close control over where they could fly and the prices they could charge. In the international sphere the system of government regulation was established by the Chicago Convention signed in 1944. This led to a complex web of bilateral agreements between pairs of countries, under which government officials and airline representatives are almost continuously involved in negotiating the exchange of traffic rights. These inter-governmental agreements have had a profound influence upon the development of air transport. Government protection of flag carriers often produced 'artificial' markets, in which the profitability of individual airlines was determined more by the number of competitors allowed on particular routes than by the quality and pricing of their services.

A series of recent developments is threatening to overwhelm the current system, in which regulatory mechanisms are increasingly coming into conflict with the objectives and aspirations of the airlines themselves. Many airlines are seeking to break free from the constraints that bilateral negotiations impose on their route networks. They are investing in foreign airlines and forming all kinds of alliances in order to gain access to traffic for which they would otherwise not be able to compete. In particular, major US airlines are making determined efforts to expand their markets by developing their international networks, because of intense competition and reduced prospects of profitability in their deregulated domestic market. At the same time the mounting cost of supporting state owned flag carriers is forcing all governments to examine the option of privatization. In some cases the prospects for privatization could be considerably enhanced if existing restrictions on foreign ownership were to be relaxed, and more and more governments are beginning to show their willingness to do this. Governments are also increasingly willing to relax controls over route entry and pricing. What they are less willing to agree to is anything that implies the surrender, or even the partial surrender, of their sovereignty in the matter of traffic rights. There lies the biggest conflict of all.

Air transport has always been a *global industry*, but one served by national firms. Some airlines now want to become *global firms*, but to do so they may in the end have to lose their nationalities, if they are going to be able to conduct their business in much the same way as global firms in other transnational industries do. This is being inhibited by governmental restrictions on foreign ownership. Governments still largely adhere to the principle that airlines should be 'substantially owned and effectively controlled' by nationals of the state in which the airline is registered. Ownership clauses in bilateral air service treaties in effect limit the grant of traffic rights to airlines registered in one or other of the two states involved. So, if an airline of one state were to take over an airline of another state, serious doubts would arise over traffic rights on international routes. The merger might invalidate the rights previously held by the airline being taken over. Other states might no longer recognize it as a national airline of its original home state. At present the risk of losing traffic rights constitutes a deterrent to full cross-border mergers; and this explains the current preference for alliances over mergers. In order to enhance 'global reach', the kinds of alliance airlines are most interested in these days are not (as in the past) those with partners based in neighbouring countries but those with airlines operating complementary networks in other parts of the world.

The book proceeds as follows. Following a survey of some key factors affecting the airline industry in Chapter 2, a number of important issues are addressed in Chapter 3 concerning the consequences of liberalizing competition. When airlines are given greater freedom, both to fly where and when they want to and to determine the levels and structure of their fares, competition has in many places become more intense. At the same time there is a marked tendency for the industry to become more highly concentrated in the hands of just a few large airlines or consortia of airlines bound together by alliances. It is explained that the trend towards increased concentration can have positive and negative effects. On the positive side efficiency may be enhanced when large airlines are able to reap certain economies not available to the same extent to smaller carriers; but on the negative side there is the fear of large carriers becoming so dominant that they can exert considerable market power. So one central issue discussed in this book is how to weigh the efficiency enhancing effects against the market power effects.

The present constraints on how airlines can configure their route networks are discussed and illustrated in Chapter 4. If there is one single most important lesson to be learnt from deregulation, it is that there are some enormous economies of scope to be derived from operating a large extensive network. The discussion in Chapter 4 explains how airlines are seeking to extend their networks, within the limitations set in bilateral agreements, by such means as franchising, codesharing and block spacing.

Airlines derive many operational advantages from scheduling services through hubs and these are discussed in Chapter 5. Here the question is examined whether the pro-competitive effects of hubs are likely to outweigh any anticompetitive ones. A crucial aspect of freer competition concerns how airlines price their services. When is it desirable for airlines to engage in discriminatory pricing and when is it not? How can it be established if airlines are engaging in a predatory manner? And where it is thought that they are, what might be done to inhibit this behaviour? All these issues are discussed in Chapter 6.

In Chapter 7, concerned with mergers and alliances, consideration is given both to the strategies being pursued by airlines and to the policies adopted by governments. When heavily regulated, airlines had a long tradition of colluding with one another; and so the question naturally arises as to whether mergers and alliances are merely going to be another way of achieving the same end result, i.e. suppressing competition. This of course is a major concern for competition authorities in adjudicating upon proposals from the four major transatlantic alliances, Star, Oneworld, the KLM/Northwest/Alitalia/Continental alliance (which might eventually be called the 'Wings' alliance, although at the time of writing this name is still to be finally confirmed) and the Swissair/Delta grouping. It is argued that the net effects of alliances upon competition may depend largely upon the particular kind of merger or alliance being entered into. In replacing agreements between airlines with complementary networks, and in substituting intra-alliance co-operation for multilateral co-operation under the auspices of the International Air Transport Association, links between airlines based in different parts of the world can generate some important pro-competitive effects. On the other hand these same links can leave alliance partners with substantial market power in certain city pair markets, especially on routes between the hub cities of the airlines involved. Hence there are trade-offs between pro- and anti-competitive effects that the competition authorities have to evaluate, as in the case of the alliance being developed between American Airlines and British Airways.

Finally, some thoughts on possible future developments in the emergence of transnational airlines are presented in Chapter 8. Here it is suggested that government imposed constraints on foreign ownership will be progressively relaxed, so that alliances may prove to be precursors to full blown cross-border mergers. Eventually the concept of an airline's nationality will lose most if not all of its significance, something which raises major questions over the bilateral system of negotiating traffic rights and whether (and how or by whom) competition between airlines can be regulated in a truly transnational context.

2 The airline industry

Altogether there are approximately 1200 scheduled airlines in the world, of which some 300 operate on international routes. Airlines exist in many different shapes and sizes. Two of the very largest are American Airlines and United Airlines. These two airlines carry over 80 million passengers annually and operate fleets of some 600 aircraft. At the other extreme one of the smallest airlines offering scheduled services on international routes is Druk Air of Bhutan, which carries less than 10 000 passengers per annum on just two British Aerospace 146 aircraft.

In terms of fleet size and passenger-kilometres flown, six of the ten largest airlines are registered in the United States (Figure 2.1). And

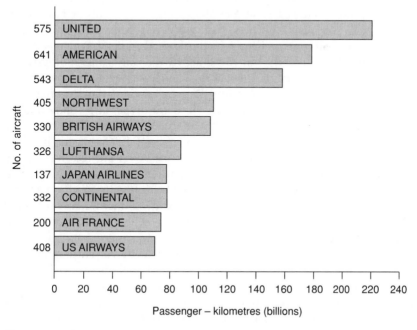

Figure 2.1 Ten largest airlines in 1997 (*Source:* International Air Transport Association)

whether it is in terms of sales revenue, passengers carried or number of employees, the list of the top 100 airlines is dominated by airlines based in North America, Western Europe and the Asia/Pacific region (Table 2.1). Beyond the top 100 there is a whole host of smaller airlines. Virtually every country in the world has its own national flag carrier and there are numerous charter airlines as well as hundreds of small regional carriers serving short haul routes.

Most national airlines depend for their livelihood on international traffic. Geographic and demographic factors justify significant domestic networks in only a few countries. The existence of so many different nationalities amongst the carriers of international traffic owes much to the bilateral bargaining process under which countries exchange route traffic rights with each other, in the form of air service agreements signed more or less as international treaties. In this process political considerations have often played a more important part than economic factors.

Airlines of nations contracting a bilateral air service agreement receive the right to enter the industry, at least on routes to and from the home countries, even though some of them would not belong in the industry on economic grounds.

Many airlines are owned by state governments. Non-scheduled charter airlines have always been privately owned but, until the trend to privatization that began in the 1980s, there was only a handful of international scheduled airlines that were not completely or largely owned by governments. Airlines in the United States have never been in government ownership; but these apart, the only other non-government firms amongst major international airlines were Cathay Pacific, Korean Air, Canadian Pacific (now known as Canadian International Cail) the French company UTA (now in state ownership following the takeover by Air France) and the Brazilian carrier Varig. All the rest were in majority state ownership, with many owned 100 per cent by their national governments. A lot of national airlines were started in the early postwar period, at a time when nationalization was fashionable and at a time when defence considerations placed a high value on the national airline as a military reserve. Without state investment many national airlines would not have been able to afford up-to-date aircraft and would have found it difficult to survive in the limited markets of the time. Governments subsidized them in order to protect local employment, to promote trade and tourism and to help the country's balance of payments. Another reason for government involvement is quite simply, prestige. A flag carrier is often seen as a status symbol, an indicator of national 'virility', especially in developing countries.

Many countries still support their airlines with state aids, but an increasing number has decided to privatize them. The number of

Table 2.1 The top 100 airlines in 1997 ranked by sales[a]. Sources: compiled from International Air Transport Association and World Airline Directory, *Flight International* (18–24 March, 25–31 March and 1–7 April 1998)

		Sales (US$ millions)	Passengers (millions)	Employees (number)
1	American	18 570	81.00	111 500
2	United	17 378	84.20	91 779
3	British Airways[b]	14 184	40.96	60 575
4	Delta	13 590	101.15	63 441
5	Lufthansa	13 354	44.40	58 204
6	Northwest	10 226	54.70	50 000
7	Air France[b]	10 185	33.50	46 385
8	Japan Airlines[b]	9 936	31.36	18 127
9	All Nippon[b]	8 798	40.83	15 200
10	US Airways	8 514	58.70	40 246
11	Swissair	7 356	10.80	16 883
12	Continental	7 213	40.00	40 000
13	KLM[b]	6 688	14.73	26 811
14	Qantas[c]	6 131	18.61	30 080
15	SAS	5 097	20.80	20 500
16	Alitalia	5 085	24.55	18 676
17	SIA[b]	4 992	12.00	28 196
18	Air Canada	4 024	14.00	21 215
19	Cathay Pacific	3 958	10.02	15 747
20	Southwest	3 817	50.40	23 974
21	Iberia	3 562	16.07	20 000
22	TWA	3 328	23.39	25 000
23	Varig	3 151	10.65	18 203
24	Thai Airways International[d]	3 120	14.38	24 186
25	Korean	3 029	25.58	17 139
26	Japan Air System[b]	2 651	19.13	6 094
27	Ansett Australia[c]	2 538	11.52	17 067
28	LTU International Airways[e]	2 349	7.20	5 159
29	CAIL	2 221	8.60	14 233
30	Air New Zealand	2 031	6.63	9 340
31	Sabena	2 012	6.87	9 500
32	America West	1 875	18.33	9 615
33	Alaska Airlines	1 863	12.25	6 477
34	China Airlines	1 740	7.40	8 490
35	Malaysia Airlines[b]	1 731	15.66	2 354
36	Vasp	1 667	4.57	7 156
37	Austrian	1 597	3.94	4 149
38	Garuda	1 571	6.69	13 727
39	China Southern	1 541	15.24	7 820
40	Finnair[b]	1 445	6.86	10 780
41	Aeroflot RIA	1 399	3.90	15 000

Table 2.1 *Continued*

	Sales (US$ millions)	Passengers (millions)	Employees (number)
42 South African Airways[b]	1 393	5.10	10 612
43 THY Turkish Airlines	1 347	10.30	8 958
44 EVA Air	1 292	4.16	5 800
45 El Al	1 220	2.90	3 407
46 Philippine Airlines[f]	1 181	7.31	13 587
47 TAP Air Portugal	1 155	4.40	8 000
48 Aeromexico	1 125	7.52	5 516
49 Emirates	1 114	3.68	4 978
50 Virgin Altantic[b]	1 075	2.81	6 400
51 Aer Lingus	1 046	5.26	5 620
52 China Eastern	1 030	6.83	6 291
53 Gulf Air	1 030	4.66	5 357
54 Olympic Airways	1 012	5.80	8 540
55 Air-India[f]	1 006	3.05	18 441
56 Aerolineas Argentinas	998	4.22	4 913
57 Mexicana	976	7.44	6 579
58 British Midland	871	5.70	4 734
59 Lan-Chile	865	2.65	4 884
60 Indian Airlines[f]	819	6.52	21 081
61 PIA[c]	817	5.88	20 977
62 American Trans Air	783	5.30	3 690
63 Braathens	763	5.71	3 840
64 Martinair	715	1.95	2 550
65 Avianca	709	3.87	3 400
66 Hapag-LLoyd	707	4.92	1 600
67 Transbrasil	680	2.90	4 201
68 Comair[b]	651	5.36	2 500
69 AOM French Airlines	641	3.37	1 020
70 Airtours International[d]	634	2.35	1 550
71 Monarch[g]	625	4.53	2 439
72 Air Europa[e]	570	6.34	2 019
73 LOT Polish Airlines	563	2.34	4 150
74 Tunisair	521	3.23	7 197
75 Mesa Airlines[d]	511	6.75	4 100
76 TAM	505	3.34	2 570
77 Tower Air	462	1.30	1 969
78 Air 2000[e]	449	4.90	1 548
79 Air Algerie	423	3.83	9 009
80 SpanAir[e]	411	4.51	1 952
81 Hawaiian	404	5.22	2 500
82 Royal Jordanian	396	1.35	4 901
83 Atlantic Southwest	385	3.78	1 487
84 Reno Air	384	5.53	5 027

85	Malev	360	1.92	2 954
86	Eurowings	350	2.50	1 611
87	Midwest Express	345	1.65	2 060
88	CSA Czech Airlines	343	1.73	2 898
89	Air Transat[e]	329	2.43	9 802
90	Meridiana	324	2.72	1 442
91	Maersk Air	309	1.81	326
92	World Airways	309	0.29	799
93	SkyWest[b]	297	2.90	2 553
94	Transaero	292	1.48	2 209
95	Air Mauritius[f]	278	0.80	1 670
96	Mesaba Airlines[b]	277	3.32	1 700
97	British Regional Airlines	271	2.16	585
98	Cyprus Airways	263	1.29	1 795
99	Air Lanka[b]	258	1.20	4 965
100	Ethiopian[c]	258	0.75	3 309

[a] The list is limited to passenger airlines. Ten cargo airlines that would be included in a top 100 list in terms of sales revenue are: Federal Express, United Parcels Service, Airborne Freight Corp., Asiana, DHL Airways, Nippon Cargo Airways, Cargolux, Premiair, American International Airways, Polar Air Cargo. Federal Express is the largest airline in terms of employees (114 636).
[b] Year to 31 March 1998.
[c] Year to 30 June 1997.
[d] Year to 30 September 1997.
[e] Year to 31 October 1997.
[f] Year to 31 March 1997.
[g] Year to 30 April 1998.

national flag carriers remaining totally in state ownership is dwindling year by year. In search of greater operating efficiency, and to reduce the burden on the public purse of financing capital investment in new equipment, more and more countries are offering shares in flag carriers both to the private sector and to other airlines. This is taking place faster in some parts of the world than in others (Table 2.2). Following recent privatizations, of for example Air Canada, the two Mexican airlines (AeroMexico and Mexicana), the Colombian carrier Avianca and also Lan-Chile, state ownership has become very much the exception amongst major airlines in North, South and Central America, especially now that both Air Jamaica and BWIA International have been partly privatized. This contrasts with the situations in Europe where British Airways and Lufthansa are still the only major flag carriers entirely without a government shareholding. Some European carriers, while not completely privatized, have substantial private shareholdings (like Swissair, SAS, KLM and Austrian) and elsewhere governments have signalled their intentions to sell their flag carriers at some time.

Table 2.2 Ownership of flag carriers, June 1998 (percentages of share capital held by national governments). *Source:* compiled from Airline Ownership Survey, *Airline Business* (June 1998)

Americas	%		
Aerolineas Argentinas	5	SIA	54
Aeromexico	0	Thai Airways International	93
AeroPeru	20	Vietnam Airlines	100
Air Canada	0		
Air Jamaica	25	*Europe*	%
American	0	Aer Lingus	100
Avianca	0	Aeroflot RIA	51
BWIA International	33.5	Air France	90.1
CAIL	0	Alitalia	67
Continental	0	Austrian Airlines	51.9
Delta	0	Balkan Bulgarian	100
Lan–Chile	0	British Airways	0
Lloyd Aereo Boliviano	48.3	CSA Czech Airlines	83.7
Mexicana	0	Cyprus Airways	80.5
Northwest	0	Finnair	59.8
Pluna	49	Iberia	92
TWA	0	JAT Yugoslav Airlines	100
United	0	KLM	25
Varig	1.2	Lot Polish Airlines	100
		Lufthansa	0
		Luxair	23.1
Asia/Pacific	%	Malev	63.9
		Olympic	100
Air China	100	Sabena	33.8
Air-India	100	SAS	50
Air Lanka	74	Swissair	21.5
Air New Zealand	0	Tap Air Portugal	100
Air Niugini	100	Tarom	100
All Nippon	0		
Biman Bangladesh	100	*Middle East*	%
Cathay Pacific	0		
China Airlines	0	El Al	100
China Eastern	61.1	Emirates	100
China Southern	68.1	Gulf Air	100
Garuda	100	Iran Air	100
Japan Airlines	0	Kuwait Airways	100
Korean Air	0	MEAL Airliban	0
Malaysia Airlines	25	Qatar Airways	0
PIA	56	Royal Jordanian	100
Philippine Airlines	14	Saudia	100
Qantas	0	Syrian Arab Airlines	100
Royal Brunei	100	THY Turkish	98.2
Royal Nepal	100	Yemenia	51

Africa	%	Kenya Airways	23
		Nigeria Airways	100
Air Afrique	70.4	Royal Air Maroc	92.7
Air Algerie	100	South African Airways	100
Air Mauritius	51	Sudan Airways	100
Air Zimbabwe	100	Tunisair	45.2
Egyptair	100		

The French government has decided upon a partial privatization of Air France, diluting its stake in the airline to 52 or 53 per cent and offering shares to the value of FF 3.5–4.0 billion to the public during the first quarter of 1999. But it may be some time before the likes of Alitalia, Olympic Airways and TAP Air Portugal can be privatized given the large deficits these airlines have been incurring. It is, of course, difficult to privatize firms that would be effectively bankrupt without the aid they receive from their government owners. This is also the case for a number of airlines in the Middle East and Africa, where governments are keen to privatize but where operating losses are likely to deter most purchasers. Privatization is proceeding apace in the Far East however, with Air New Zealand and Japan Airlines already transferred in toto to the private sector and with MAS and SIA, in which private shareholders already hold substantial stakes due to join them. And the process of airline privatization has also started in the People's Republic of China. In that country the two largest regional airlines, China Eastern and China Southern, have between 30 and 40 per cent of their share capital listed on stock exchanges. It is possible that further partial privatization will soon follow of two other Chinese regionals China United and China Yunnan, and perhaps in the long term of the flag carrier Air China.

Of the top 100 airlines listed in Table 2.1, 62 are in 100 per cent private ownership, 18 are partially privatized and the remaining 20 are in full state ownership or very close to it. The predominance of privately owned carriers is greater still when one looks at the ranking by sale: only four state owned airlines appear in the top 25; and privately owned airlines take nine out of the top ten positions. Airlines in full state ownership account for only a tenth of total sales made by the top 50. This of course is influenced by the inclusion of ten large airlines from the United States, but even without the US carriers privately owned airlines still predominate over state owned carriers, especially when one considers the non-scheduled (charter) sector and the many hundreds of small regional airlines almost all of which are in 100 per cent private ownership.

Accompanying the trend towards privatization is a trend towards foreign ownership. Foreign ownership is not something entirely new. In the 1940s and 1950s some well-established US and European airlines often took stakes in foreign airlines just starting up. For example, Pan American took minority stakes in many Latin American airlines; Air France bought shares in a number of African airlines, especially those in former colonies; and the two British airlines, BEA and BOAC, often did the same, not just in Commonwealth countries but in other countries as well: at one time BEA held 40 per cent of Alitalia and BOAC 50 per cent of Egyptian Airways and also 47 per cent of Middle East Airlines. The airline ownership map was then redrawn on more nationalistic lines, so that in the 1960s and 1970s few airlines held a stake, even a minority stake, in the airline of another country. This is now changing again, with many privatized airlines seeking to take equity stakes in airlines based in other countries that have complementary networks (see Table 7.5 in Chapter 7).

What is new in foreign ownership is the holding of shares in privatized airlines by people living outside the country in which the airline is registered. For instance, when British Airways was floated in February 1997, some 17 per cent of its shares was purchased by foreign nationals. By March 1992 the figure had grown to the maximum permissible level of 41 per cent, although it then slipped back to 22 per cent by March 1997. Over the same period share ownership of the airline has become more concentrated, the total number of shareholders falling from 1.1 million at flotation to around 230 000 in 1997. A large proportion of BA shares held by foreign nationals are held in the United States, although the nationality spread amongst shareholders as a whole covers more than 100 countries throughout the world (British Airways, 1998)

A further trend in the ownership of airlines is an increase in employee participation. This is most noticeable in the United States where a number of major carriers have swapped shares in the company in return for concessions on wages, pensions and working rules. The first to do so was Northwest, which exchanged $886 million worth of concessions for one-third of the shares in the company and three seats on the board of directors. The buyout of United Airlines left employees with 55 per cent of shares and three directors. The deal struck by TWA gave employees 45 per cent of shares and four directors in return for $660 million of concessions. And USAir agreed to turn over 20 per cent of its shares to its pilots in return for a 21.6 per cent pay cut.

Employee ownership is not limited to the United States and there are signs that it is spreading to Europe and elsewhere. Employees were given preferential terms in the purchase of British Airways shares when the airline was privatised in 1987; and priority was given to employee participation when the German government sold its remaining share in

Lufthansa in 1997. When Aeroflot became a joint stock company in March 1997, the Russian government retained a majority 51 per cent of the shares, with all the remaining 49 per cent passing to the airline's employees. And about 25 per cent of the ownership of Air France is likely to pass into employees' hands following the expected partial privatization in 1999.

2.2 Growth and distribution of traffic

Air transport is a high growth industry. Very few industries, if any, have enjoyed such growth for such a long period of time. Since 1945 world passenger traffic has grown at an average annual rate of 12 per cent, although this figure is influenced by particularly high growth from a small base in the early part of the postwar period when the industry was still relatively immature. Since 1960 passenger traffic has grown at an average rate of 9 per cent per annum. Freight and mail have also grown rapidly, at average rates since 1960 of 11 and 7 per cent per annum, respectively. Total output of world air transport, measured by tonne-kilometres performed, grew by a factor of nearly 20 between 1960 and 1995, over which period the output of the total world economy, measured by gross domestic product (GDP), only grew by a factor of just over three.

The rate of growth is slowing down as the industry gets larger and becomes more mature. But world passenger traffic still increased at an average annual rate of 5 per cent over the decade 1985-95, although it recorded its first ever decline in 1991, at the height of the Gulf War, and experienced relatively slow growth in the extended economic recession that followed it. Growth between 1992 and 1993 was only 2.3 per cent, but recovered to achieve rates of between 7 and 9 per cent up to 1997-98. In recent months the industry has been affected by the turmoil in the world's financial markets and the possibility of another recession is very likely to reduce once again short-term growth rates. Forecasts vary of how air traffic will grow in the long-term future, but most predictions are for average annual growth rates of between 5 and 7 per cent. One forecast, from the International Civil Aviation Organization, is given in Figure 2.2, and this predicts growth of 5.5 per cent up to 2005. At this rate of growth, world air traffic will almost triple in the next 20 years.

Figures on total traffic conceal variations from one part of the world to another (Table 2.3). There has been burgeoning growth in the Asia/Pacific region, with more modest growth in Europe and Africa. The rapid growth of Asian airlines, such as Cathay Pacific, Malaysian

Table 2.3 Growth in world passenger traffic (passenger-kilometres performed by scheduled airlines of ICAO contracting states). *Source:* International Civil Aviation Organization

Region of airline registration	1985 (billions)	1995 (billions)	2005[a] (billions)	Average annual growth rate (per cent) 1985–95	1995–2005[a]
Africa	36.7	51.0	77	3.3	4.0
Asia/Pacific	222.3	549.7	1260	9.5	8.5
Europe	428.2	549.3	870	2.5	4.5
Middle East	42.7	67.0	115	4.6	5.5
North America	569.2	902.7	1310	4.7	4.0
Latin America/Caribbean	68.3	107.9	175	4.7	5.0
World	1367	2228	3807	5.0	5.5

[a]Forecast.

Airlines and Singapore International Airlines (SIA) has effected some considerable changes in the structure of the international industry. Twenty-five years ago airlines of the Asia/Pacific region were responsible for not much more than 10 per cent of the world's air traffic but now account for something over 20 per cent. Future growth is expected to continue being rather uneven, although the recessionary impact on the Asia/Pacific region is in the short term likely to be greater given the effects of 'Asian Flu' and the recent sharp downturn in the so-called 'tiger' economics of the Pacific Rim.

One possible explanation for the variation in growth rates by region is that regions are at different stages in the life cycle of the industry (Figure 2.3). A possible hypothesis is that growth follows an S-shaped pattern over time: slow to begin with, then very rapid and finally slow again when the industry reaches maturity. On this interpretation, Africa would appear to be at the beginning stage, Asia in the rapid growth stage, and Europe and North America about to enter the mature stage.

2.3 Demand for air travel

Three fundamental factors affecting passenger demand are incomes, fares and service levels (Figure 2.4). Broad estimates of aggregate elasticities imply that demand is highly elastic with respects to income, rather less elastic with respect to fares and relatively inelastic with respect to service levels.

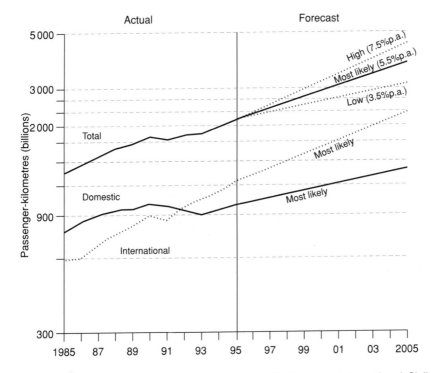

Figure 2.2 One forecast of world passenger traffic (*Source:* International Civil Aviation Organization)

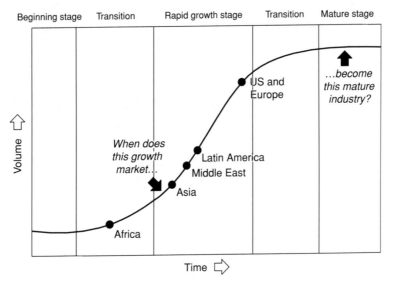

Figure 2.3 Market life cycle (*Source:* Boeing)

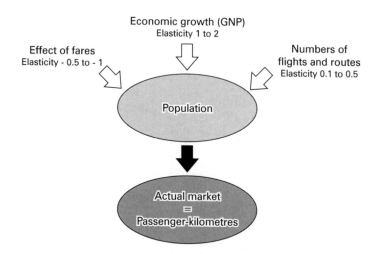

Figure 2.4   Components of air travel demand (*Source:* Airbus Industrie)

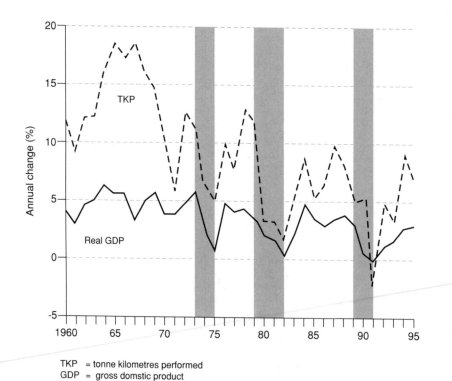

TKP = tonne kilometres performed
GDP = gross domstic product

Figure 2.5   Relationship between economic activity and the growth in air travel (*Source:* International Civil Aviation Organization)

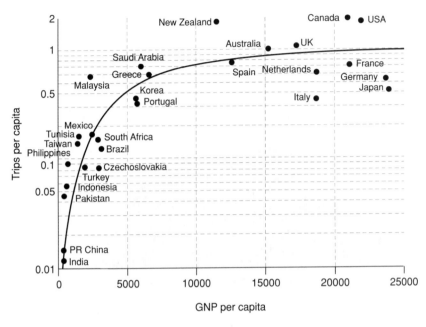

Figure 2.6 International comparisons of air travel related to economic activity, 1990 (*Source:* Boeing)

The high income elasticity can be seen in the short-term time series relationship between economic activity and air travel demand (Figure 2.5). Although air travel tends to grow faster than GDP, it still follows very closely the cyclical pattern in GDP. High income elasticity is also evident in cross-section international comparisons from which a long-term relationship between economic activity and air travel can be discerned (Figure 2.6). In North America high average income levels are reflected in each person making at least two air trips per annum, whereas in countries like China and India, at the opposite end of the income spectrum, only one in every hundred people take an air trip. It is mainly the rich people who fly. There is a pyramidal structure to the penetration of air travel in different income bands (Figure 2.7). In the United States for example, three-quarters of people in the top income band (those earning $100 000 or more) take an air trip each year as compared with only 11 per cent in the lowest band (those on $10 000 or less). The fact that air travel demand comes first and foremost from high income passengers is also evident in data relating to the United Kingdom: average annual incomes of passengers using London airports in 1996 were found to lie between £35 000 and £65 000 (Figure 2.8); and in comparisons of propensities to fly between UK planning regions there

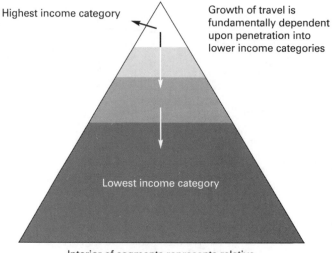

Highest income category

Growth of travel is
fundamentally dependent
upon penetration into
lower income categories

Lowest income category

Interior of segments represents relative
population at each income level

Example of air travel penetration (%) in the United States

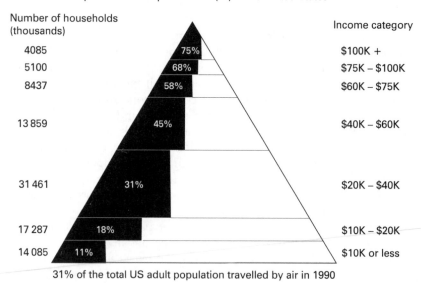

Number of households
(thousands)

Income category

Number of households (thousands)	Penetration	Income category
4085	75%	$100K +
5100	68%	$75K – $100K
8437	58%	$60K – $75K
13 859	45%	$40K – $60K
31 461	31%	$20K – $40K
17 287	18%	$10K – $20K
14 085	11%	$10K or less

31% of the total US adult population travelled by air in 1990

Figure 2.7   Air travel and income categories (*Source:* Boeing)

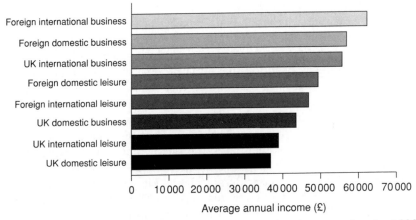

Figure 2.8 Average income by passenger type at London area airports, 1996 (*Source:* Civil Aviation Authority Survey)

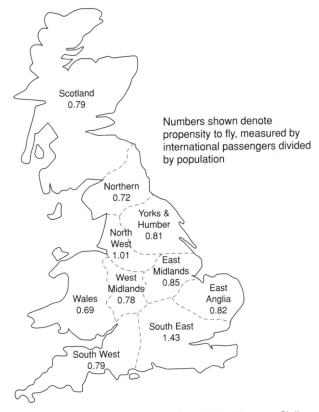

Figure 2.9 Propensity to fly by UK Planning Region, 1996 (*Source:* Civil Aviation Authority Survey)

is a clear north-south divide just as there is in many other respects, the frequency at which international air journeys are taken being very much higher in the south-east than in other parts of the country (Figure 2.9).

Most forecasts of future demand are based upon extrapolation of past trends and on the assumption that a mature market is one that grows at the same rate as GDP. It is recognized that the lower rates in the more mature markets apply to far higher levels of traffic. But 'maturity' in this sense implies a decline to unity in income elasticity of demand; and who is to say exactly when this stage has been reached, even in most developed markets? It is sometimes suggested that some markets are approaching saturation, but there are good reasons to doubt this, for there are indications of considerable latent demand in even the most mature markets. In the United States a Gallup/Air Transport Association survey revealed that almost a quarter of the US population have never flown, and only a third have flown in the previous twelve months (Air Transport Association, 1993). In the United Kingdom the proportion of people who have never flown is certainly much higher, probably around 50 per cent.

What constitutes a saturation level may itself rise over time in response to economic, social and demographic developments. For instance, the increasing proportion of relatively healthy and prosperous retired people in the population should contribute some increase in the demand for leisure-related air travel. In many empirical studies of air travel demand, the income factor has been represented simply as current income, with no recognition of the effect that wealth or assets (financial and non-financial) has on demand. When wealth, or 'permanent' income, is included the effect can be quite significant, as Alperovich and Machnes (1994) found in estimating demand elasticities for international routes to/from Israel. Ageing populations in some mature markets could contribute significantly to air traffic growth insofar as older people tend to have both greater personal wealth and more time available for travel. But there is another side to this: with people living longer, greater expenditure tends to be made on medical care, leaving that much less of discretionary income, or wealth, to be spent on things like travel. Wheatcroft and Lipman (1990) have attributed to increased spending on medical care the fact that for the last 15 or 20 years the percentage of spending by US consumers on travel and recreation has remained remarkably constant, at 6.8 per cent. This means that expenditures on travel have increased only at the same rate as the increase in consumer incomes, implying an income elasticity of no more than unity, the indicator of a mature market. Wheatcroft and Lipman noted that the proportion of US consumer expenditure spent on medical care rose from only 4.7 per cent in 1950 to over 13 per cent by 1990, but considered that expenditure on medical care will likely reach a peak allowing other expenditures, including recreation and travel, to increase somewhat more rapidly in the future. This is possible, at least in a country like the United States where provision for medical care has been largely a matter for private finance for a long time. In European countries, where there has always been more of a tradition of state support for health and pensions, a rise in consumer expenditure on such things might be expected, as the number of governments seeking to shift part of the finance burden from public to private funds increases.

However, there are other socio-economic factors that might cause saturation levels to rise. A decline in average family size should encourage a shift in the air/surface modal split, since intercity trips by smaller travelling parties are more likely to be made by air. A continued increase in paid holidays and in the number of two-income families should bring more people into the category of those able to afford at least one, and perhaps two, overseas holidays a year. The influence of increased higher education should also have a positive impact on air travel demand, especially if the globetrotting activities of university students (another group with more time for travel than most!) is anything to go by. The growing economic integration in North America and Europe might exert some positive effect on the demand for air travel within those regions, as might increasing liberalization of airline competition, provided that congestion problems, both in the air and on the ground, can be overcome without some very sharp increase in costs.

Leisure travel has been growing more rapidly than travel on business and this is something that affects the aggregate price elasticity of demand. The demand for leisure travel is price elastic, but that for business travel is price inelastic. Across the world as a whole the leisure/business breakdown is now approximately 80/20, virtually reversing the position as it was in the early postwar period, when it was business travel which predominated. The business travel share varies widely, being very much higher on domestic routes. It also varies a lot by airline. On an airline like Swissair for example, business passengers represent far more than 20 per cent of total passengers. But the declining proportion of business travellers in total demand means that demand has in aggregate been getting more price elastic over time.

Business travellers are very important to the airlines. For it is mainly these passengers who pay the high fares (first, business or full economy) that yield a lot of revenue. The proportion of total revenue earned from the high-fare passengers can be quite large. In the case of British Airways for example, passengers travelling in business class on long haul routes (which the airline markets as its 'Club World' product) account for just 5 per cent of BA's total passengers but generate as much as 25 per cent of the airline's total revenue.

There has been some discussion recently about the possible effect on business travel of dramatic improvements in global electronic communications, through such innovations as e-mail, the information super-highway, video teleconferencing, etc. Such innovations have already reduced the need for some business travel and might be expected to continue to do so as electronic communications systems are refined and introduced more widely. But electronic communications are unlikely to prove to be anything more than a partial substitute for business air travel. Far from air travel, the kind of 'journeys' most influenced by these developments have so far been visits within company establishments from one office to another, with external marketing trips, visits to suppliers and journeys to customers to provide technical sales service much less affected. Indeed it is not beyond the realms of possibility that new forms of electronic communications may act more as a *complement* to air travel and rather less as a substitute for it. Some years ago it was suggested that greater use of telephones, and then fax machines, would largely replace postal and courier services. But of course nothing of the kind has taken place, these two forms of communications having grown in parallel with each other. Similarly, e-mail, super-highways and teleconferencing may actually stimulate some kinds of business travel, especially international travel. This was one of the points to emerge from an earlier study undertaken by the author into the demand for supersonic air services (Hanlon, 1973). A survey of large companies heavily involved in international business travel revealed that the purpose of overseas visits was such that they could not be replaced simply by fax message or videoconference. Day-to-day routine matters can be dealt with through such media, but important decisions and technical problems usually require face-to-face contact on the ground, as does the search for new business. Air travel and telecommunications tend to reinforce one another in this respect. Both have played a part in making it easier for large multinational companies, with a presence in many different countries across the world, to centralize many functions that would otherwise require staff on the spot. Business travel may now be a much smaller proportion of total travel, but this is because leisure travel has been growing so much faster. Business travel is still growing in absolute terms, despite periodic downturns in times of economic recession. It is possible that a lot of the recent growth in the use of electronic means of communication has been due to firms responding to recessions – and also to greater competition in final product markets – by cutting travel costs rather than to any great increase in business efficiency from these means of communications. In the longer term the increased globalization of business in general is likely to foster the continued growth of both travel and telecommunications.

2.4 Factors affecting airline operating costs

One of the most crucial factors affecting airline operating costs is the average stage length over which it flies its aircraft. Other things being equal, the longer the stage length the lower the cost per unit. Unit cost declines rapidly as stage length increases because many of the costs in operating a flight are incurred in take-off, landing, climb and descent. Also higher block speeds and better fuel economy are achieved on the longer sectors. The L-shaped relationship between unit cost and stage length is a fundamental characteristic of airline economics, and the airlines with the lowest costs per seat mile, or cost per tonne kilometre are those operating large aircraft over long stages, like Virgin Atlantic, Qantas, SIA, etc. (Figure 2.10).

Allowing for stage length it is clear that airlines in Europe have relatively high costs. This was one of the main problems identified by the Comité des Sages (1994). European airlines' unit operating costs are between 40 and 50 per cent higher than those of comparable airlines in the United States. It is widely believed that high social charges associated with employment are mainly responsible for this. But in fact there is not much difference between European and US airlines in salary and social charge levels. In 1992 the average salary was \$40 543 in the US industry and \$44 493 in Europe, while the average social charge was actually slightly higher in the United States at \$11 722 as against \$10 513 in Europe.

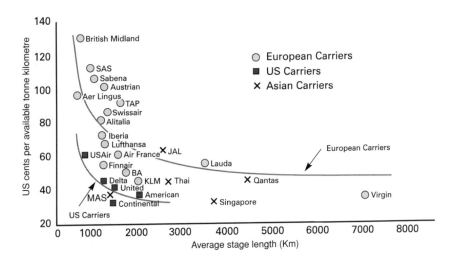

Figure 2.10 Unit operating costs as a function of stage length (*Source:* Comité des Sages, 1994)

Table 2.4 Average annual remuneration for different categories of airline staff (year ended 31 December 1996 to nearest $100 at current exchange rates). *Source:* International Civil Aviation Organization

	Pilots and co-pilots	Cabin attendants	Maintenance personnel	Ticketing, sales and promotions staff
North America				
United	150 100	46 500	—	36 500
USAir	134 200	36 400	42 400	36 400
Delta	134 000	35 800	—	34 300
Northwest	131 600	31 100	52 800	51 100
American	121 000	30 500	32 200	33 100
Continental	108 600	31 400	73 500	—
Southwest	106 900	27 000	53 800	35 500
TWA	95 600	23 900	35 700	—
Air Canada	94.600	29 600	34 200	23 700
CAIL	92 800	33 200	31 800	30 300
America West	82 600	20 300	35 800	23 100
ValuJet	53 500	16 000	21 100	—
Kiwi International	52 200	27 300	49 300	24 700
Atlantic Southeast	33 000	16 000	27 100	32 400
Trans States A	25 000	22 400	20 900	—
Latin America/Caribbean				
Transbrasil	138 300	53 400	39 000	21 300
Austral	87 900	16 190	32 500	21 800
Varig	81 300	34 100	20 600	20 900
Nordeste	73 600	29 000	25 200	16 000
Mexicana	62 500	13 800	13 700	13 100
Faucett	53 600	12 000	10 900	7 800
Saeta	39 000	9 300	9 400	14 200
LAB	24 200	6 200	6 100	6 100
Sansa	13 300	5 000	—	7 700
Cubana	6 700	3 300	3 100	2 500
Europe				
Air France[a]	220 100	64 100	51 400	51 600
Aviaco	195 400	64 900	54 300	44 000
Iberia	185 700[b]	68 000	44 900	44 300
Austrian	175 100	44 500	63 100	55 300
SAS	173 400	67 400	64 300	63 900
Lufthansa	136 400[b]	49 900	—	—
Meridiana	132 800	63 600	50 400	43 600
TAP Air Portugal	124 200	42 100	18 500	45 000
British Airways	111 200	29 700	40 700	34 700
Finnair	102 900	33 400	41 600	37 000
Eurowings	86 600	42 900	52 000	33 000

Tyrolean	85 000	32 400	43 800	37 300
British Midland	82 800	23 100	39 200	29 800
Virgin Atlantic	76 100	18 000	37 800	29 700
Air UK	49 800	15 800	24 400	20 100
Brymon Airways	41 900	17 900	19 000	32 000
THY Turkish	41 300	14 500	12 000	23 100
CityFlyer Express	32 900	13 100	35 900	21 500
Asia				
Japan Asia[a]	229 300[b]	48 200	191 200	96 200
Japan Airlines[a]	213 400[b]	84 000	—	—
SIA	183 100	48 600	56 400	—
All Nippon[a]	179 600	45 200	—	—
Thai Airways International	124 100	19 400	22 100	39 300
Asiana	95 400	37 600	39 300	46 000
Korean	72 800	30 200	34 300	43 200
Malaysian[a]	53 000	23 500	18 100	27 900
Philippines A	43 700	5 700	8 500	11 300

— Not available.
[a] Year ended 31 March 1997.
[b] Includes flight engineers.

There is considerable variation in salary levels from airline to airline (Table 2.4). Too much should not be read into the precise figures here, since the comparisons of averages are affected by, amongst other things, currency fluctuations, cost-of-living differences, the mix of staff, and so on. The variation is especially wide for pilots, and this is only partly explained by differences in the aircraft they fly or in their average ages and seniority levels. In North America, where airlines buy their labour in a single market, salaries tend be fairly similar across airlines, but in Europe and Asia there are large differences between airlines based in neighbouring countries. For example, the average pilot salary in Air France is almost twice that in British Airways; and Thai Airways pilots are paid 2.3 times as much as pilots flying for Malaysian Airlines. As they stand the figures on salaries point up some extraordinary comparisons: pilots employed by America West, Varig, British Midland, Korean Air and many other carriers all earn less on average than cabin attendants working for Japan Airlines! Wide international differences like this are possible only because of restrictions on the employment of non-nationals. The increasing globalization of airline companies, whether through outright mergers or through alliances, may well lead to some easing of these restrictions and to a certain levelling out of salaries across airlines. The process is already underway.

Airlines based in high-wage hard-currency countries have begun to move some of their activities to countries where labour costs are much lower. Swissair and Lufthansa have transferred part of their aircraft overhaul requirements to Shannon Aerospace in Ireland. It is quite possible that many more airlines will subcontract work to partners based in low-wage economies – 'outsourcing' as it is known – and that more airline jobs will be exported out of high-wage economies in the future. The process is likely to be accelerated by the growth in airline alliances. As a possible early example of what might become a more general phenomenon later on, it is reported that Sabena is considering moving its pilots' contracts to Switzerland in order to avoid high social security taxes and charges in its home country of Belgium. The airline might also employ its cabin crew from Switzerland. The employees would not be asked to move to Switzerland, but their contracts would be issued in that country and they would pay their taxes and charges there. This would result in some significant savings to Sabena, which has an alliance with Swissair, whose parent company, the SAir Group, has a 49.5 per cent equity stake in Sabena. (For a similar reason, Virgin Express, which is based in Brussels, has warned that it may move to the UK or Ireland in order to reduce social taxes on employment.)

It used to be the case that US pay levels were significantly above those in Europe but now, following pressures unleashed by deregulation and deals struck with unions, US levels are often lower. But so far as labour costs are concerned the real difference between the United States and Europe lies in physical productivity, as measured by available tonne kilometres (ATK) per employee (Table 2.5). European productivity levels are very much lower, leading to labour costs per ATK up to 40 per cent higher. There are many qualifications that should be made in comparisons of labour productivity (to account for difference between airlines in stage lengths, organizational structures, product quality, the extent to which maintenance is subcontracted to other companies, etc.). But nonetheless the US–Europe productivity 'gap' is a wide one; and the gap is an even wider one between European and Asian carriers, which have the advantage of lower salary levels as well. Given that labour costs make up something in the region of 30 to 35 per cent of total operating costs, European airlines need to increase their efficiency levels in this area, if they are to remain competitive on the global scene. A start has been made in that the 1988–92 percentage productivity increases achieved by most European airlines were significantly greater than the improvements effected by their US counterparts, but European airlines have still a long way to go in this respect.

After labour, the next major component of operating costs is fuel. Across the world's airlines as a whole fuel can represent something between 10 and 20 per cent of total operating costs depending on the

Table 2.5 Labour productivity of US and European airlines. *Source:* Comité des Sages (1994)

	ATK per employee (1992)	% change (1998-92)
Europe		
Aer Lingus	144 136	7.76
Air France	289 170	1.52
Alitalia	279 617	7.64
British Airways	298 939	6.91
Iberia	172 244	5.18
KLM	325 635	6.41
Lufthansa	291 196	2.92
SAS	172 650	6.69
Swissair	220 204	4.89
TAP	132 557	3.11
United States		
American	332 256	2.38
Continental	412 181	−2.37
Delta	330 888	2.70
United	357 454	2.20
US Air	248 505	1.23
Southwest	372 482	5.21

international price of oil. Fuel costs also exhibit marked variation between airlines, not only because of factors like stage length but also on account of the costs of transporting fuel to the airline's main airports and local rates at which tax is levied on it. Indeed for some particular airlines fuel can be the largest single item of cost, an extreme example being Indian Airlines, a carrier which has to pay both federal and state government taxes on its purchase of fuel (Hanlon, 1986). Airlines in Europe tend to suffer from relatively high fuel costs too, having to pay about 15 per cent more per gallon than airlines in the United States.

In the past the unit operating cost of air transport declined as a result of aeronautical innovation. From the Douglas DC-3 to the introduction of jets there was a gradual fall, in real terms, in the unit cost of aircraft operation of some 30 per cent. A fall of roughly the same magnitude came with the appearance of the first generation of jet aircraft; and there were further reductions when turbo-fan and wide-bodied jets were introduced. These falls in unit cost came partly from increases in speed, but mainly from increases in aircraft size. But there are now indications that innovation in aircraft types is, in these respects, running into diminishing marginal returns. Aircraft technology is constantly improving, but no major technological leap has occurred recently and none is on the horizon. Various advances leading to reduced operating costs are still possible. In aerodynamics, developments are currently focused on airflow control to effect significant reductions in drag, by drilling tiny holes in wing skins to suck away the secondary layer. So far as airframe structures are concerned, there is potential for greater use of composite materials, stiffer and lighter than the present metallic structures, which could reduce the empty weight of an airliner by as much as 30 per cent, which in turn could reduce fuel consumption. The use of improved materials could also result in better engine performance. But none of these kinds of development seem to offer the prospect of a large discrete fall in unit cost in the way that earlier innovations did. For further reductions in unit cost airlines will need to look more at improvements in managerial efficiency rather than relying on technological innovation.

The financial crisis that the industry experienced in the early 1990s placed a sharp focus on the need to cut costs. Airlines have made substantial reductions in staffing, cutting something like 100 000 jobs worldwide. Orders for new aircraft were either cancelled or deferred. Some routes were dropped. And many airlines have been reviewing their administrative and operational functions with a view to eliminating any practices found to be not strictly necessary.

2.5 Financial performance of the industry

The years 1990–94 proved to be very difficult ones for the airline industry. It is not hard to see the reason for this. First and foremost there was the economic recession and the downturn in major world economies that began in 1990 and which was accentuated by the Gulf War in 1991. As explained in Section 2.3, air travel demand has a high income elasticity and is extremely sensitive to fluctuations in the level of economic activity. Fear of airlines becoming targets for terrorist attacks exacerbated the fall in traffic. Many airlines were caught a little by surprise by the depth and duration of the slump in demand. In anticipation of continued air traffic growth they had bought and introduced many new aircraft in the late 1980s. Hence the industry generally had too much capacity for the available traffic. Traffic revenues fell sharply and downward pressure on fares was increased by the liberation of competition that was sweeping across the world at broadly the same time. Airlines found it difficult to rein their costs at anything like the same speed as their revenues were falling, especially since many had to meet bills for new aircraft recently acquired. The inevitable result was that some substantial financial deficits were encountered.

For scheduled airlines of ICAO Contracting States, the net result (after allowances for non-operating items, subsidies and taxes) was negative in each year from 1990 to 1994. As percentages of operating revenues, the deficits were –2.3 in 1990, –1.7 in 1991, –3.6 in 1992, –1.9 in 1993 and –0.1 in 1994. Thereafter, the resumption of higher growth rates in traffic led to positive net results of +1.7 in 1995 and +1.9 in 1996, and the improvement continued into 1997, when the operating result was 5.7 per cent of revenues – the highest since 1988 (International Civil Aviation Organization, 1998). Midway through 1998 the effect of the Asian currency crisis and pessimism in western economies once again set the industry on the downswing of the economic cycle, and the indications are that 1999 is going to be another difficult year, especially since many airlines are facing sharp reductions in first and business class travel which, as noted above, account for a disproportionately large share of airline revenues.

Some airlines have shown themselves able to weather financial crises better than others. The ten most profitable airlines in 1997 are given in Table 2.6 and the ten heaviest loss-makers in Table 2.7. The successful carriers are those which are efficiently managed, have their costs under control, have good yield management procedures and generally have responded well to the more competitive environment. It is noticeable that seven of the ten most profitable airlines are from the United States, which reflects the economic boom that characterized the US economy at this time. In the other direction, the Asian downturn clearly had its impact in that five out of the ten heaviest loss-makers were Asian carriers. The downturn in Asia also had the effect of causing SIA to drop from first to sixth place in terms of net profit, but this airline still managed the highest net margin, in terms of profit as a percentage of sales revenue.

Table 2.6 Ten most profitable airlines, 1997. *Source: Airline Business*, September 1998

		Net profit (US$ millions)	Net margin (net profit as % of sales)
1	US Airways	1025.0	12.0
2	American	985.0	5.3
3	United	949.0	5.5
4	Delta	845.0	6.2
5	British Airways	755.0	5.3
6	SIA	671.2	13.4
7	Northwest	596.5	5.8
8	Lufthansa	481.7	3.6
9	Continental	385.0	5.3
10	Southwest	317.8	8.3

Table 2.7 Ten heaviest loss-making airlines, 1997. *Source: Airline Business,* September 1998

		Net loss (US$ millions)	Net margin (net loss as % of sales)
1	Japan Airlines	767.0	–7.7
2	Korean Air	234.0	–7.7
3	PIA	119.7	–14.7
4	TWA	110.8	–3.3
5	Philippine Airlines	95.2	–8.1
6	Air-India	82.7	–8.2
7	Malaysia Airlines	69.8	–4.0
8	Sabena	67.0	–3.3
9	South African Airways	60.1	–4.3
10	Aer Lingus	59.9	–5.7

In comparing airline profitability across different regions or across different countries, recognition should be given not just to differences in economic conditions but also to differences in the degree to which states support their national flag carries with subsidies and other forms of aid. This is particularly relevant in Europe, where seven airlines – Sabena, Air France, Iberia, Aer Lingus, TAP Air Portugal, Olympic Airways and Alitalia have been in receipt of substantial state aids in the 1990s (Table 2.8). With an increasing number of airlines being privatized and thus expected to conduct their business entirely without financial assistance from their governments, aid granted to state owned carriers is potentially a significant distortion of competition. In Europe all cases of state aid have to be submitted to the European Commission for approval.

The Comité des Sages reviewed the whole question of state aids and concluded that, in a competitive market, access to finance should be equitable and not based on ownership. It also held that a state which owns an airline should neither favour that carrier nor disadvantage it by failing to assume the responsibilities of a commercially orientated shareholder. The surest way of phasing out privileged treatment of state owned carriers would be to privatize them; and the need to operate in an increasingly competitive global market also implies privatization. Of course it is difficult to privatize firms that would in effect be bankrupt without the aid they receive from their governments. So the Comité felt that states should be given a 'one time, last time' opportunity to put their airlines on a normal commercial footing, and that state aids should be allowed to continue for a brief transitional period, subject to certain conditions. The conditions include the submission of a radical restructuring plan for commercial viability and ultimate privatization; a prohi-

Table 2.8 State aids to EU airlines. *Source:* European Commission

Year	Airline	Subsidies (ECUs millions)	Subsidies as % of annual sales revenue	Loan guarantees (ECUs millions)
1991	Sabena	833	85.3	–
1991–2	Air France	843	20.3	–
1992	Iberia	929	37.4	–
1993	Aer Lingus	224	47.2	–
1993	Air France	228	4.9	–
1994	TAP Air Portugal	914	139.9	900
1994	Olympic Airways	1900	276.6	300
1994	Air France	3000	61.6	–
1995	Iberia	674	n.a.	–
1997	Alitalia	2.75[a]	n.a.	–

[a] Trillion lira.

bition on the use of public money to buy or take over another carrier; and restrictions on the use of state aids for financing an increase in capacity.

The question of state aids is highly political and highly controversial. Without some assistance from their government, some of the airlines involved would simply go out of business, with a massive loss of jobs and with the industry becoming more and more concentrated in the hands of fewer and fewer airlines. To some this justifies one last chance to rescue the situation: to others it is merely delaying the inevitable. Following EC approval of state aids for three carriers in July 1994, but in particular following the large FF20 billion package of aid approved for Air France, loud protests were made by governments in the United Kingdom, Germany, Scandinavia and the Netherlands. The Commission defended its position by arguing that distortions of competition would be prevented by the strict conditions imposed on the recipient airlines. But the UK government decided to take the Air France case to the European Court of Justice, seeking to get the Commission's approval annulled. British Midland filed its own objection with the Court and a group of six other airlines – British Airways, Air UK, KLM, Maersk Air, SAS and TAT – filed objections with the lower European Court of First Instance, all seeking to overturn the Commission's ruling. The European Court of Justice concluded that the subsidy to Air France was illegal and called for its annulment; and the European Court of First Instance upheld two of the complaints raised by the airlines (one relating to Air France's purchase of 17 new aircraft and one concerned with the implications for competition on Air France routes beyond Europe). However, the Commission responded by tightening the conditions under which the aid was given and still allowed its approval to stand.

Elsewhere in the world airlines recently in receipt of state aids have included Air Afrique, Air-India, Balkan Bulgarian Airlines, Cayman Airways, CSA Czech Airlines, Estonian Air, Kenya Airways and Middle East Airways. In the United States no airline receives any direct financial assistance in the form of state aids, but the federal government does provide some subsidies under its Essential Air Service programme, which ensures air links with remote and rural areas. However, even this kind of subsidy is being progressively withdrawn and the US government continues to cut the allocated budget for it each year (e.g. the $33 million allocated to the programme in 1995 was cut to $23 million in 1996).

Another factor that is relevant when comparisons are being made of the profitability of international airlines is the influence of foreign exchange rates. An international airline typically earns a large proportion of its revenue, and incurs a large proportion of its costs, in its own national currency, the currency of the country in which it is based. But whilst large, these proportions are not necessarily dominant (Hanlon, 1981). Some airlines can earn more than half their revenues in foreign currencies while incurring the vast majority of their costs in their national currency. So when exchange rates fluctuate this can have a significant impact upon an airline's profit and loss situation. Airlines based in countries with 'hard', appreciating, currencies are disadvantaged by a rise in the exchange value of their national currencies, while the opposite is the case for airlines based in countries with 'soft', depreciating, currencies. Airlines whose profitability might have been adversely affected in this way include Lufthansa, Swissair and Austrian Airlines. On the other hand, the relative softness of sterling must, in much of the 1970s and 1980s, have been of significant advantage to British Airways, although more recently the high exchange values of the pound must have had quite the opposite effect (and a similar reversal of effects must apply in the case of Japanese carriers, due to falls in the external value of the yen).

In the future, the effects of market liberalization and globalization could mean that such currency gains and losses largely disappear, or at least become much less significant, as airlines get greater freedom to switch their costs out of hard currencies and also greater freedom to enter what have hitherto been traditionally regarded as national carrier's 'home' markets. The introduction at the beginning of 1999 of the new European Union currency, the Euro, is going to reinforce this trend, while at the same time ensuring greater transparency in the relative levels of air fares charged in different countries.

3 Competition issues

3.1 The regulation versus competition debate

For many years air transport was a closely regulated industry, both domestically and internationally. Government had a whole host of reasons why they were not prepared to leave the industry entirely to the forces of free and unfettered competition. This regulation versus competition debate spawned a large literature in the 1960s and 1970s (see Richmond, 1962; Caves, 1962; Wheatcroft, 1964; Levine, 1965; Kahn, 1970; Keeler, 1972; Douglas and Miller, 1974; and White, 1979). All that is presented in this section is some brief discussion of the fundamental issues involved.

Governments traditionally regarded air transport as, in some sense, a public utility. Strictly speaking, it is not. Economists prefer to reserve the term 'public utility' to enterprises that have characteristics of natural monopoly. Natural monopolies exist where the advantages of size are so great that a service can only be provided at least cost if it is supplied by one, and only one firm. A single firm becomes a monopolist because the average cost of providing the service reaches a minimum only when an output rate large enough to satisfy the entire market has been reached. In a situation of this sort competition will not be sustainable. If there is more than one firm, each of them must be producing at a higher-than-minimum level of average cost; and so each will have a motive to cut price to raise output and thereby reduce average cost. The result is likely to be economic warfare, the outcome of which will be the survival of just one firm, the natural monopolist. The monopolist may then in the interest of maximizing its own profits, raise price and restrict output, producing at a rate at which costs are not minimized. Hence the rationale for government regulation: to prevent the firm from using its monopoly market power to move away from satisfying total market demand at least cost by charging a higher-than-competitive price for the service.

There is general agreement on the need for regulation in natural monopoly industries. These are industries in which the ratio of fixed (inescapable) to variable (escapable) cost is often very high. The fixed costs are often associated with heavy infrastructure investment, which often generates some enormous economies of scale, with average costs falling as output expands. Telecommunications, gas and electricity distribution, and water supply are often cited as examples of natural monopolies. If there were several firms supplying a given local area, this would result in multiplication of cables, transformers, pipelines and so on. Consequently it is much more efficient if local monopoly rights are granted to just one firm. But to prevent this firm exploiting its monopoly position, regulation is required to restrain prices. This is why the UK government, having decided to privatize telecommunications, power and water utilities, also decided to impose upon them price caps related to the rate of general price inflation. It is also the reason why similar public utilities in the United States are subject to rate-of-return constraints in their pricing.

The UK government applied the same principle when privatizing the British Airports Authority, and imposed caps on the charges the BAA can make for aeronautical activities at Heathrow, Gatwick and Stansted. Similar caps have been applied at Manchester Airport. It is recognized that there are elements of natural monopoly in the supply of airport facilities. But are there any in airline operations? Where airport authorities supply runways and terminals, where navigation and air traffic control facilities are supplied by governments, and where the 'track', or airspace, is god-given, airlines are very much in the position of having their infrastructure provided for them. They have no heavy investment to make in fixed assets with inescapable or sunk costs. The major investment an airline has to make is in the acquisition of a fleet of aircraft. An aircraft is a sophisticated, hi-tech piece of equipment and as such can be a rather expensive asset to acquire, costing many millions of dollars to purchase. But an airline does not necessarily have to purchase aircraft; it can lease them. And even if it does purchase aircraft, the costs involved are by no means inescapably sunk, in the same way as infrastructure investment often is. For by its very nature, an aircraft is a very mobile asset, and can be considered as 'capital on wings'. There is a well developed market for second-hand aircraft and, to be disposed of, an aircraft can be flown to the other side of the world if need be. Hence an aircraft is in no sense a fixed asset and can be redeployed relatively easily.

It is generally accepted that the airline industry is characterized by a relatively low fixed-to-variable cost ratio. Most of the costs incurred are escapable. This is not to say that there are no sunk costs at all. As discussed later expenditures on advertising are, to all practical intents and purposes, sunk costs. Nor is it true to say that there are absolutely no elements of natural monopoly in the airline industry. Investment in sophisticated computer reservations systems involves a great deal of capital expenditure and the average cost of running a system falls sharply as the number of bookings increases. This too is discussed later in the book. But generally speaking, the *a priori* expectation is that sunk costs in the airline industry are very low by the standards of many other industries. Also there is no particular *a priori* reason to expect the long-run average costs of airline operation to fall with increases in output. Nor does the empirical evidence suggest this. A whole army of scholars in the United States has over a long period been engaged in testing this hypothesis (Crane, 1994; Koontz, 1951 and 1952; Proctor and Duncan, 1954; Cherington, 1958; Caves, 1962; Gordon, 1965; Straszheim, 1969; and White, 1979). The general findings of these studies was that the average cost per seat-mile bore no statistically significant relationship to the total number of seat-miles flown, or that long-run average cost was more or less constant with respect to output levels. Caves (1962) concluded that, once some minimum efficient size has been attained, scale of operations plays an insignificant role in determining average costs, and that very large size may even be slightly disadvantageous. Both theory and evidence strongly suggest that the industry is characterized by constant returns to scale, at least so far as the costs of airline operation are concerned. On this view, large airlines would have no cost advantages over small airlines and therefore the latter would face no insuperable entry barriers.

Airlines may not qualify as public utilities under an economist's natural monopoly definition, but governments have often treated them as though they do, regarding them as 'quasi' public utilities (Wheatcroft, 1964). There are a number of reasons for this. The most general argument is that civil aviation, like other transport industries, generates important external benefits. The returns from air transport are not limited to those accruing to the industry itself, but encompass wider effects on the economy at large. Governments often see airlines as instruments to promote special national interests. The national airline can be looked upon purely and simply as a prestige symbol; or as a means of encouraging trade and foreign investment; or as a way of stimulating the development of tourism; or as an important source of foreign exchange; or as a vehicle for providing support to home industries in the aerospace sector; or as a way of guaranteeing the availability of a standby fleet, with fully trained crews, in the event of an emergency. Governments have many different objectives to pursue, and there can often be conflicts between these and the commercial objectives of airlines themselves. So countries have often tried to avoid these conflicts by conferring monopolies on their national airlines, protecting them from free and unregulated competition on international routes. The importance governments attach to these nationalistic and mercantilist objectives may have been declining somewhat over time, but they are still highly significant.

In discussions of airlines as quasi public utilities, the question of safety is often the question raised. Air transport is a fail-dangerous activity, a fail-extremely-dangerous one. It has always been regarded as having

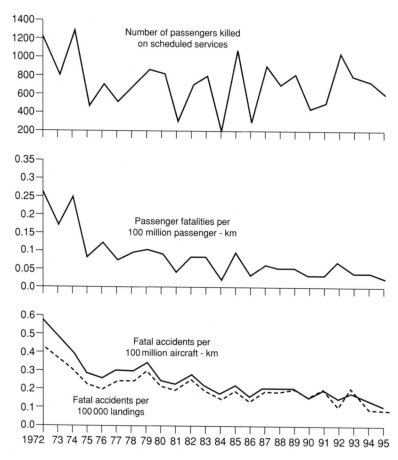

Figure 3.1   Fatal accident rates on scheduled airlines, 1972-95 (traffic of ICAO contracting states excluding the Russian Federation) (*Source:* International Civil Aviation Organization)

unique safety problems because of the nature of its vehicle. There is a widely held view that market forces alone cannot be expected to elicit from all airlines a sufficiently high and consistent degree of attention to safety standards. It is true that airlines have strong commercial self-interests in safe operations. Nobody will want to fly on an airline with a poor safety record. But most people would prefer to prevent accidents by regulation, rather than wait for an airline to lose passengers' confidence. While the airline may be acquiring a reputation for unsafe operations, many people could actually be killed. The need for technical regulation of safety is one of the few things on which governments have reached unanimous agreement. Under the aegis of the International Civil

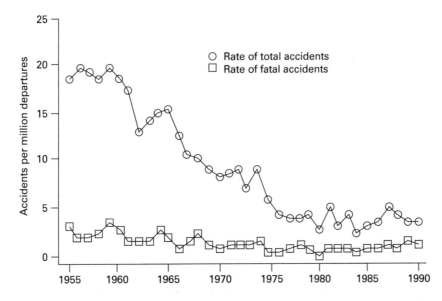

Figure 3.2 Total and fatal accident rates for US scheduled airlines, 1955-90 (*Source:* Rose, 1992)

Aviation Organization, governments have agreed standards of airworthiness, maintenance, aircrew qualifications, flying hours limitations and other operational requirements. It is fair to say that technical regulations of this kind have met with a fair measure of success. The number of passengers killed has fallen over time, despite substantial growth in traffic; and accident rates, however these are measured – per passenger-kilometre, per aircraft-kilometre or per landing – all show considerable declines (Figure 3.1). Across the world in 1995 there were 22 accidents on scheduled services, involving 557 passenger fatalities. This is equivalent to one death for every three billion passengers-kilometre flown, a rate eight or nine times better than that which prevailed in the early 1970s. On the whole scheduled airlines' safety record is impressive both in its own right and in relation to other modes. But there are some wide variations by country (Taylor, 1988). One of the best records is the United States, where deregulation since 1978 does not, on the face of it, appear to have had any significant effects on total or fatal accident rates, which have continued to fall (Figure 3.2).

Another argument advanced in favour of regulation is that the airline industry, if not a natural monopoly, is naturally oligopolistic, at least at the level of the individual route market. Oligopolistic industries are ones in which most of the output is produced by just a few large firms. When there are only a few firms in the industry, each firm, when deciding on price and other marketing strategies, must take the likely reactions of its competitors fully into account. A price cut, for example, may be advantageous to one firm considered in isolation, but if this results in other firms also cutting their prices to protect their sales, then all firms might suffer reduced profits. Consequently, oligopolists are expected to avoid price competition, colluding to co-ordinate their prices either with one firm acting as price leader or with all firms joining a cartel. In those situations the oligopolists can seek maximum joint profits, setting prices at levels similar to those that would prevail under monopoly. In avoiding price competition, the oligopolists then channel most of their competitive efforts into various forms of non-price competition, advertising and other kinds of product differentiation. Price cutting may be seen as a fairly dangerous thing to do, since it can start a price war that may have grave consequences for the stability of the industry, while advertising and product differentiation may be viewed as much less risky ways of winning customers away from competitors. But expenditure on such non-price forms of competition may only have the ultimate effect of raising the costs of the entire industry, because of mutually offsetting effects, one firm's efforts in this direction being cancelled out by those of another; and the higher costs may be passed on to the customer in higher prices. Hence, to prevent firms colluding, or to prevent the instability caused by price wars, it was argued that oligopolistic industries like the airline industry should be regulated, with prices set by a government regulatory authority.

A similar argument questions whether a deregulated air transport market can be viable in the long term, or whether the inherent characteristics of the industry are such that competition would ultimately prove destructive. This is an issue that has been around for a long time and it is one that tends to attract more attention during economic recessions. Air transport markets often exhibit a lot of instability over time, due to high income elasticities of demand, as discussed in Chapter 2. But in addition to this there is the question of the existence or not of a so-called 'empty-core' (Telser, 1978; Button, 1996). Simply put, a core implies that competition leads to the optimal level of supply in the market, but where there are indivisibilities competition could destabilize the market and lead to a suboptimal level of supply or no supply at all. The core is then said to be empty. For example, in the present context, a route might ideally, given the level of demand, be served by one and half flights a day, but naturally only one or two flights can in fact be flown. One airline might operate a single flight but its high profits might attract a second carrier. Two airlines on the route might not be able to generate sufficient revenue to make a profit, so that one or both might abandon the route. The result might be no flights at all or just one operated as a local monopoly. If such an empty core exists there can be benefits for both the airlines and their passengers if the airlines get together and co-operate with each other. But if airlines are permitted, or more than that encouraged, to co-operate, it might be difficult to distinguish between situations in which such co-operation is desirable for the establishment of stable market equilibria and when it merely serves a cloak for anticompetitive collusion to enable the carriers to earn monopoly profits. If any kind of collusive behaviour is to be sanctioned by government authority, it is important to consider how best to regulate such collusion once it is allowed.

Arguments about external benefits, safety, market stability, etc., led to the establishment in 1938 of the US Civil Aeronautics Board, which for the next forty years regulated the prices charged by scheduled airlines operating interstate domestic routes in the United States and also controlled entry to these routes. There was much criticism of regulation by the CAB (Caves, 1962). Much of this criticism centred on the CAB's entry policies: between 1938 and 1977, the CAB permitted no entry at all into city pair markets that already had two or more carriers, and even in markets with no non-stop service or where there was only one carrier, there was little new entry. The critics argued that new entry was important for promoting competition and stimulating efficiency. There was also criticism that airline fares were considerably higher than they would have been under competition. This was largely attributed to airlines competing mostly in terms of frequency of service and in-flight frills like gourmet meals and not in terms of fares. Some economists (Douglas and Miller, 1974) suggested passengers would gladly trade frequency and frills for substantially lower fares. At the same time more and more people began to question the merits of regulation when they could see what appeared to happen when regulation was absent. CAB regulation only applied, at the federal level, to interstate routes. Routes within individual states were unregulated and fares there were very much lower than on interstate routes, some comparisons throwing interstate fares into a bad light. In particular, reference was made to the so-called 'Californian experience' (Levine, 1965). Some very cheap fares were available on routes like San Francisco–Los Angeles and these fares (and also some on routes within Texas) compared very favourably with equivalent fares on interstate routes of approximately the same distance on the East Coast. For example, standard coach class fares for intrastate routes in California were often about half (and sometimes less than half) those for interstate routes from cities like Chicago, Boston and Detroit (Table 3.1). Many people blamed regulation for the high fares on interstate routes, so the Federal Government decided to deregulate interstate routes, passing the Airline Deregulation Act in 1978.

The above arguments were clearly very influential in persuading the US government to deregulate when it did. But there were also perhaps

Table 3.1 Comparisons of fares on interstate and intrastate routes within the United States, 1975. *Source:* Civil Aeronautics Board

City pair		Distance (miles)	Coach class one-way fare ($)
Los Angeles–San Francisco	(intra)	338	18.75
Chicago–Minneapolis	(inter)	339	38.89
Los Angeles–Sacramento	(intra)	373	20.47
Boston–Washington	(inter)	399	41.67
San Francisco–San Diego	(intra)	456	26.21
Detroit–Philadelphia	(inter)	454	45.37

some other, more underlying, factors involved. The effect that the suppression of price competition had in channelling airline competition into aspects of service quality had implications for airlines' choice of equipment and thus for aircraft manufacturers. At a time of rapid technological advance in aircraft design, airlines stood to lose market share unless they matched their competitors in using the latest type of aircraft available, because the most up-to-date aircraft had greater passenger appeal.

The advent of pressurized cabins, the replacement of piston-engined aircraft by turbo-props and then the substitution of turbo-props by jets, all tended to mean that aircraft were retired from front line service before they were fully amortized in the operator's accounts, having been rendered prematurely obsolescent by more advanced types. For this reason airline executives sometimes complained that the rate of aeronautical innovation was too fast for the financial health of their companies. Had airlines been free to compete in terms of fares, it is possible that the rate of innovation might have been appreciably slower. But each technological leap in aircraft design brought with it a substantial gain in productivity, reducing seat-mile costs; and the pressure on airlines to adopt new aircraft had important advantages for the manufacturing sector. If there appeared to be no significant economies of scale in airline operations, there certainly were some enormous ones in aircraft manufacture. The cost per aircraft declines very steeply as the rate of output of a particular type increases, as development and set-up costs are spread over more and more units and as the manufacture moves down the 'learning' curve. From this point of view the main beneficiaries of regulation may well have been not the airlines themselves but rather their suppliers. But that was then. The circumstances now are somewhat different. Since the introduction of the first wide-bodied airliner powered by turbo-fan engines there have been regular improvements in aircraft design, but no major advance has occurred recently and there is no new technological leap on the horizon. For the first time in the history of the industry, aircraft are being retired more because they have reached the end of their physical lives than because of obsolescence. Diminishing marginal returns have set in the field of aeronautical innovation and there are fewer external benefits from regulation to flow from this direction: hence the shift in focus to efficiency in airline operations, sought by deregulation and by allowing greater price competition.

If, as some have argued, the airline industry is naturally oligopolistic, would the outcome with deregulation simply be that firms would recognize their mutual interdependence and continue to avoid price competition through collusion? This is where another set of arguments, made in reference to the theory of contestable markets, came in.

3.2 Contestable markets

The theory on contestable markets was developed in the early 1980s. They key point in this theory concerns the *threat* of competition, as distinct from *actual* competition. According to the theory, firms in oligopolistic industries will still price at the same levels as they would in more competitive industries, provided a threat of competition exists. For the threat of competition to be credible and for a market be classed as contestable a number of pre-conditions must be met (Baumol, 1982; Baumol, Panzar and Willig, 1982). First, there should be no barriers to the entry of new firms to the market. What this means in economic terms is that there should be no extra costs borne by new entrants that are not borne by incumbent firms already in the industry. If for instance incumbent firms enjoyed economies of scale, as in a natural monopoly situation, new entrants would be at a cost disadvantage, and then the threat of their entry would not be all that credible. The second condition is that there should be no heavy 'sunk' costs. A sunk cost is a cost that, once incurred, is inescapable. For its entry to be a real threat, a new firm must be able, if it wants to, to engage in 'hit-and-run' entry. It must be able to go into the market, make profits for a brief period of time and, if things look as if they are not going to work out on a long-term basis, get out of the market again without having irrevocably committed a lot of resources and without losing a lot of money. If hit-and-run competition is profitable, any attempt by incumbent firms to raise price above competition levels will provoke entry. But entry to some industries does involve substantial costs. In manufacturing, for instance, investment in fixed plant and equipment, such as a factory, is a heavy sunk cost; and for this reason many manufacturing industries are not contestable markets. What is also necessary for successful hit-and-run entry is a third condition, which is that the time it takes incumbents to respond to new entry by varying their prices is longer than the time the new firm needs to make its entry profitable. In other words there must be some delay in the reaction of incumbent firms; otherwise the incentive for entry, i.e. the existence of prices above competitive levels, could be withdrawn as soon as entry takes place, making entry an unattractive proposition.

How far are these conditions met in markets for air travel? As discussed earlier, there appear to be no elements of natural monopoly in the airline industry, nor much evidence of significant scale economies. Hence new entrants would not on these accounts be at any cost disadvantage compared with existing firms and the condition that there are no entry barriers might appear to be met. Then what about the condition that there should be no sunk costs? If a new airline wants to enter the industry, it is going to need some aircraft. An aircraft is a sophisticated, hi-tech piece of equipment and as such can be a rather expensive asset to acquire, costing many millions of dollars to purchase. But expenditure on aircraft is not a sunk cost in the same way that plant and equipment in manufacturing is. For an aircraft may be considered as 'capital on wings' and by no means a fixed asset but, by its very nature, a highly variable one. It is something that can be disposed of fairly easily, flying it to the other side of the world if need be. The main fixed assets used by airlines are in fact provided for them by governments and airports. So can new entrants succeed in hit-and-run competition? It was thought that the entry/exit process could be a rather quick one and certainly quick enough in relation to incumbents' ability to change fares, alter schedules, etc., since in the past such changes had always been subject to some delay.

So, with all three conditions apparently met, the proponents of contestability considered the airline as almost a textbook example of a contestable market (Bailey and Baumol, 1984) If that is so, it does not matter so much if there is little actual competition on a particular route, so long as there is plenty of potential competition, with a lot of new entrants ready to come in if incumbent airlines exert market power and charge high fares. But a decade and a half of experience with deregulation in the United States and elsewhere has cast a lot of doubt on this proposition.

3.3 Experience of deregulation

There have been many studies of US deregulation (Civil Aeonautics Board, 1982; Bailey *et al.*, 1985; Brenner *et al.*, 1985; Levine, 1987; Kahn, 1988; US Department of Transportation, 1990; Keeler, 1991; Dempsey and

Goetz, 1992; and Williams, 1993). These all provide detailed accounts of the effects on airline costs, fares and profits, on industry concentration, on the intensity of competition, etc. and so only a very brief commentary focusing on the fundamental issues is presented here. There are also studies covering the effects of deregulation in Canada and Australia (Button, 1991), but since the effects in Canada and Australia have been very similar to those in the United States, the discussion here focuses on US experience.

At first it seemed that the advocates of deregulation were to be vindicated by events. Deregulation brought in a lot of low-cost new entrant airlines and released airlines hitherto confined to intrastate routes. Airlines like People Express, AirCal, Air Florida and so on began challenging the established trunk airlines on interstate routes. This had a dramatic impact on industry structure. The number of carriers offering scheduled services on trunk routes rose from 36 in 1978 to over 120 by 1985; and by 1985 the top five carriers accounted for 57 per cent of the US industry's output, compared with 69 per cent in 1978. So industry concentration fell; fares and costs also fell; and profits rose, as airlines became more efficient. All in all, things looked good. Two economists at the Brookings Institution in Washington DC (Morrison and Winston, 1986) set out to estimate the benefits of deregulation, comparing the situation in 1983 with that in 1977, one year before the airline Deregulation Act was passed. They made the comparison by constructing a 'counterfactual' 1977 scenario, developing a model to give a picture of how the industry would have looked had there been no regulation in 1977. The results of this study indicated annual gains to passengers of at least $6 billion and to airlines of at least $2.5 billion (both figures at 1977 price levels). Given all this, deregulation was hailed as an unqualified success in the mid-1980s. But what happened then?

From 1985 onwards the industry entered a period of consolidation. Fierce competition pushed a number of airlines into bankruptcy or merger. Many of the established airlines, shaken in the early years of deregulation, by now had recovered, having cut costs and having learnt to exploit some of their advantages to force competitors out. Aggressive pricing and scheduling behaviour proved to be more effective competitive weapons than some advocates of deregulation had foreseen. Concentration in the industry began to rise again. Hardly any of the original new entrants survived as independent operators; and the industry has become more oligopolistic than it was before deregulation, the top five carriers now accounting for 70 per cent of the industry's output.

Does this show that contestability no longer applies? Or was it not really applicable in the first place? US experience of deregulation suggests that, contrary to earlier *a priori* reasoning, none of the pre-conditions for contestable markets is met in the airline industry. The theory is no longer regarded as credible in the air transport context. Some of the leading figures who initially suggested that air transport may be 'naturally' contestable subsequently changed their minds:

> We now believe that transportation by trucks, barges and even buses may be more highly contestable then passenger air transport.
>
> (Baumol and Willig, 1986)

To see why a different view is taken now, let us reconsider the conditions for contestability, taking them in reverse order.

What is now abundantly clear is that new entrants cannot really engage in hit-and-run entry, but only 'hit-and-get-hit-back' entry. It is not realistic for new entrants to expect some delay before incumbent airlines respond to their entry. Where there is any delay, it is getting shorter and shorter all the time. Under regulation there were relatively few fares and these changed relatively infrequently. But, as everyone now knows, in liberalized markets fares can be changed many times, almost at a moment's notice, the changes being notified to travel agents more or less instantly via extensive networks of computer reservation systems. The number of fare changes airlines make is rising rapidly. In the past, the Airline Tariff Publishing Company, a co-operative venture between airlines to process changes in ticket prices, considered 25 000 changes a day to be a large number. But by 1988, somewhere between 40 000 and 60 000 was not unusual (and in one peak week nearly 600 000 were processed, United Airlines alone filing around 30 000 a day (Hamilton, 1988)). It is clear that incumbent airlines can now react very swiftly when they see any of their traffic threatened by a new entrant. Or they can even forestall entry by announcing fare changes in advance of the entrant commencing operations on the route or routes in question, something discussed further in Chapter 6 (section 6.8).

It is also questionable whether the no-heavy-sunk-costs condition is met. The costs of acquiring aircraft may not be sunk costs, but there are other items of airline expenditure that are, such as advertising expenditure. Money spent on advertising cannot be recouped if the airline decides to withdraw from the industry. It is inescapably sunk. And this can now be quite a heavy sunk cost. One result of deregulation has been to increase the relative importance of advertising and sales promotion in general. For reasons discussed below, to be a major carrier in deregulated markets, an airline needs a fairly extensive network of routes. It is possible for some airlines to operate as 'niche' carriers, specializing on certain types of routes for certain types of traffic; but to enter into competition with the large network airlines, a new entrant would need to commit a lot of non-recoverable resources to advertising the launch of a network and thus would have to incur a lot of sunk costs.

Sunk costs in advertising and difficulties with the idea of hit-and-run entry are serious enough objections to the notion of contestability in air transport. But the most compelling reason for rejecting its application to airline competition is the discovery that there are some 'new' forms of entry barrier. The airline industry may not be like public utilities in having strong elements of natural monopoly, nor like capital intensive manufacturing industries in having significant economies of scale in production; but there are nonetheless some very important advantages in large firm size in this industry. There is no particular advantage in large size *per se*, as some airlines have discovered (e.g. Aeroflot, Pan American, TWA and Air France, perhaps) and the benefits of large size derive not from conventional economies of *scale* as such but from greater opportunities to reap economies of *scope*.

The distinction between economies of scale and economies of scope can be explained as follows. With economies of scale, the average cost per unit of output declines as the level of output increases. Where economies of scope exist the cost of producing two (or more) products jointly is less than the cost of producing each one alone. Formally, if C denotes cost and Q output, economies of scale mean that C/Q falls as Q expands. Economies of scope can be gauged from the relation:

$$S = \frac{C(Q_1) + C(Q_2) - C(Q_1 + Q_2)}{C(Q_1 + Q_2)}$$

Where $C(Q_1)$ is the cost of producing Q_1 units of the first product alone, $C(Q_2)$ is the cost of producing Q_2 units of the second product alone, and $C(Q_1 + Q_2)$ is the cost of producing Q_1 units of the first product in combination with Q_2 units of the second product. Where there are economies of scope $S > 0$ because the cost of producing both products together is less than the cost of producing each alone, i.e. $C(Q_1 + Q_2) < C(Q_1) + C(Q_2)$. The larger the value of S the greater the economies of scope.

The scope economies large airlines are able to reap lie mainly on the marketing side, most of them related to network size. Airlines serving large and widespread networks can more easily afford large-scale marketing campaigns which are much more efficient than promotions of individual routes, but which are beyond the means of many small airlines. Quantity discounts in media purchasing mean that advertising costs rise much less than in proportion to the number of city pair markets served. Also, advertising an entire network gives large airlines a strong sense of identity in the public mind. The marketing advantages of large networks are reinforced by the use of sophisticated computer reservations systems and loyalty marketing schemes. Computer reservations systems generate economies of scope, insofar as they permit the booking system to be centralized and they also have useful some spin-offs like, for example, facilitating the airline's yield management procedures. These are discussed in section 3.5. Loyalty marketing schemes, in the form of frequent flyer programmes, travel agency commission overrides and corporate discounts, require extensive networks to be most effective, and these are discussed in section 3.4. But the most important source of economies of scope – and arguably the most profound change induced by deregulation – are the economies of route traffic density airlines can reap by configuring their networks in the hub and spokes pattern. By combining passengers and groups of passengers an airline can carry the total more cheaply than if it carried the passengers separately. This is what might be achieved by routing through hubs, which has the effect of increasing traffic on each sector flown. The impact of hub and spokes networks is discussed more fully in Chapter 5.

If economies of scope have become so important in deregulated air transport, why were they not evident before? They were not uncovered in the many studies referred to above that investigated relationships between size and efficiency in air transport. There are two possible explanations. First, the researchers were examining the influence of output level Q, on average cost, C/Q, and not directly seeking a measure of scope economies, S. Second, it could have been that regulation itself prevented large airlines from exploiting their size advantages, given that route entry was controlled and airlines had limited freedom to pursue scope economies by reconfiguring networks.

If economies of scope give large airlines significant advantages over smaller ones, thereby reducing contestability, how has this affected the benefits of deregulation? There is no doubt that average fares paid by passengers have fallen in real terms, after allowing for inflation (Figure 3.3). What is a little less clear is how far this is due to deregulation and how far it is the result of other factors. Dempsey and Goetz (1992) believe it has less to do with deregulation and rather more with falls in the level of real fuel prices and with the continuation of a long-term trend established in the pre-deregulation period. A more widely supported view is that expressed by Pickrell (1991), an economist at the US Department of Transport, whose review of various estimates of deregulation's effect on fares led to the conclusion that on average fares paid are some 15 per cent lower than they would have been if the regulatory regime had continued in force. One reason average fares have fallen is that many more passengers are travelling on discount tickets (Figure 6.6). Both the proportion of total traffic flying at discounts and the average size of the discount have risen appreciably: over the period 1982–92 the proportion at discounts rose from 75 to 90 per cent; and in relation to full fares, the average discount increased from around 45 to something over 60 per cent. There is clearly far more price discrimination in the deregulated environment and the implications of this for competition are discussed in Chapter 6.

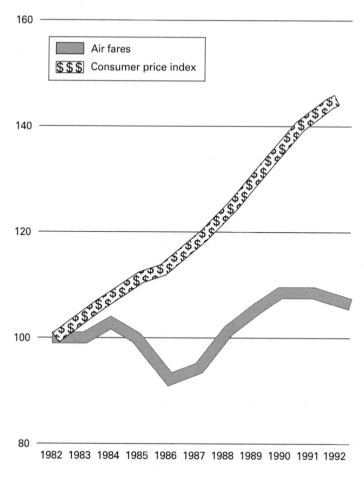

Figure 3.3 Air fares on US domestic routes compared with consumer prices, 1982-90 (*Source:* Air Transport Association)

If fares have fallen this should be reflected by growth in passenger demand. Passenger traffic has indeed grown strongly, its level in the mid-1990s being about double what it was in the mid-1970s. However, traffic growth on US domestic routes has not been exceptional when compared to growth on domestic or international routes elsewhere in the world (Figure 3.4), a point made by the UK Civil Aviation Authority (1993), raising the question of how large estimated gains from deregulation to US consumers can be reconciled with traffic demand only increasing at rates commensurate with the growth in air travel across the world as a whole, when outside the United States regulation still very largely prevailed. There are of course many factors determining passenger

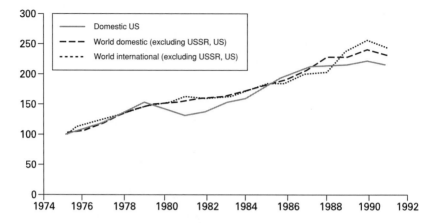

Figure 3.4   Traffic on US domestic routes compared with traffic growth elsewhere in the world (*Source:* Civil Aviation Authority)

demand and those affected by deregulation (primarily fares and service frequencies) could have been outweighed by other more exogenous factors. For example, the US market for air travel is one of the most mature and in mature markets one might expect growth rates in passenger demand to be lower then elsewhere, as explained in Chapter 2. So, the fact that US traffic has grown at approximately the same rate as world traffic could still be, at least in part, a positive result of deregulation.

In an updated application of their 'counterfactual' methodology for estimating the welfare effects of deregulation, Morrison and Winston (1995) found that travellers' benefits were accruing at an annual rate of US $18.4 billion (at 1993 price levels). Accordingly these authors reject calls for the industry to be re-regulated, notwithstanding the instability, lack of profitability and impediments to competition observed in the first half of the 1990s.

What the airlines might consider a negative outcome of deregulation is the financial insecurity that seems to go with it. Bankruptcy has claimed over 100 airlines including such previously strong carriers as Braniff, Eastern and Pan American. Three others, America West, Continental and TWA were able to continue, but only under Chapter Eleven bankruptcy protection; and in addition, both Northwest and USAir (now renamed as US Airways) experienced some serious financing difficulties during the economic recession at the beginning of the 1990s. Of the large airlines, only American, United and Delta seemed financially strong enough to weather economic downturns.

Some very heavy losses were incurred in the period 1990–93 (Figure 3.5. The industry lost around US $5 billion in 1993 alone, and the sum

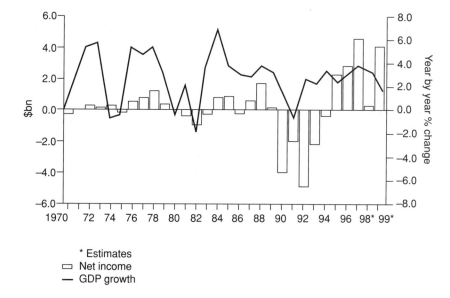

Figure 3.5 Net income of US scheduled airlines (*Source:* Air Transport Association)

total of deficits incurred during this period could be seen as exceeding all profits made since the invention of powered flight, as it was put in some press articles. No surprise then if, seeing this, airlines elsewhere began to view the prospect of deregulation with something less than unbounded enthusiasm.

The financial position of US airlines in the fist half of the 1990s brought into question whether the two goals set for President Clinton's National Commission to Ensure a Strong and Competitive Airline Industry (Clinton Commission, 1993) are compatible: is it possible to achieve both a strong and a competitive industry at one and the same time? In the depths of recession there were a number of spectacular 'price wars' which lent some credence to the view that the industry is susceptible to destructive competition. The Clinton Commission received a lot of complaints about the way in which the bankruptcy laws are administered, in particular the 'Chapter Eleven' provision, under which a firm is permitted to shelter from its creditors and is given time to re-organize its affairs in an attempt to stay in business. It was submitted that Chapter Eleven bore a heavy responsibility for the industry's poor financial performance, insofar as it served to artificially prolong the lives of 'failed' carriers, giving them temporary relief from the need to service their debts and encouraging them to offer deep discounts on fares just in order to generate sufficient cash flow to keep going. This, it was argued, obliged other carriers to follow suit, the ensuing price wars plunging the whole industry into losses. The Clinton Commission did not altogether accept this, although it did conclude that some reform to bankruptcy provisions is desirable, to reduce the time bankrupt airlines are given to file re-organization plans. Other possible causes of price wars may have been the (longer than expected) economic recession and also the tendency for competitive expansions of capacity in periods of growing not to be followed by appropriate reductions in capacity when demand falls during a slump. But Chapter Eleven may have been at least partially responsible for the lengthy price wars that took place, when the protection it gave was prolonged for a considerable period of time. Airlines not in bankruptcy complained that they were being forced to compete with carriers whose cost levels had been artificially reduced. On the other hand, there has been the suggestion that the biggest and most powerful airlines priced aggressively in the hope of driving smaller and weaker airlines from the market, by engaging in predatory pricing, a matter considered in Chapter 6.

Morrison and Winston (1995) subjected the question of how far the industry's financial losses could be attributed to the pricing behaviour of carriers operating under Chapter Eleven bankruptcy protection to econometric analysis. Their conclusion is that the effect was quite small. Interestingly, it was found that the net revenues of some airlines were actually enhanced through the tarnished image of its bankrupt competitors (e.g. Delta in competition with Eastern and Continental) although those of some of the others were actually damaged by the lower marginal costs and fares of competitors in Chapter Eleven bankruptcy (e.g. American and United competing against TWA).

However, an underlying concern about the financial problems besetting the industry is the fear that only a few large airlines may in the long term survive. Smaller airlines are already conscious of the market power that large carriers derive from the size and spread of their extensive networks. The commercial strategies large airlines are adopting are designed to reinforce this market power, and one of these strategies includes the use of loyalty marketing schemes.

3.4 Loyalty schemes in airline marketing

Loyalty schemes form part of an airline's overall marketing strategy, and expenditure on loyalty schemes is much like expenditure on other forms of marketing such as advertising. Marketing expenditure has two fundamental purposes. One is to increase the airline's share of passenger demand; the other is to make that demand less price elastic. These objectives are illustrated in Figure 3.6

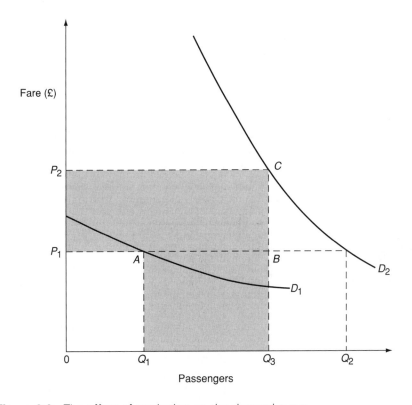

Figure 3.6 The effect of marketing on the demand curve

The original demand curve, before anything is spent on marketing, is respresented by D_1. On this schedule, if the fare charged by the airline is P_1, the number of passengers carried by the airline is Q_1. Following a marketing compaign the demand curve shifts to the right and acquires a steeper slope. The rightward shift allows an increased number of passengers (Q_2) to be attracted to the service at the original price, and the steeper slope enables the airline to raise the fare and still have a substantial increase in passengers. Thus, in Figure 3.6, the fare can be raised to P_2, at which passenger demand is Q_3, still well above the original level of Q_1.

The airline benefits both from an increase in passengers and from a higher fare per passenger; its total gain in revenue is the shaded area, area Q_1ABQ_3 from the increase in passengers plus area P_1BCP_2 from the increase in fare. So long as this additional revenue is greater than the costs associated with the marketing campaign, the airline increases its profit.

Reducing price elasticities is an underlying objective that loyalty schemes have in common with advertising and other forms of marketing. Advertising is an attempt to reduce elasticities by persuading passengers that one airline's service is much superior to those of others, whereas loyalty schemes seek to achieve the same effect by raising passengers' 'switching' costs, making it relatively expensive, in term of lost rewards, to transfer their patronage from one airline to another. If price elasticities or more particularly cross-price elasticities are reduced, this lowers the incentive for competitive price cutting and increases the scope for enhancing revenues by raising fares.

Loyalty schemes can often be more profitable then other forms of marketing. It often costs more in marketing terms to generate new customers than to retain existing ones. A major advantage in loyalty schemes is that they provide a valuable source of data about customers on whom the greatest amount of profit is earned, enabling firms to target these customers that much more effectively (Reichheld, 1996).

Airlines tend to focus loyalty schemes on passengers whose demand is already less price elastic; that is, on passengers prepared to pay premium fares for first, business and fully flexible economy class travel. To these passengers, price is usually a far less important factor than factors related to the quality of service, factors like frequency, seat access, convenience in making/changing bookings, in-flight comfort and so on. And the fares such passengers pay are often some multiple of the fares paid by passengers from price elastic segments of the market, passengers who travel on promotional fares like the advance purchase excursion (apex), passengers for whom price is the most important factor. In Chapter 6 an example is given of the variation in fares on British Airways' services from London to New York (Figure 6.2). In November 1998 fares ranged from £5234 for first class, through £2954 for business class, £844 for unrestricted travel in economy class and down to £357 for passengers travelling on an apex fare. Thus, in relation to the apex fare, the unrestricted economy fare is more than twice as expensive, the business class fare around eight times as expensive and the first class nearly fifteen times as expensive. Because the amounts they pay are so much higher, passengers travelling on first, business and unrestricted economy class fares typically contribute a disproportionately large share of the airline's total revenue. This was noted in Chapter 2. For major international airlines it is fairly typical for high fare passengers to contribute around 30 per cent of total passengers but generate as much as 70 per cent of total revenue. The share they contribute to airline profits can be even more disproportionate. The profit per passenger is often much greater in the higher fare categories, and passengers seated towards the front of the aircraft are usually those on whom the lion's share of airline profit is earned.

Hence it is towards the high fare traffic that airlines mainly direct the marketing of their loyalty schemes, of which there are essentially three kinds: frequent flyer programmes, corporate discounts and travel agency commission overrides.

Frequent flyer programmes

A frequent flyer programme (FFP) is a purchase incentive plan which rewards the passenger for repeat patronage of the services of a particular airline. For each eligible ticket bought, the passenger accumulates mileage points according to distance travelled and according to the type of ticket bought, first and business class passengers receiving points at multiples of the basic rate. Once earned the passengers can exchange the mileage points for rewards in the form of free or discounted tickets, upgrades from one class of travel to another, special concessions on car hire and hotel accommodation and other benefits in the form of free gifts, dedicated lounges at airports and so on.

The first FFP was launched by American Airlines in 1981 and this was so successful that other US airlines decided to follow suit. American's 'Advantage' programme now has 16 million members, while United Airlines' FFP 'Mileage Plus' has around 12 million and Northwest's 'Worldperks' about 10 million. All told some 30 million US residents are now members of a FFP, almost one in every eight people in the United States. The popularity of the programmes run by US airlines meant that European airlines had to introduce schemes of their own, albeit somewhat reluctantly at first. The first European carrier to have one was British Airways, with its 'Air Miles' scheme, followed by Lufthansa with its 'Miles and More' programme. Now, almost all major airlines have FFPs, under their own distinctive brandnames, such as KLM's 'Flying Dutchman', Swissair's 'Qualiflyer', British Midland's 'Diamond Club Destinations', Virgin Atlantic's 'Freeway' and so on.

A recent survey by *Official Airline Guides* found that 90 per cent of the world's business travellers participated in a FFP. Participation is highest in the United States where travellers participating in FFPs belong to an average of 4.6 schemes each. In Europe the highest participating rates are to be found in France, the Netherlands and the UK, and the lowest in Belgium and Germany.

It is known that business travellers are heavily influenced by their FFP membership in choosing the flights of a particular airline. A survey undertaken by the US General Accounting Office (1990) found more than half the responding travel agents reporting that travellers always or almost always choose their flights in order to build up FFP mileage points (Table 3.2), the GAO concluding that FFPs 'tilt the playing field on which carriers compete'. In a number of ways FFPs encourage travellers to choose the airline on which they are most likely to fly in the future. This is especially so for FFPs marketed by airlines dominating particular hubs. Frequent flyers in the hub city could become virtually 'captive' to the hub airline. Multiple membership of several different FFPs is always possible, but the rewards are usually structured in a non-

Table 3.2 The influence of frequent flyer programmes. *Source:* US General Accounting Office

Number of times business travellers choose flights in order to build up mileage points	Percentage of travel agents reporting
Always or almost always	57
More than half the time	24
About half the time	9
Less than half the time	4
Rarely if ever	2
Other	3
	100

linear fashion such that their marginal value increases as the passenger builds up more and more points on a single airline. Indeed, some airlines have created 'elite' levels in their FFPs at which additional bonuses over and on top of any existing entitlements are awarded to members chalking up total mileages of 25 000, 30 000, 50 000 or 60 000 within some specified period (e.g. the Silver and Gold levels in BA's Executive Club, the Gold and Platinum levels in American's Advantage scheme and the SilverWing and RoyalWing in KLM's Flying Dutchman). These additional bonuses serve to increase passengers switching costs still more.

Conditions applying to mileage points and rewards can often be rather complex, making it difficult to compare one FFP against another. European FFPs are often somewhat less generous than their counterparts in the United States, insofar as they tend to award points only for travel at premium fares (first, business or full economy) whereas US FFPs allow points to be earned on all travel, albeit at different rates depending on the fare category. Where European and US carriers are in direct competition, as on transatlantic services, European FFPs have to be more generous to remain competitive and so they give special bonuses. The FFPs of European airlines are much more closely targeted at business travellers. Of European business travellers 86 per cent are members of at least one scheme; among those making more than twenty trips per year, the figure is as high as 97 per cent.

It used to be thought that airlines could possibly be storing up trouble for themselves in operating FFPs. What might happen if there were suddenly to be a 'run' on awards, a lot of passengers seeking to redeem accumulation mileage points all at one and the same time? Under ordinary circumstances only something between 15 and 30 per cent of accrued points is actually redeemed. Although the possibility exists of a surge in the take-up rate, as happened when in 1984 Pan American suddenly imposed a relatively short cut-off period for redemptions and the take-up rate soared to 85 per cent. But other airlines are now conscious of the dangers in doing something like that and most FFPs have standard cut-off dates set a long way in advance, sufficiently distant from the time mileage points are accrued to prevent redemptions coming in a rush.

Another issue concerning FFPs is whether they generally have the effect of increasing airlines' total expenditure on marketing. Shenton (1993) points out that FFPs are only one form of marketing expense and that their growth has not been associated with increased marketing costs in total, because at the same time expenditure on media advertising has declined. Shenton cites data showing that US airline media advertising declined by 35 per cent between 1982 and 1992, while airline revenues more than doubled. In 1982 media advertising was equivalent to 1.15 per cent of revenues and dropped to 0.73 per cent by 1992, a 'saving' of $300 million, more than enough to pay for FFPs, Shenton argued. This may seem a reasonable argument and it is one apparently endorsed by the UK Civil Aviation Authority (1993b). But perhaps it needs more support-ing evidence, since there could be other reasons to explain the fall in the advertising/revenue ratio, as a brief reference to economic theory might show. In economic theory, the advertising/revenue ratio is known as the 'advertising intensity' ratio and it has been demonstrated that the optimal (profit maximizing) advertising intensity is achieved when the ratio of advertising expenditure (A) to sales revenue, the product of price (P) times quantity sold (Q), is the same as the ratio of advertising elastic-ity of demand (E_a) to price elasticity of demand (E_p):

$$\text{advertising intensity} = \frac{\text{advertising expenditure}}{\text{sales revenue}} = \frac{A}{P.Q} = \frac{E_a}{E_p}$$

where

$$E_a = \frac{dQ}{dA} \cdot \frac{A}{P} \text{ is the advertising elasticity of demand}$$

and

$$E_p = \frac{dQ}{dP} \cdot \frac{P}{Q} \text{ is the price elasticity of demand.}$$

It is commonly observed that $A/P.Q$ tends to remain broadly constant over time for a particular firm or industry, but this is only the case where the magnitudes of E_a and E_p, and the relationship between them, also remain constant over time. Where there are significant changes in elastic-ity magnitudes, one rising relative to the other, then one should expect to see some change in the advertising intensity: if demand becomes relatively more price elastic and relatively less elastic with respect to advertising expenditure, the amount spent on advertising as a proportion of revenue will fall. This is quite possibly what has been happening in the deregulated US airline industry. With greater price competition and indeed, as discussed above, price wars, the magnitude of E_p must have been rising over time, if not for the industry as a whole, then certainly for the individual airline; and even if E_a remained constant, the value of the ratio would fall, leading to a fall in the advertising intensity, revealed by advertising expenditure falling as a percentage of revenue. It is quite likely that FFPs are partly substituting for media advertising, but just as likely that falls in advertising intensity are the result of price elasticities generally increasing.

A more serious criticism is that FFPs put small airlines with relatively few routes, or routes just within one particular geographic area, at a big disadvantage when competing for the loyalty of premium fare passengers. This was recognized by airlines like British Midland and Virgin Atlantic. Neither have very extensive networks and so when they launched their respective FFPs, they sought to minimize their disadvantages in various ways. British Midland attached to its FFP the label 'Destinations', presumably in an attempt to distract passengers' attention away from the fact that its network is limited to short haul domestic and European routes between large cities and has no long haul services nor many flights to holiday resorts. And the rewards in Virgin Atlantic's 'Freeway' FFP initially concentrated on non-travel benefits (like golfing weekends), possibly seeking to offset the disadvantage of a network restricted to barely half a dozen long haul routes and appealing to those frequent travellers whose desire for further overseas travel had diminished or been sated by having flown on so many overseas trips already. Factors like this led the European Commission to the view that '*a priori*, FFPs may be considered a barrier to entry for new entrants with a small network' (Commission of the European Communities, 1993b).

It has been shown in theoretical terms that FFPs erect entry barriers on the demand side of the market by creating artificial linkages between different services, so that they deter entry by creating a need for airlines to establish from the outset a network of a certain size (Cairns and Galbraith, 1990). The only real way of offsetting the disadvantage of a small network is for the airline to link its FFP with those of other carriers. This is what many airlines with limited networks have done. British Midland for example, has entered into reciprocal FFP arrangements with Air Canada, SAS and United, while Austrian Airlines has similar pacts with Delta and Swissair. But at the same time many of the larger airlines are also combining their FFPs, especially those grouped in one of the emerging global alliances. As the Chairman of Lufthansa, a member of the Star Alliance, put it:

It [the combined FFP] is the glue to hold the alliance together.
(Jurgen Webber, quoted in *Airline Business*, August 1997, p. 34)

And the six principal members of the Star Alliance have promoted the advantages of its combined FFP in the following terms:

Be recognized as a frequent flyer on not one, but six airlines – SAS, Air Canada, Lufthansa, Thai, United Airlines and Varig. Apply mileage points from qualified flights on any of the six airlines towards your overall frequent flyer status....Redeem miles for reward travel on any of our six carriers, giving you more than 600 destinations around the world to choose from.

(Advertisement placed in *The Economist*, 5 September 1998)

As two members of the Oneworld Alliance, British Airways and American Airlines want to combine the Air Miles and AAdvantage schemes to permit full reciprocity. So it is clear that alliances are attaching a great deal of importance to jointly marketed loyalty schemes. And it is not hard to see why: the more extensive the network to which the FFP applies, the greater the advantage large airlines which are members of a global alliance will have over smaller non-alliance carriers in competition for high yield business travellers.

It has been argued (Levine, 1987) that, in targeting their FFPs primarily at business travellers, airlines are seeking to take advantage of the 'principal–agent' problem that arises when the traveller (the agent), monitored imperfectly by his or her fare-paying employer (the principal), makes inefficient choices between fares/travel times and additional FFP mileage points. It has been suggested that FFPs encourage unnecessary travel, or travel at higher fares than necessary, or travel over more circuitous routings, just so that the traveller, who does not meet the costs involved, can increase the number of FFP points he or she can thereby accumulate. An advertisement taken out by the low-cost carrier easyJet reproduced a finding of a MORI survey that:

some travelling executives were choosing flights, which earned maximum points, rather than sticking to airlines offering the most economic flights.
(*Financial Times*, 7 October 1996)

And raised the question:

Have you calculated the *real* cost of airline loyalty schemes to your company? (emphasis in the original)
(*The Times*, 6 December 1996)

If this is perceived as a large problem – and as yet there is no evidence on the overall size of the problem, just anecdotal reports – then it is possible employers will put a lot of pressure on airlines to direct the benefits from FFPs to them rather than to the individual traveller.

Corporate discounts

Some are already doing so. Several large companies in Germany are trying to trace all the accumulated mileage bonuses outstanding to employees flying Lufthansa, as a first move towards asking for them to be handed over. In Sweden leading companies like Saab–Scania, Electrolux and Volvo are pressing SAS to award benefits from its 'Eurobonus' FFP directly to the companies and not to the travellers.

One airline that has already responded to the call is Virgin Atlantic. Virgin has given companies the option of taking the accumulated mileage credits as part of its 'Corporate Freeway' FFP; and some 250 companies have taken up this offer since it was introduced in 1994. In America almost 10 per cent of companies insist that business travellers hand back their benefits so that they can be used to obtain free or reduced price tickets for other staff. Companies that do this claim to have saved between 12 and 15 per cent on their air travel budgets. Among British companies, some have banned the use of FFPs altogether, while others take the view that the benefits should be shared by all employees and not just those who travel. Even some UK local authorities are beginning to take an interest in FFP benefits, it being recently reported that Birmingham City Council, for example, is demanding that all councillors making civic trips overseas hand over all mileage points so earned. Some organizations appreciate the positive effect FFP benefits have on travellers' morale and because of this are quite prepared to let their individual employees continue to enjoy them. But there are now so many FFPs in existence that their translation into some kind of corporate discount scheme would mean some significant savings for employers who spend a lot on air travel. Hence it might be expected that more and more employers will press for the loyalty bonuses to be earned on a corporate rather than an individual basis.

The corporate discount schemes that already exist tend to be cast in terms of ascending thresholds according to the number of journeys made, or the amount of money spent, on the services of a particular airline within a specified period of time. If purchases by a company or organization exceed these thresholds, then deeper discounts progressively apply, so that the discounts given rise in a non-linear fashion in a similar way that the benefits of FFPs do.

As airlines extend their networks in the process of globalization, the more able they are to offer corporate bodies comprehensive travel packages, using not just their own online services but the services of alliance partners as well. Some alliance groupings may soon be able to offer companies worldwide service through the medium of codesharing and also through the use of franchise operators on regional routes.

Travel agency commission overrides

Travel agency commission overrides (TACOs) are to travel agents what FFPs are to individual travellers and corporate discounts are to companies. Airlines reward travel agents for directing more passengers to them, and TACOs are designed to encourage agents to concentrate bookings on a single carrier. TACOs are paid over and above standard rates of commission, normally around 9 per cent (although some airlines have been reducing their standard rates recently). The overrides may be paid, either in absolute or percentage terms, on an agent's sales for a particular airline, either in total or for a particular set of routes. They are triggered by reaching some target threshold level of sales determined in relation to the level of sales the agent achieved for the airline in the previous year. Once the threshold has been reached, the additional commission is paid not just on additional sales beyond that point but on those already made within the year in question as well. Hence the effective rate of commission on incremental sales beyond the threshold is well above the standard 9 per cent, depending on the volume of incremental sales and the proportion this bears to the threshold sales volume, usually set somewhat above the agent's sales for the previous years.

At first sight TACOs appear to tie agents to much the same extent that FFPs tie passengers and corporate discount tie firms. But there is a bit of a difference here. While FFPs and corporate discounts are offered to the airline's end-customers this is not the case with TACOs, which are deals with intermediaries. Deals with travel agents are less exclusive and have less direct influence on the travel decision. Agents can earn TACOs from a number of different airlines at the same time. And, as the Civil Aviation Authority (1994) has explained, agents may in the long run at least, have little to gain from boosting the sales of any one dominant airline. For if in one year the agent diverted as much traffic as possible to one particular carrier, this could have the effect of making the following year's override commissions that much harder to achieve.

Are airline loyalty schemes anticompetitive?

All three kinds of loyalty scheme create strategic advantages for airlines with high market shares and reduce the potential for competition. They go a long way towards making an extensive network almost a *sine qua non* for serious participation in the valuable premium fare market. The advantages of network size for a FFP are fairly clear. A large network gives passengers more opportunities both to earn the mileage points and to use them once they have earned them. An airline with relatively few routes is doubly disadvantaged here. The same applies, perhaps *a fortiori*, to corporate discount schemes. Corporate discounts may pose a threat to competition, possibly more so than FFPs if large airlines exploit the advantages of their networks in such a way that small competitors find it difficult, if not impossible, to respond. The UK Civil Aviation Authority (1994) has argued that discount incentives directly linked to overall use of an airline's global network are likely to be anticompetitive, against which effective action can only be mounted at a supra-national level, involving both the European Commission and the US authorities.

Recently Virgin Atlantic made representations to the European Commission about British Airways' corporate discount schemes, claiming that they are in breach of Article 86 of the Treaty of Rome which refers to an abuse of a dominant position. BA responded that its discounting policies are standard practice, not just in the airline industry but also in hotels and car rental companies. Virgin countered that the mere fact of other firms following similar policies does not make the practice right and entered the specific complaint that BA unfairly persuades companies to use its services by offering a combination of discounts for different routes. Companies whose staff travel on routes on which BA faces little or no competition – such as from the United Kingdom to South America – are, it is said, offered additional discount if they also agree to use the airline to fly on routes served by many carriers. If true, this would be tantamount to a form of price discrimination, which can certainly have anticompetitive effects. Price discrimination is a topic discussed in Chapter 6.

Small airlines contend that they are also put at a disadvantage by the TACO schemes operated by their larger competitors. Once the initial override threshold has been reached some airlines allow the agent further overrides in exchange for still further growth in sales, on a sliding scale above the threshold level. The incremental commissions earned by the agent can become very high at particular points on this scale, on which there are significant discontinuations, known in the industry as 'spikes'. These spikes occur at sales levels at which the airline believes the agent will need the biggest incentive to further increase the sales of its tickets. As a result of this the agent's incremental commission can go up to something in excess of 50 per cent of an airline's additional sales revenue. In principle this should not necessarily be to the disadvantage of small airlines but sometimes it can be, depending on the formula used to calculate the TACOs. In particular small airlines have complained when large airlines have calibrated TACOs in relation to market shares, rewards to the travel agent being based on comparisons of sales between those for the airline paying the commission and those on other airlines the agent is dealing with. This issue was raised a few years ago in the United States, when Morris Air complained to the Clinton Commission about the kind of TACOs that Delta was paying agents located in Salt Lake City. The complaint was that Delta's overrides were related to agents' percentage sales on Delta rather than simply sales growth. It might be argued that commission payments like this are in the nature of 'kickbacks' that have anticompetitive effects and thus justify intervention by the regulatory authorities.

Sales agents in other industries receive different rates of commission on different products or brands and so naturally tend to be biased towards the high-commission sale. The same might be expected of travel agents. There may be no general reason to regulate travel agents' commissions, but, since agents often hold themselves out to the public as unbiased conveyors of travel information, there may be a case for at least some controls over the way in which TACOs are structured. Otherwise there is some risk of the incentives to favour one airline over others becoming so great that, abandoning all sense of impartially, agents might increasingly lead unsuspecting travellers to sub-optimal choices between travel alternatives merely in order to meet override targets.

All loyalty schemes tend to reduce demand elasticities. That indeed is their underlying purpose. Perhaps the most serious implication for airline competition would be a general decline in the magnitude of cross-elasticities, including those with respect to the quality factors. If loyalty schemes succeed in rendering premium fare passengers more or less captive to particular airlines or to particular alliances, or to particular alliance groupings, other independent airlines are going to find it difficult to compete, not just in the premium fare segment of the market, but for promotional fare passengers as well. The non-linear incentive structures built into the schemes are designed to achieve just that.

Policy issues

If it is accepted that loyalty schemes have anticompetitive effects, what if anything should government competition authorities do about them? This question is becoming more and more pressing as time passes. Whether there are going to be two, three or four main global alliances the future success, or even the future survival, of independent airlines remaining outside these grouping may depend crucially upon how much of the premium fare traffic becomes captive to the alliance carriers. The marketable networks of alliance carriers are set to expand greatly and this will make their loyalty schemes very much more attractive to passengers; and this, together with the non-linear reward structures built into the loyalty schemes, could diminish cross-elasticity magnitudes still further. Hence independent airlines will find it extremely difficult to win the traffic back, and without the revenue from premium fare passengers many of these independent airlines may have to withdraw from some of the most important markets. Concerns of this kind have led to a number of suggestions being put forward for government policy on airline loyalty schemes; and some of the main ones are discussed briefly below.

Outright prohibition?

Some people have raised the question of whether loyalty schemes should be banned if they can be shown to be reducing competition. A total ban might seem a rather draconian measure and one likely to evince the response: why ban them in air transport, when they are in such common use in other industries?

Loyalty schemes are used a lot in retailing, by supermarket chains (in the UK, Sainsbury, Tesco, Asda and Safeway) and a whole host of other retail outlets besides (in the UK, Boots the Chemist and W. H. Smith). The fact that firms in other industries market loyalty schemes is because they see the same competitive advantages in them as airlines do. Loyalty schemes marketed in other industries also have the effect of reducing price elasticities of demand. There is, for instance, some suggestion that supermarket chains in the UK have been able to use their purchasing power to squeeze discounts out of their suppliers but have not been passing on the cost savings to customers in the form of price cuts. Supermarkets' price-cut margins have been tending to rise. One possible explanation for this is that the widespread use of loyalty cards has reduced supermarket customers' price elasticities of demand, perhaps to such an extent that supermarkets' total revenue would fall if they cut prices. Hence the fact that loyalty schemes exist in other industries may not, in itself, be a good enough reason to justify their use in air transport.

Is it practicable for them to be banned outright? Is it not too late for this? Many air travellers have already clocked up mileage points which they have not yet redeemed. At best the schemes could only be phased out, perhaps over a fairly long period of time. But even if they were, would they not reappear in some other guise? And exactly how far would a ban go? Would it cover 'two for the price of one' offers and other similar promotions?

In short, an outright ban would be very difficult to apply and might smack of re-regulating an industry which is supposed to be in the course of deregulation. It is not really a practical proposition, certainly not at the present time.

Government controls?

If it is not possible to prohibit loyalty schemes, is it possible to replace them in some way to remove, or at least reduce, their anticompetitive effects? As mentioned previously in relation to TACOs, some control over reward structures might do something to lessen the dominance of individual airlines of alliance groupings, but such controls would also amount to a fair degree of re-regulation, and as such may be considered unacceptable, not just by the airlines, but by the travelling public as well. The whole thing could easily become a regulatory mess. The successful application of 'codes of conduct' in the use of computer reservation systems (which are discussed in section 3.5) demonstrates that some government intervention can still be useful in an otherwise deregulated industry, but controlling things like FFPs and corporate discounts could turn out to be an administrative nightmare. Levine (1987) concluded that government control over loyalty schemes are likely to succeed only in creating other problems and would entangle regulatory authorities in a morass of complex marketing decisions about which they have little specialized knowledge and expertise.

Taxing rewards?

There is an argument that rewards from airline loyalty schemes, especially where they are received by passengers not paying their own fares, should be taxed as non-pecuniary income, a taxable benefit of employment in much the same way as the use of company cars often is. A number of governments have been considering this. It has at various times been seriously considered by the Internal Revenue Service in the United States. But once again, there would be particular difficulties in implementation. The tax authorities would have to find some way of distinguishing between awards from personal travel (not to be taxed, since passengers pay their own fares) and those earned from business travel (when employers meet the cost of the tickets). Also, as Humphreys (1991) has pointed out, accruing FFP points is not the same as using them, and so there would be some tricky administrative problems in measuring the taxable benefit. What exactly would the value of the benefit be, when numerous restrictions apply to when and how awards can be redeemed; when the monetary evaluation of a free flight will vary according to the destination chosen and the fares structure applying at the time; and when redemption is subject to capacity controls, so that there will be a question of whether the valuation should be in relation to the fare the passenger would have had to pay to get the same seat on the flight, or the actual cost to the airline of carrying this additional passenger on a space-available basis (which would be much less)?

The idea of taxing rewards might be supported on equity grounds and is a response to the principal–agent problem, but it would require some intricate solution to some ticklish administrative problems, in income tax systems which are already over-burdened with complexities. On top of everything else, the fact that awards accrue to passengers from many different countries (see, for example, Figure 5.4 in Chapter 5) is bound to generate a lot of anomalies and possible distortions, unless there is going to be an unprecedented degree of tax harmonization across countries.

Third party access?

To protect competition in markets for premium fare passengers, one policy option that is worthy of serious consideration is that of requiring each loyalty scheme to grant 'third party access'. In essence what this means is giving other airlines the same arrangements that exist online or between alliance partners. This could reduce the tendency for high fare passengers to become captive to particular airlines or to particular alliances, which in turn could reduce the tendency for cross-elasticities to fall.

The US General Accounting Office (1990) supported the idea of requiring mileage points to be transferable from one FFP to another. The view of the UK Civil Aviation Authority (1994) is that, if regulation of some kind proves necessary, it should take the form either of large airlines being required to accept small carriers as participants in their FFPs or of FFP awards being made transferable. The German Cartel Office (the Bundeskartellamt) has on one occasion actually ordered third party access when, in 1997, it required Lufthansa to grant it to one of its small competitors, Eurowings. This followed a complaint from Eurowings that Lufthansa's Miles and More FFP violated the strict German competition laws by giving Lufthansa an 'unfair' advantage on German domestic routes, encouraging business travellers to choose Lufthansa rather than Eurowings simply on account of FFP bonuses rather than on the basis of price or service. When Lufthansa agreed to open its FFP to Eurowings, under 'fair and reasonable conditions', the Cartel Office stopped its proceedings. The European Commission has also used the third-party access condition as a kind of *quid pro quo* for approving airline mergers and acquisitions. It did so when approving Air France's equity stake in Sabena (a stake which has since been relinquished) and when approving British Airways' investment in TAT European (Commission of the European Commission, 1992a and 1992b).

There are, however, a certain number of problems with third party access. One of them is that the honouring of points earned on other carriers' services could seriously disadvantage airlines whose networks include many routes to desirable holiday destinations, routes on which many passengers might seek to redeem rewards in other carriers' schemes. This might be overcome by a suitable adjustment in inter-airline revenue prorating but a rather heavy burden of transactions cost is likely to be incurred. When one airline sells tickets on which FFP mileage points are earned and these points are then redeemed on the services of another carrier, a fairly complex form of inter-airline account-ing has to be employed to arrive at an appropriate division of the relevant costs and revenues. There could often be great imbalances between sales and redemptions, from one airline to another. Government regulation to ensure that third party access is in fact granted could also prove costly in administrative terms.

Secondary trading?

Loyalty schemes are by no means a new idea. They have been marketed by many firms in many industries for many years. One of the best known schemes in the United Kingdom used to be the Green Shield trading stamps scheme, which was at its peak during the 1970s. Under this scheme customers collected stamps at a whole host of retail outlets, like grocery stores and petrol stations, and redeemed them for catalogued goods distributed through a separate chain of shops run by the Green Shield Company. The stamps were a kind of common currency bonus which could be earned in a great many different places. But collecting and redeeming them meant some fairly heavy transactions cost to the customer; and since they were not bespoke to particular companies, they did little to reduce cross-price elasticities demand for the products of individual firms. The Green Shield stamps scheme did not make customers 'captive' to particular businesses and consequently it did little to suppress price competition. It eventually died out because firms sought increased market shares by offering price reductions instead.

Airline loyalty schemes might also in the long term die out, if they too led to rewards of a common currency kind, i.e. if the rewards could be redeemed on any carrier and were not bespoke to particular airlines or particular airline alliances. This could be achieved if passengers were able to buy and sell loyalty scheme rewards as traded goods, i.e. if a secondary trading market could be set up in which passengers were able to exchange rewards earned with one airline or alliance for those of another.

The idea seems more relevant to FFPs than to either corporate discounts or TACOs. A secondary market in FFP mileage point appears increasingly possible with increased use of the Internet. At present FFP mileage points can have different marginal values to different passengers, depending on their proximity to points thresholds that have to be reached to qualify for rewards. To passengers only a few points away from a threshold the marginal value of some extra points can be much greater than it is to passengers needing many more points to reach this threshold. Also, where the rewards structure is non-linear, passengers who have built up a large number of points in a particular FFP can benefit more from a few extra points than passengers whose points tally is much lower. So, because the marginal value of additional points can vary a lot between passengers, there is plenty of scope for profitable exchange, especially where some passengers are members of two or more FFPs and are closer to rewards thresholds in some FFPs than they are in others.

Consider a simple example. Suppose a passenger is a member of two FFPs, one marketed by Airline X, the other by Airline Y. To qualify for, say, a free holiday, the passenger needs 40 000 mileage points in the Airline X FFP or 30 000 points in the FFP of Airline Y. So far the passenger has collected 10 000 points in the Airline X FFP but 28 000 points in the Airline Y FFP. At the same time a second passenger, who is seeking an upgrade from economy to business class, for which the threshold is 8000 points on Airline X and 6000 points on Airline Y, has accumulated 5000 points in the Airline X FFP and 2000 points in the Airline Y FFP. If the two passengers could trade with each other and exchange 3000 points in X for 2000 in Y, both could achieve their rewards without having to notch up further points on either FFP.

If it were possible to trade FFP mileage points in this way, passengers would feel more encouragement to collect points across a number of different FFPs rather than skew their travel decisions in favour of one airline merely because they are closer to a rewards threshold with that airline. They would make their choice of airline more on the basis of relative price and service qualities, and cross-elasticities of demand with respect to these factors would correspondingly increase.

It is true, as mentioned above, that quite a number of frequent flyers have multiple FFP memberships; but often this is more because they have to use the services of different airlines on account of the restrictions on traffic rights (which are discussed in Chapter 4) rather than due to passengers preferring to earn rewards in a number of different FFPs. One of the objectives in alliance formation is to overcome these restrictions on traffic rights; and the purpose of alliance members extending reciprocal FFP membership to each others' passengers is to promote loyalty to the alliance as a whole. Passengers are thus given a rewards incentive to concentrate their flying on carriers within a particular alliance and the more global the networks of the alliances become, the less need there will be for passengers to use non-alliance carriers. Hence cross-elasticities of demand, for the services of one alliance relative to the service of non-alliance carriers in general, could fall quite sharply. But if secondary trading in FFP rewards were to be permitted, with passengers able to exchange points earned on alliance FFPs for points earned on FFPs outside the alliance, the incentive for passengers to concentrate bookings within the alliance, purely because of FFP rewards, could be much reduced.

Some trade in FFP rewards has in fact taken place, especially in the United States, where independent agents have provided a brokering service. Sometimes passengers have exchanged FFP rewards for cash. But it was all on a fairly small scale and airlines successfully took action against it through the courts (Braden, 1990). The airlines' case was that tickets are not transferable from one person to another and that this also applies to the FFP rewards earned by purchasing them. It was submitted that non-transferability is a condition of sale, and that airlines have the right in law to prevent secondary trading in both tickets and FFP rewards. Although courts might accept this as a correct legal interpretation, is there not a case for amending laws here? There may be good operational and safety reasons for making tickets non-transferable, but it is difficult to see any compelling reasons why non-transferability should be extended to FFP rewards, and it is interesting that some airlines are beginning to relax restrictions on the transfer of FFP rewards. Witness the promotion currently being marketed by Air France under which members of its Frequence Plus FFP can nominate any person of their choosing to receive the 'Rewards' tickets earned within the FFP. There are of course certain qualifications to this offer, but it does at least demonstrate that it is not impossible for airlines to permit transferability in the matter of FFP rewards.

Although the airlines are likely to oppose its general introduction, secondary trading of FFP rewards is not only possible but also highly desirable on competition grounds. If it catches on in a big way, it might even mean the phasing out of FFPs altogether. However, it is less easy to see how secondary trading could apply in the case of corporate discount schemes. The same principle might apply, but the practical problems of arranging a market between firms might be huge. And it is likely that, if secondary trading causes FFPs to lose much of their function in blunting cross-elasticities of demand, airlines will increasingly turn to corporate discounts to achieve much the same effect.

3.5 Computer reservations systems

If government authorities have so far left matters like FFPs, corporate discounts and TACOs largely unregulated, this is not the case with computer reservations systems (CRSs). When first developed in the 1960s and 1970s, CRSs were seen simply as devices for saving time and labour in handling large and growing amounts of flight reservations data. Airlines that invested in CRSs made their system publicly available and in the regulated era, when route entry and fares were tightly controlled, these airlines did not see any particular market power advantages from CRSs. All that changed with deregulation. In deregulated markets passengers have very many more options for their journeys, in terms of carrier, fares, routeing, etc. and they can no longer rely upon any one individual airline to provide them with a list of the available alternatives. For that they have to go to travel agents, the vast majority of whom are linked into one or other of the powerful CRSs owned or hosted by major carriers. By using CRSs agents can focus swiftly upon the multiplicity of flights, fares and seat availabilities on any given route.

It is well known that around 80 per cent of all flight bookings are made through CRSs operated with the aid of visual display units (VDUs) located in travel agents' shops. Of these about three-quarters are made from the first screen page to appear on the VDU and about half from the first line of the first page. Access to the first screen page, and if possible to the top line, has become an extremely important factor in airline competition. So how does an airline get its flights listed near the top of the first screen display? It does of course help if what the airline is offering is fairly close to what the passenger wants to buy. But airlines owning or controlling CRSs soon realized it was possible to programme the computer so as to bias the selection of flights in favour of those they operate themselves. There was certainly a lot of this taking place in the 1980s, some clear examples being identified by Lyle (1988) and by the House of Commons Transport Committee (1988). A competitor's flights often appeared on a later screen page than the flights of the CRS owner, even when the competitor's flights were more convenient and less expensive. There were also fears that CRS owners would be able to charge some very high prices for services provided to other airlines. These concerns led to calls for airlines to be divested of CRS ownership. But governments preferred to regulate them instead. Codes of Conduct have been introduced by the US government, the European Commission and the European Civil Aviation Conference. These codes explicitly forbid display bias and require charges to be reasonable and non-discriminatory. It is fair to say that regulatory intervention has removed most of the initial concerns, but it is difficult to eliminate bias and discrimination altogether, given that airlines owning or controlling CRSs are adept at finding loopholes in any set of rules. One development that presents a challenge to the Codes of Conduct is the growth in codesharing, something discussed in the following chapter (section 4.6). It is possible that one explanation for the recent proliferation of codesharing is that airlines are seeking display advantages by cluttering CRS screens with repetitive displays of the same service, pushing other airlines' services further down the screen page or onto the next page, a practice referred to as 'screen padding'. This practice is allowed under the US Codes of Conduct, but is restricted under the EC Code to two combinations of codesharing flights.

There has also been some concern about the possibility of the CRS industry becoming more and more oligopolistic or even monopolistic. In the operation of CRSs there are some very high fixed costs, but marginal cost is close to zero. Hence there are some enormous economies of scale, with average cost declining continuously as the number of bookings dealt with increases. There may be no natural monopoly in airline operations, but it is possible there is one in CRS operations. There is no technical reason why global demand for CRS services cannot be met by one single mega-system.

There had been fears that CRS markets would be dominated by the two largest systems in the United States, namely American Airlines' Sabre and United Airlines' Apollo/Covia, conferring on the two 'host' airlines some enormous market power. To meet the threat this posed, airlines in other regions of the world grouped together to establish their own large systems, such as Galileo and Amadeus in Europe and Axess and Abacus in the Far East. Within the United States two major CRSs, Delta's Datas system and the Pars system controlled by TWA and Northwest, merged to form Worldspan. So now instead of just two, there are four 'super' CRSs – Galileo International, Sabre, Amadeus and Worldspan – which together account for 80 per cent of CRS locations and 85 per cent of CRS terminals (Table 3.3). Market shares vary by region (Table 3.4). In the United States the largest share is taken by Sabre, especially in terms of terminals (this reflecting the fact that Sabre is used a lot by large travel agents who tend to have more than one terminal in their shops). In Europe Amadeus has approximately half the market, in terms of both locations and terminals, followed by Galileo International with about a third. But regional data tends to conceal the degree to which CRS markets are concentrated in individual countries. Market shares within European countries are given in Table 3.5, from which it is clear that CRSs dominate in the countries of the host airlines involved, 'Amadeus' countries being France, Germany, Scandinavia and Spain and 'Galileo' countries being Austria, Ireland, Italy, the Netherlands, Portugal, Switzerland and the United Kingdom.

Sabre and Worldspan have significant market shares in some European countries, but the Amadeus/Galileo shares are often greater than 80 or 90 per cent. In 1990–91 negotiations took place between Amadeus and Sabre about the possibility of forming a marketing alliance, with Sabre taking an equity stake in Amadeus. Nothing

Table 3.3 Computer reservations systems terminals and locations[a] (September 1993). *Source:* Humphreys (1994)

	Location		Terminals	
	Number	*%*	*Number*	*%*
Galileo International	31 760	29.0	102 864	30.0
Sabre	24 522	22.5	100 269	29.3
Amadeus	19 413	17.8	47 441	13.8
Worldspan	11 792	10.8	40 912	12.0
System One	7 780	7.1	29 786	8.7
Axess	5 840	5.3	10 130	3.0
Abacus	3 000	2.7	8 000	2.3
Infini	2 250	2.1	3 000	0.9
Gets	3 000	2.7	–	–
Total	109 357	100.0	342 402	100.0

– Not available.

[a] Figures relate to travel agencies and exclude airlines offices and airports.

Table 3.4 Market shares of major CRSs[a] (%, September 1993). *Source:* Humphreys (1994)

		US	*Latin America*	*Europe*	*Far East*
Galileo International	Locations	32.1	7.6	29.8	17.7
	Terminals	27.2	8.9	33.5	21.3
Sabre	Locations	32.9	19.0	10.9	18.7
	Terminals	38.8	20.3	11.3	26.0
Amadeus	Locations	–	53.9	51.8	–
	Terminals	–	42.9	49.6	–
Worldspan	Locations	19.5	–	7.4	–
	Terminals	19.1	–	5.5	–
System One	Locations	15.4	19.5	–	0.4
	Terminals	14.9	27.9	–	0.5
Axess	Locations	–	–	–	33.3
	Terminals	–	–	–	25.0
Abacus	Locations	–	–	–	17.1
	Terminals	–	–	–	19.8
Infini	Locations	–	–	–	12.8
	Terminals	–	–	–	7.4

[a] Excludes Gets (which is particularly strong in Latin America).

Table 3.5 CRS markets shares in European countries (% of locations, 1993). *Source:* Humphreys (1994)

	Amadeus	Galileo	Sabre	Worldspan
Austria	34.8	60.4	3.1	1.6
Belgium	21.1	30.1	16.0	32.8
Denmark	54.2	14.1	6.9	24.8
Finland	98.1	–	1.7	0.2
France	81.7	4.1	10.1	4.1
Germany	91.6	1.4	4.7	2.3
Greece	–	39.9	34.9	25.2
Hungary	–	97.6	2.4	–
Ireland	–	84.6	6.0	9.4
Italy	–	76.9	17.8	5.3
Luxembourg	57.1	–	42.9	–
Netherlands	–	61.6	10.3	26.8
Norway	74.5	11.2	7.7	6.6
Portugal	6.0	65.5	0.2	28.3
Spain	88.7	5.2	2.6	3.5
Switzerland	–	87.7	9.9	2.4
Sweden	77.0	–	13.0	10.0
UK	0.2	65.6	20.0	14.2

– Less than 0.1%.

ultimately came of this deal but the structure of the CRS industry is still evolving and it is possible that it will end up much more oligopolistic than the airline industry itself.

Increased concentration among the super CRSs and the close marketing and technical links that exist between them and the other CRSs (Figure 3.7) raise questions about market power and the possible need to strengthen regulation to preserve competition. But another development could assuage some of the worst fears in this direction. With the exception of American Airlines' Sabre system, all CRSs are now jointly owned. And in one case, that of System One, there is a substantial non-airline investor in the shape of Electronic Data Services, a subsidiary of General Motors, which holds a 50 per cent stake. Multiple ownership is encouraging the emergence of independent 'no host' systems that give no preferential treatment to any particular one of the owners. Worldspan, Amadeus and Galileo have adopted the no-host technology, and other CRSs are following suit. Also, some new systems are designed to meet the needs of smaller airlines seeking access to a cheaper and less sophisticated system, the principal example being Gets, which is run by Societe Internationale des Telecommunications Aeronautiques. For these

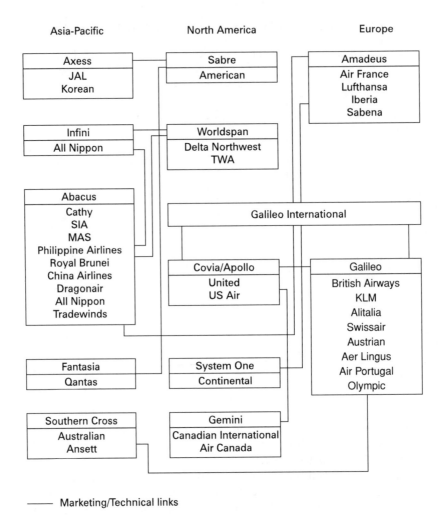

— Marketing/Technical links

Figure 3.7 Ownership and interrelationships of computer reservations systems, 1992 (*Source:* International Air Transport Association)

reasons CRSs are becoming increasingly independent of their airline owners, operating more and more as businesses in their own right.

In which case, does that mean government regulation is now less necessary? Joint airline (and non-airline) ownership may reduce the chances of CRSs being biased in favour of one particular airline, but the dominance of CRS companies in particular countries or markets gives them considerable market power which they may use to charge high prices and earn high profits. When Sabre and Apollo dominated CRS activity in the US domestic market, they were extremely profitable. According to the US Department of Transportation (1988) these two systems earned for their airline owners some very high rates of return on investment: in 1985 and 1986 Apollo earned something over 100 per cent. The very large profits once earned by Sabre and Apollo have fallen with the increase in competition within the US domestic market, but there is always the possibility of an increase in concentration in the global market with the growth of Amadeus and Galileo International, each with strong positions in individual countries, and there is still some concern about the fees charged for CRS participation, especially among the smaller airlines.

In 1994 the European Commission received a formal complaint from a group of five UK airlines (British Midland, Loganair, Jersey European, Manx and Air UK) about the pricing policies followed by Galileo International in Europe. The five UK airlines complained that Galileo was using its dominant position to increase its fees and that their distribution costs were rising by some 30 per cent a year. The carriers wanted their complaint against Galileo to be treated as a test case, promising further complaints against Amadeus, Sabre and Worldspan as well (Humphreys, 1994). CRS fees are charged on a per booking basis irrespective of the fare paid. As such they are bound to have a relatively greater impact on airlines with high proportions of low-fare passengers (i.e. those operating short haul routes and those with relatively high percentages of excursion passengers travelling on discounted fares). One argument put forward is that they should vary by the value of the journey booked, if they are not to prove discriminatory against some small airlines. But CRS costs do not vary with the value of the booking, the costs involved in processing a first class fare from London to Tokyo being much the same as those in processing an economy fare from London to Amsterdam. To avoid their fees impacting relatively more heavily on low-fare airlines CRS companies would have to discriminate positively in their favour.

Some low-fare airlines are seeking to escape high distribution cost by withdrawing from CRSs and introducing ticketless travel. One is easyJet. Its booking system is similar to those used by hotels and car hire firms. A passenger making a booking is given a confirmation number, all that is needed for baggage handling and flight check-in which takes place at the gate. There is no seat allocation process, passengers being given re-usable boarding passes numbered in sequence and boarding the aircraft in order of arrival at check-in. Not only has this substantially reduced queues at check-in and speeded up boarding, it has also eliminated any of the costs of handling tickets. It has been estimated that the cost of producing a single ticket (including labour, printing and travel agency commissions) come to between $15 and $30 (Nuutinen, 1994). Ticketless travel is now possible because of automation and the widespread use of credit cards. Some major carriers are now considering doing something similar, because distribution costs have been increasing as a proportion of total operating costs. Complete ticketless travel may not be so appropriate for the major airlines, which are more likely to adopt some form of electronic ticketing using smart cards and self-service vending machines. But one way or another 'paperless' travel is likely to be an important development in the years to come.

Another aspect of CRSs with important implications for airline competition is the huge volume of marketing data they generate. Such information can be very useful for estimating price elasticities of demand and for managing revenue yields (discussed in Chapter 6, section 6.3). The US and European Codes of Conduct both require CRSs to release the same marketing data to all participating carriers without discrimination. But to make full use of this data, airlines need to invest substantial sums in computer facilities themselves. British Airways, for example, has in recent years spent annual amounts of around £150 million on computers and the associated information technology for this purpose (Humphreys, 1994). But expenditure on that scale is often beyond the resources of many smaller carriers who are thus at something of a disadvantage in this respect.

3.6 Increasing concentration

It is widely expected that the global airline industry is going to become more and more highly concentrated. Forecasts vary of just how many airlines will survive and of how far the industry will be dominated by some very large carriers. One forecast produced by the Boeing Airplane Company is given in Figure 3.8. Boeing predicts that by the year 2010 the top 20 airlines in the world will account for around two-thirds of world air traffic (measured in terms of passenger-kilometres), their share having risen from about 50 per cent in 1982.

Increasing concentration raises the question of what will happen to inter-airline competition. Will it become more or less intense? Before addressing this issue it may be helpful to consider some theoretical points.

On one view high levels of concentration in any particular industry facilitate collusion and lead to higher prices for consumers and higher profits for firms. An opposing view is that a direct relationship between concentration and profits is more likely to reflect more efficient firms gaining market share and thereby becoming more profitable. Much depends on the relationship between concentration and prices. Even

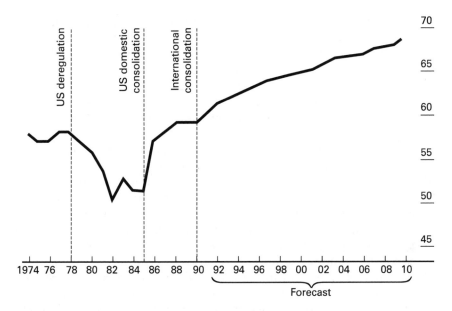

Figure 3.8 Top 20 airlines' share of world passenger-kilometres, 1974-2010 (*Source:* Boeing)

where increasing concentration is simply the result of efficient firms becoming more dominant, once they achieve this greater dominance they will enjoy a greater degree of monopoly market power, which they may then use to raise prices. Hence there may be a trade-off to consider, if increasing concentration leads both to greater efficiency and to some enhancement in the monopoly market power exercised by dominant firms.

In a frequently cited paper the economist Oliver Williamson (1968) analysed this trade-off and showed how the balance between market power and efficiency effects depends crucially on the price elasticity of demand for the good or service in question. Without entering too deeply into the technicalities of microeconomic theory, it is possible to summarize Williamson's arguments as follows. In theory the degree of monopoly market power exercised by a firm is shown by its price–cost margin, which is represented by the ratio:

$$\frac{\text{price} - \text{marginal cost}}{\text{price}}$$

A ratio of zero would apply to firms with no monopoly power at all; that is, to firms operating under conditions described in microeconomic theory as perfect competition, where all firms have to accept that they can charge no more than marginal cost. Under imperfect competition, firms do have some measure of monopoly market power, and the closer the ratio is to one, the greater that power is. The effect of a price–cost margin greater than zero is to reduce the profit-maximizing equilibrium output below the level it would be set under perfect competition. When output falls there is a loss of consumer benefits and the magnitude of this loss depends upon the elasticity of demand; the more elastic the demand, the greater the loss of benefits. But the overall effect of an increase in market power depends on how the event that gives rise to it (e.g. a merger or an alliance) affects the level of marginal cost. If the marginal cost level falls (e.g. as a result of economies of scale/scope) then it is possible for cost savings to the firm to outweigh the loss of benefits to consumers and the net overall outcome could be positive. Whether or not the outcome is positive depends on the size of the cost reduction relative to the magnitude of the demand elasticity. In this respect it is important to note that a much smaller proportionate reduction in cost is required to offset a given loss in consumer benefits, since the cost reduction applies to the whole of the firm's output whereas the loss in benefits only relates to the restriction from the competitive output level. Williamson demonstrated this by performing a number of simulations, at varying demand elasticities, to show the percentage cost reductions sufficient to offset given price–cost margins. For example, he found that, at a demand elasticity of –1, a 10 per cent margin would be offset by a cost reduction of only 0.5 per pent; and that, at an elasticity of –2, a cost reduction of just 4 per cent would be sufficient to offset a margin of as much as 20 per cent. The conclusion from this is that, if there are any non-trivial savings in costs, the margins from monopoly market power have to be rather substantial for the net overall effect to be negative.

The Williamson trade-off is illustrated in Figure 3.9 in terms of the standard price–output diagram used in microeconomics. Under perfect competition the price–cost margin is zero with price, P_1, set at marginal cost, at which price the output level is Q_1. If as a result of concentration the firm gains market power, it can set a price, P_2, above marginal cost, which will have the effect of restricting output to Q_2. The losses from market power are then the reduction in consumer benefits, area P_2ABP_1 less the increase in profits to the firm, area P_2ACP_1, or the triangle ABC. If at the same time increased concentration leads to increased efficiency, this will have the effect of lowering marginal cost (which is assumed in the diagram to be constant with respect to output level, so that it is equal to average cost and can be represented as a horizontal straight line). If the reduction is from marginal cost 1 to marginal cost 2 the total saving in cost is the fall in cost per unit times the number of units, which is represented by the rectangle P_1CEF. Whether area P_1CEF is greater or less than area ABC depends crucially on the slope of the demand curve,

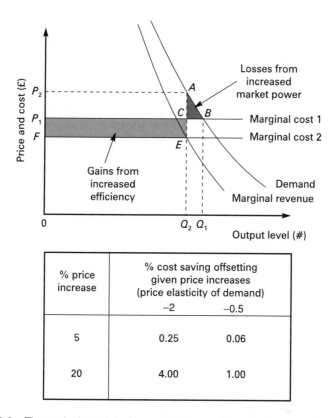

Figure 3.9 Theoretical model of potential trade-offs with increased concentration)

% price increase	% cost saving offsetting given price increases (price elasticity of demand)	
	−2	−0.5
5	0.25	0.06
20	4.00	1.00

which in turn determines how large the restriction of output, Q_1-Q_2 is in relation to the original output level Q_1. Other things being equal, the steeper the demand curve, the smaller the output restriction and the more likely it is that the efficiency gains (area P_1CEF) will outweigh the losses from market power (area ABC).

The above analysis is subject to a number of important qualifications. First of all, no allowances are made for the relative timing of the market power and efficiency effects; and it can be quite important to consider the shapes of their respective time streams. For instance, the stream of consumer losses may start immediately once the firm gains an increase in market power, whereas the reduction in cost may take some years before it is fully achieved. In this case the relevant comparisons would be in terms of equivalent present values, with future effects on costs and benefits discounted at an appropriate rate of interest. The comparison may also require some adjustment where the cost saving accrues to just one firm, but where the market power effects carry over to other firms in the industry. Other firms may take advantage of the opportunity afforded by increased concentration to increase their prices as well, under a kind of 'umbrella' effect. When this occurs, there may be a whole series of losses from raised prices to be set against a saving to just one firm, and so some kind of weighting factor may have to be introduced to reflect this. There may also be questions about distributional equity. It may, for instance, be argued that losses in benefits to consumers should be weighted more heavily than cost reductions for the firm. In this case £x of consumer losses would no longer be regarded as being compensated for by £x of additional profits (i.e. the rectangle P_2ACP_1 in Figure 3.9 would no longer be regarded as a neutral 'transfer payment' in this respect). In other words in one of Williamson's simulations referred to above, if one were to weigh consumer losses at, say, twice the rate of the gains in profits, a 20 per cent rise in price at an elasticity of –2 would require a compensating cost saving, not of 4 per cent, but of 12 per cent.

All this is on the premise that the firm's cost level does actually fall when its market power increases. If instead it rises, then there would of course be no trade-off to consider at all, and the increase in cost should be added to the consumer losses in measuring the net outcome overall. The question of what happens to the cost level is crucial. So if increased concentration leads to greater market power, what does it do to the cost level?

So far as the airline industry is concerned there are grounds for believing that increased concentration does indeed lead to lower cost levels, not through economies of scale but through economies of scope. In particular, in creating larger networks, increased concentration can result in greater market power on some routes, but at the same time can generate some significant economies. This can be illustrated in terms of the close relationship that exists between market concentration and the development of hub and spokes route networks. The development of hubbing is discussed in detail in Chapters 4 and 5 and only a brief discussion of the possible trade-offs is presented here.

The market power effects of hubs derive from the fact that for passengers with origins and destinations in hub cities there is often little choice but to travel on the airline based at the hub. Hub airlines are often very dominant in their hub cities partly because airport capacity constraints (especially at peak periods) seriously inhibit competition from new entrants. There is no doubt that they enjoy considerable market power and it has been very clearly demonstrated that they have been using this power to charge higher fares on routes to/from hubs compared to routes of similar distance elsewhere. A number of econometric studies found significant positive correlations between higher fares and the degree of concentration. Some of the market power hub airlines enjoy comes from having a larger presence in a given city, something that enhances the customer loyalty effects of their FFP and TACO strategies.

But hubbing can also lead to some significant reductions in costs. In funnelling traffic onto a smaller number of routes, hubbing has the effect of increasing route traffic density. It is well known that marginal cost declines with increases in route traffic density, as a number of empirical studies has shown (Caves, Christensen and Tretheway, 1984). Hence there can be some cost savings to set against the losses from higher fares to/from hubs. However there is a further trade-off to consider. As explained in Chapter 5, the increased concentration on routes to/from hubs may be accompanied by reduced concentration in through markets served via the hubs. It is sometimes the case that when competition *at* hubs falls, that *between* hubs rises. And the significance of Williamson's analysis here is that often the price elasticity of demand is higher for travel in through markets than in point-to-point markets to/from hubs (see section 5.7).

All these points tend to be concealed when comparisons are made of changes in aggregate industry concentration, such as for example in the graph in Figure 3.8, which shows the share of total industry output accounted for by the top 20 airlines. A rise in aggregate concentration does not necessarily imply a fall in the intensity of competition. In Chapter 2 it is noted that there are some 1200 scheduled airlines in the world, but because of restrictions on route entry, not many of these are in direct competition with each other. With route entry being liberalized, it is certainly possible for the total number of airlines to fall, for aggregate concentration to rise, and for competition intensities to increase, all at one and the same time.

Of more relevance than aggregate industry concentration is concentration in particular city pair markets. Market concentration can be measured in a number of different ways. Two principal measures are the n-firm concentration ratio (CR_n) and the Hirschman–Herfindahl Index (HHI). These are illustrated in Figure 3.10. The CR_n is calculated as the sum of the market shares of the n largest firms, where n is chosen fairly arbitrarily. For example, in the diagram:

$CR_3 = 90\%$ in market A
$CR_4 = 60\%$ in market B
$CR_5 = 70\%$ in market C

Reading off the vertical axis on which market shares are cumulated. The CR_n is a popular measure because of its limited data requirements, all it needs being the total market sales and sales made by the n largest firms. The drawbacks are that it only considers the largest firms and takes no account of disparities in firm sizes. The greater the number of firms and

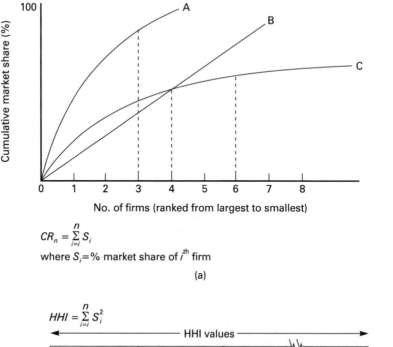

$$CR_n = \sum_{i=i}^{n} S_i$$

where $S_i = \%$ market share of ith firm

(a)

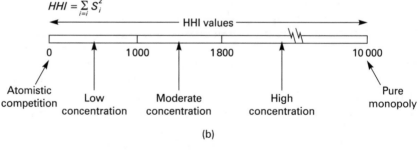

$$HHI = \sum_{i=i}^{n} S_i^2$$

(b)

Figure 3.10   Two measures of market concentration. (a) Concentration ratio (CR); (b) Hirschman–Herfindahl Index (HHI))

the more uniform they are in size, the greater the degree of competition likely to be present. A measure of market concentration should ideally capture both these elements, the total number of firms *and* their size distribution. These are the advantages of the HHI measure, which is calculated as the sum of the squared market shares of all firms in the industry. The process of squaring gives greater weight to the larger firms, and the more unequal the size distribution of firms, the higher the value of the HHI. The HHI is zero when there is a very large number of equal-sized firms and it reaches its maximum value of 10 000 (or 100^2) under pure monopoly. Because it more appropriately reflects the intensity of competition, the US Department of Justice (DoJ) bases its antitrust policy on the HHI measure, which it uses as a screening criterion in deciding whether or not to challenge a proposed merger. If a merger would leave the relevant market with a HHI of less than 1000 (regarded as 'low' concentration) the Department of Justice will not challenge it; but where the post-merger market would have an HHI of more than 1800 ('high' concentration) all significant mergers will be challenged. In the 'grey' area in between, where 1000 < HHI < 1800, the DoJ challenges mergers that have the effect of increasing the HHI by 100 or more.

The HHI has also been used in studies charting changes in concentration over time and changes following deregulation or liberalization. When used for this purpose it is important that the 'market' to which the HHI relates is properly defined. In air transport a market is made up of all passengers who want to travel from a specific origin to a specific destination, and of all airlines that provide service from that origin to that destination. In this respect there is an important distinction between a city pair market and a route: a route is the physical path an aircraft takes between take-off at one airport and landing at another; whereas a market is the pairing of the airports at which the passenger's journey originates and terminates. In hub and spokes networks many passengers travel on several different routes but participate in only one market. The most relevant basis on which to measure concentration is the origin–destination (O–D) city pair market rather than the individual route.

Earlier in this chapter it was observed that US deregulation had the effect of causing aggregate industry concentration to fall and then subsequently to rise again. The same pattern has been seen in econometric studies examining concentration on individual routes. But what happened to concentration in O–D city pair markets? This was examined in a study by Belobaba and Van Acker (1994) who calculated average HHI values for the top 100 O–D city pairs in the US domestic industry from 1979 to 1991 (Figure 3.11). What they found was that the average HHI fell from a level of 4920 in 1979 to 3360 in 1985 and subsequently increased again to 4020 by 1991, repeating the experience of aggregate industry and route concentration. But the 1991 level was 900 (or 18 per cent) below the 1979 level, indicating that concentration in O–D markets is still significantly less. About 70 per cent of the top 100 markets experienced an overall decrease in concentration between 1979 and 1991. Although the HHI values appear high in relation to the US DoJ merger guidelines, it should be noted that the sample of city pairs to which the averages relate is not representative of the industry as a whole. The Belobaba and Van Acker study also found that concentration is higher in those O–D markets where at least one of the endpoints served as an airline hub. It also provided some evidence that concentration is higher in the large O–D markets and that the gap between these and the smaller

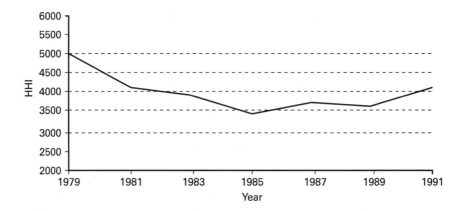

Figure 3.11   Values of Hirschman–Herfindahl Index for top 100 US domestic city pair markets, 1979-91 (*Source:* Belobaba and Van Acker, 1994)

markets appears to be widening over time. Had it been possible for Belobaba and Van Acker to consider other markets outside the top 100, it is likely that they would have found concentration in markets linking non-hub cities to be falling more.

What is emerging is that competition in through markets is becoming fiercer over time, a point that has relevance not just to hubbing but also to the questions raised by mergers and alliances, which are considered in Chapter 7. Depending on the relative magnitudes of price-cost margins and price elasticities of demand, the effects of increased competition for through traffic could offset, or more than offset, the effects of any reduction in competition on point-to-point routes. This is very largely an empirical question and is something that can vary quite a lot from one market situation to another.

4 Route networks

Most route patterns have an affinity to one or other of three basic types: line, grid or hub and spokes. These are illustrated in Figure 4.1.

In a line network the aircraft sets out from its base airport and makes a number of intermediate stops en route through to its ultimate destination. The intermediate stops are made either to refuel or to pick up traffic. Without stops some long haul services would not be operationally or economically viable. As aircraft range increases, or as the volume of long haul traffic grows, the need for intermediate stops becomes that much less. Although there are still plenty of airlines around the world that operate route systems like this, the emphasis has shifted very much away from line networks. For they have disadvantages on both the cost and revenue sides. Costs tend to be high, because station expenses are spread over just a few flights using each airport, maybe just one or two a week. This also means that local marketing is difficult and rather expensive in terms of average cost. At the same time cockpit cabin crews often have to have long stopovers or alternatively have to be ferried to their next flights; and in some cases long haul aircraft can be very inefficiently employed on relatively short sectors operated at low load factors at tail ends of the route. On the revenue side yields are often poor, because the low frequencies at which services on line routes tend

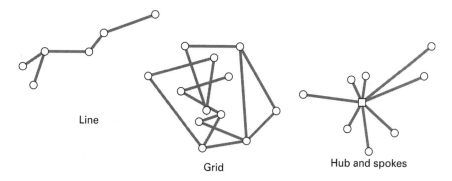

Figure 4.1 Network patterns

to be operated do not appeal to business travellers paying the higher fares. Nor do the journey times on such multisector routes. The Scandinavian airline SAS used to serve no less than four intermediate stops (Lisbon, Rio de Janeiro, Sao Paulo and Montevideo) on its service between Copenhagen and Buenos Aires; and the Brazilian carrier Varig currently makes three intermediate stops (Sao Paulo, Johannesburg and Bangkok) on its service between Rio de Janeiro and Hong Kong.

Grid networks have often been a characteristic of domestic air transport. A prime example used to be the United States where, before deregulation, many airlines operated grid networks, especially on the eastern seaboard (e.g. the former Eastern Airlines). A current example is India, where the domestic airline's network is very much in the pattern of a grid, based as it is on the 'diamond rectangle' of Bombay/Delhi/Calcutta/Madras. The main advantage of grid networks is that they make it easier to achieve high rates of utilization, of both aircraft and crews. Flights can be scheduled to operate on a number of different routes without backtracking, which helps to minimize the time for which aircraft are idle on the ground and which also means that crew stopovers and slippage can be minimized. Traffic-flows through stations are higher than they are in line networks, but the sales effort is still rather dispersed, a disadvantage that becomes that much more serious in deregulated or liberalized air travel markets.

An important advantage in hub and spokes networks, in which routes radiate from a central hub airport to a number of outlying spoke airports, is the effect they have in multiplying by permutation the number of city pairs an airline can serve. When airports are linked via a hub, the number of available city pairs is much greater than when they are linked directly, as shown in Figure 4.2. If for example five direct services, each linking a single city pair are replaced by connecting services from the same group of cities via a hub, there is an elevenfold increase in the

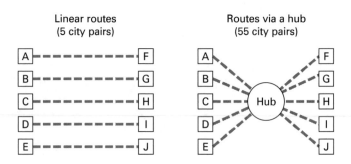

Figure 4.2   Leverage of a hub

Table 4.1: Markets in a hub and spokes system

Number of spokes	Maximum number of connecting markets	Number of local markets	Maximum number of city pair markets
n	$n(n-1)/2$	n	$n(n+1)/2$
5	10	5	15
10	45	10	55
25	300	25	325
50	1225	50	1275
100	4950	100	5050

number of linked city pairs from a mere doubling in the number of sectors operated. One additional spoke would raise the number of possible linkages by a further eleven city pairs. Mathematically, if there are n spokes, an airline can provide through connecting services for up to a theoretical maximum of $n(n-1)/2$ city pairs. When these are added to the n city pairs to/from the hub itself, the total possible city pair markets is $n(n+1)/2$; and the way in which total city pairs rise with the number of spokes is illustrated in Table 4.1. In practice, some city pairs may require too great a deviation to attract traffic, and some may not be served because they are already well supplied with direct services. But the leverage of hubs in generating city pair linkages was a prime motive for the thoroughgoing change from line and grid networks in the deregulated US domestic market.

Figure 4.3 illustrates two main kinds of hub, the 'hourglass' hub and the 'hinterland' hub (Doganis and Dennis, 1989). Through an hourglass hub flights operate from one region to points broadly in the opposite direction; and through a hinterland hub, short haul flights feed connecting traffic to the longer trunk routes. An hourglass hub usually only caters for connections in two directions, outbound and return, whereas a hinterland hub serves as a multi-directional distribution centre for air travel to and from its surrounding catchment area. Flights through an hourglass hub are usually operated by the same aircraft, whereas connections through a hinterland hub often require a change of gauge (e.g. from regional aircraft to long range jets). Both kinds of hub have become common in the deregulated US domestic market.

Hub and spokes networks may now be a familiar feature within the United States, but they have in fact been the predominant pattern in international operations for some considerable time, although for different reasons. With each state claiming sovereignty over the services above its territory, international services can be flown only with the consent of

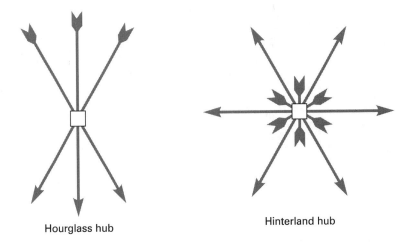

Hourglass hub

Hinterland hub

Figure 4.3   Two kinds of hub

the governments involved. In this matter governments negotiate with each other on a bilateral basis, one state with another; and governments draw up air service agreements specifying the routes that designated airlines from each of the two countries can fly. The way in which this has developed has meant that only airlines registered in the states involved are licensed to enter the routes. As a result national airlines have tended to operate the vast majority of their international routes to and from their home country, in and out of their main hubs, usually located in their capital or largest cities, e.g. London for British Airways, Paris for Air France, Frankfurt for Lufthansa and so on. But these primarily star-shaped networks often did not generate anything like the multiplier effects on city pairs linkages as the hub and spoke networks that developed in the United States following deregulation. This was partly because of the way international services were operated, but mainly due to restrictions in inter-governmental bilateral agreements.

4.2 Freedoms of the air

Air service agreements are negotiated by governments within the framework of the five 'freedoms of the air' defined in the Chicago Convention. Governments negotiate the exchange of overflying rights, the first freedom; rights to land for technical reasons, the second freedom; rights to carry traffic to/from the home state, the third/fourth freedoms; and rights to carry traffic to/from third countries en route, the fifth freedom.

Except where special political or military difficulties apply, mutual exchange of the first and second freedoms usually takes place as a matter of course. But in the exchange of the remaining three freedoms, governments bargain hard with each other.

In negotiating traffic rights all governments are concerned about the market shares secured by their own national carriers. In the past some protectionist governments have insisted upon a minimum share of 50 per cent whereas some more liberal governments have been willing, within limits, to let market shares be determined through airline competition. A traditional view has been that bilateral agreements should result in an 'equitable exchange of economic benefits' (Loy, 1968). But the question of what constitutes an equitable exchange has long been open to a number of interpretations, especially when a large country is negotiating an agreement with a small country. Market shares have been the cause of many disputes, and many bilateral agreements have included restrictions on airline capacity levels, especially in relation to fifth freedom services. The philosophical basis on which traffic rights are exchanged is essentially mercantilist. Governments expect reciprocity. This can be a problem for the government of a small country, with relatively little traffic-generating potential but with big ambitions for its national flag carrier. One way in which such a country might enhance its participation in air travel markets is to trade other benefits in exchange for traffic rights. Another is to engage in the carriage of what has become known as 'sixth freedom' traffic.

The sixth freedom of the air, which was neither recognized nor defined in the Chicago Convention, refers to the carriage of traffic between two foreign states via the state in which the airline is registered. As an example, if British Airways carries a passenger from New York to London, where the passenger transfers to another BA flight on which he travels to Bombay, the airline is engaging in the carriage of sixth freedom traffic. The notion of a sixth freedom is one on which there has been considerable controversy. Some states have considered the sixth freedom to be a special form of the fifth freedom, because neither the origin nor the destination of the traffic concerned is in the state of registration. Accordingly these states have argued that sixth freedom traffic should be subject to the same restrictions that apply to fifth freedom traffic. This has been rejected by other states on the ground that the sixth freedom is implicit in the grant of a pair of third/fourth freedoms. Not surprisingly, the latter view was often taken by countries whose locations present their airlines with good opportunities to carry sixth freedom traffic; and the opposing view has tended to be held by countries which originate or attract large volumes of traffic, but which are not particularly well placed on the world's air routes so far as capturing sixth freedom traffic is concerned.

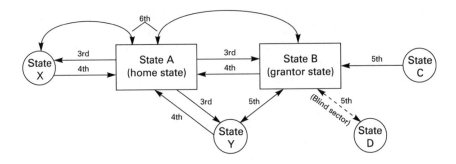

Figure 4.4 Freedoms of the air

The main point at issue is illustrated in Figure 4.4. This shows the traffic rights enjoyed by an airline registered in State A whose government has negotiated the exchange of third and fourth freedoms with both State B and State X, as well as fifth freedom rights between States C and D. By combining the pair of third/fourth freedoms, the airline of State A can carry traffic between States B and X. The question that has often been raised concerning this traffic is whether or not it should be classed as fifth freedom, to be negotiated for and restricted in the same way as fifth freedom rights to/from States C and D.

Negotiations on fifth freedom rights have often been very protracted, not least because there are always at least three countries involved. The fact that fifth freedom rights require the simultaneous agreement of three or more states has often in practice meant that only a small proportion of rights traded bilaterally can in fact be used. It is possible to distinguish – and in some bilateral agreements this distinction is in fact drawn – between three kinds of fifth freedom: intermediate-point, beyond-point and behind-point.

- The intermediate-point is exercised when an airline carries traffic between a grantor state and another foreign country located somewhere between the home and grantor states. In Figure 4.4, the airline of State A has intermediate-point rights between State B and State Y.
- Beyond-point rights are enjoyed when the airline is allowed to carry traffic on routes beyond the grantor state, between State B and States C and D in Figure 4.4.
- Behind-point rights may be held to apply to the carriage of through traffic on routes behind the home state, for example between States A and X.

Whatever their kind, potential grantor states have tended to view fifth freedoms as encroachments upon their 'natural' third/fourth freedoms.

But the economic viability of through services on long haul routes on which traffic is thin often depends on the airline being able to carry traffic to/from foreign countries en route. Hence a compromise often had to be reached. Sometimes the fifth freedom carrier was restricted to carrying no more than a relatively small proportion – of the order of, say, 10–15 per cent – of the total capacity offered by third/fourth freedom carriers. And sometimes the compromise has involved the granting of so-called 'blind sector' rights. A blind sector is one on which the airline has fifth freedom rights only in respect of stopover traffic. That is, the airline of State A has blind sector rights between States B and D, if the only traffic it can pick up in B and set down in D (or, vice versa, pick up in D and set down in B) is traffic which originates in A (or in D) and is making a stopover in B en route.

From time to time there were attempts to use the question of stopovers to resolve disputes over sixth freedom traffic. One idea was to classify X to B via A traffic, or C to A via B traffic, as fifth freedom, if the length of time the passenger spends at the point of transit is less than some specified period (e.g. 12 or 24 hours), and as a combination of third/fourth freedoms if the stopover is longer than this (Hanlon, 1984). But no general agreement has ever been reached on the definition of stopover traffic; and the only restriction that individual countries have ever successfully placed on sixth freedom operations has been to prevent them being advertised as through services under a single flight number. In practice this restriction is often not a meaningful one. Flight numbers can be amended with letter suffixes, passengers can be transported to their final destinations on the same aircraft and, to all practical intents and purposes, advertisement of a through sixth freedom service can be both overt and widespread.

Two further freedoms, also not specified in the Chicago Convention, are the 'seventh' and the 'eighth'. An airline has the seventh when it is permitted to operate stand-alone services entirely outside the territory of its home state, to carry traffic between two foreign states. For many years a US airline had such rights when operating a shuttle service between Tokyo and Seoul. The eighth freedom is where an airline is given the right to carry traffic between two points within the territory of a foreign state. This is more commonly known as 'cabotage', a term that originated in shipping (and derives from the French *caboter*, which means 'to sail around the coast'). In commercial air transport the term applies to traffic on domestic routes, or on routes between the grantor state and its overseas territories or former colonies (for example, UK–Bermuda or UK–Hong Kong). Cabotage rights are usually reserved for national carriers and only very rarely granted to foreign airlines. But there have been some instances of foreign airlines operating on cabotage routes. For example, for many years Air France was granted cabotage rights on internal domestic routes in Morocco; and even the US has on occasion permitted cabotage, such as in 1979 on routes to/from Honolulu (although in this case only when US airlines were affected by a strike and by the temporary grounding of DC-10 aircraft). But these exceptional cases apart, sovereign states have steadfastly refused to trade cabotage rights and have insisted that domestic routes can be operated only by airlines registered in the home state. The result of this is that, for example, Swissair has no rights to domestic traffic between London and Manchester, just as British Airways has no rights to Geneva–Zurich traffic. But some of the restrictions on cabotage are now being lifted, at least at regional level.

One effect of the third package of liberalization measures which came into effect in the European Union in 1973 was to grant access to international routes to all EU airlines. Airlines registered in any member state became eligible for fifth and seventh freedom rights on international routes throughout the Union, except for a number of 'lifeline' routes on which public service obligations were imposed and some thinly trafficked routes on which new services had just been introduced. Cabotage eighth freedom routes were also fully liberalized, but this concession did not come into effect until 1997. Between 1993 and 1997 member states could still refuse cabotage to airlines of other EU states, unless it was 'consecutive' cabotage, with the domestic sector operated as an extension to an international route. A list of new freedoms taken up under these EU liberalization measures is given in Table 4.2. In most cases, new fifth or seventh freedom rights have led to new competitors entering routes dominated by national carriers, like Debonair's flights from Germany to Spain and Italy and Virgin Express's Spain–Italy routes. But a few of the new routes are monopolies, such as Portugalia's service between Madrid and Turin and Regional Airlines' services on the Bilbao–Lisbon and Stuttgart–Venice routes. By December 1997 fifth and seventh freedom services within the EU accounted for 1195 international round trip flights a month, 2 per cent of the total (Civil Aviation Authority, 1998). Eighth freedom cabotage services are less significant – representing about 1 per cent of total domestic services within the EU – but they are increasing. There were twenty-six services in December 1997, ten of which were on routes in Spain, although most were either on thin monopoly routes or provided only a small part of the total frequency on relatively dense routes.

There are signs that the new freedoms may become less exceptional in the future. It may, for instance be possible for seventh freedoms to be exercised on international routes. Under the so-called 'Heathrow Agreement' of 1991, in return for the UK government agreeing to United and American taking over rights previously held by TWA and Pan American, the US government granted UK airlines seventh freedom

Table 4.2 New freedoms taken up under EU liberalization measures by December 1997.[a] *Source:* Civil Aviation Authority

Airline (and country of registration)	Sector [origin/destination on through routes]	Freedom
Aero Lloyd (Germany)	Lanzarote–Fuerteventura–Linz	7th
	Linz–Tenerife	7th
	Linz–Las Palmas	7th
	Malaga–Vienna	7th
Alitalia (Italy)	Malaga–Barcelona–[Milan]	8th
	[Rome]–Barcelona–Seville	8th
British Airways (UK)	[Manchester]–Brussels–Rome	5th
	Helsinki–Stockholm–[London]	5th
British Midland (UK)	[London]–Cologne–Dresden	8th
Debonair (UK)	[London]–Dusseldorf–Munich–[Barcelona]	8th
	Dusseldorf–Munich–[Barcelona]	8th
	Dusseldorf–Munich–[Madrid]	8th
	[London]–Dusseldorf–Munich	8th
	Dusseldorf–Munich	8th
	Barcelona–Munich–[Dusseldorf]–[London]	7th
	Barcelona–Munich–[Dusseldorf]	7th
	Madrid–Munich–[Dusseldorf]	7th
	[London]–Munich–Rome	5th
	Munich–Rome	8th
EasyJet (UK)	Amsterdam–Nice	7th
Finnair (Finland)	[Helsinki]–Barcelona–Madrid	8th
	Amsterdam–Gothenburg–[Helsinki]	5th
	Barcelona–Dusseldorf–[Helsinki]	5th
	Berlin–Stockholm–[Helsinki]	5th
	London–Stockholm–[Helsinki]	5th
	Manchester–Stockholm–[Helsinki]	5th
	Brussels–Stockholm	7th
	Copenhagen–Stockholm	7th
	Dublin–Stockholm–[Helsinki]	5th
	Milan–Stockholm–[Helsinki]	5th
	Oslo–Stockholm	7th
	[Helsinki]–Stockholm–Vienna	5th
GB Airways (UK)	[London]–Valencia–Jerez	8th
	[London]–Murcia–Valencia–[London]	8th
Golden Air (Sweden)	Bergen–Skien	8th
Hamburg Airlines (Germany)	[Hamburg]–Lyon–Toulouse	8th
Hapag Lloyd (Germany)	Lanzarote–Fuerteventura–Luxembourg	7th
	Fuerteventura–Mulhouse	7th
Iberia (Spain)	[Barcelona]–Hamburg–Helsinki	5th
	[Madrid]–Hamburg–Oslo	5th

Table 4.2 *Continued*

Airline (and country of registration)	Sector [origin/destination on through routes]	Freedom
KLM (Netherlands)	[Amsterdam]–Lisbon–Porto–[Amsterdam]	8th
Lauda Air (Austria)	[Vienna]–Barcelona–Lisbon	7th
LTU (Austria)	Salzburg–Lanzarote–Fuerteventura–Salzburg	7th
	Salzburg–Las Palmas	7th
Luxair (Luxembourg)	Munich–Saarbrucken–[Luxembourg]	8th
	Lanzarote–Fuerteventura–[Luxembourg]	8th
Muk Air (Denmark)	[Copenhagen]–Kristianstad–Ronneby	8th
Portugalia (Portugal)	Barcelona–Bilbao–[Porto]–[Lisbon]	8th
	Palma–Valencia–[Lisbon]–[Porto]	8th
	Bilbao–Madrid–[Lisbon]–[Porto]	8th
	[Lisbon]–Las Palmas–Tenerife–[Lisbon]	8th
	Hanover–Madrid–[Lisbon]–[Porto]	7th
	Hanover–Mulhouse–[Lisbon]–[Porto]	7th
	[Porto]–[Lisbon]–Madrid–Mulhouse	7th
	[Lisbon]–Madrid–Turin	7th
Olympic (Greece)	Marseille–Naples–[Athens]	7th
Regional Airlines (France)	Munster–Stuttgart–[Venice]	8th
	[Munster]–Stuttgart–Venice	5th
	[Bordeaux]–Bilbao–Lisbon	5th
	[Toulouse]–Madrid–Porto	5th
Ryanair (Ireland)	London–Glasgow	8th
	London–Sandefjord	7th
	London–Stockholm	7th
Sun–Air (Denmark)	Geilo–Oslo–[Billund]	8th
TAP Air Portugal (Portugal)	[Lisbon]–Lyons–Nice–[Lisbon]	8th
	[Lisbon]–Berlin–Hamburg–[Lisbon]	8th
	Athens–Rome–[Lisbon]	5th
	[Funchal]–[Lisbon]–Copenhagen–Oslo	5th
	[Porto]–[Lisbon]–Copenhagen–Oslo	5th
	[Faro]–[Lisbon]–Copenhagen–Oslo	5th
	[Porto]–[Lisbon]–Munich–Vienna	5th
Tyrolean (Austria)	[Vienna]–Gothenburg–Oslo	5th
	Lanzarote–Mulhouse	7th
	Las Palmas–Mulhouse	7th
	Luxembourg–Tenerife	7th
	Mulhouse–Tenerife	7th
Virgin Express (Belgium)	Barcelona–Rome	7th
	Madrid–Rome	7th
VLM (Belgium)	London–Dusseldorf	7th

ᵃ The list does not include the traffic rights enjoyed by wholly owned subsidiaries (such as British Airways' subsidiaries Deutsche BA and Air Liberté).

rights to operate stand-alone services to the USA direct from France, Germany and several other European countries. This could, for example, mean British Airways being able to fly non-stop between Paris and New York or between Frankfurt and Chicago. At present these rights cannot be exercised, awaiting as they do the consent of the relevant European governments, just as rights to operate UK-USA services held for many years by certain European airlines still await the approval of the UK government. At the moment traffic rights between EU states and third countries outside Europe are still the subject of bilateral negotiations, although the European Commission would like to acquire sovereignty in this matter, something which is referred to as 'external competence'. Similar liberalization measures have been taken in other regional groups of states. The states of the Andean Pact agreed in 1991 to establish an 'open skies' area in which the five freedoms of the air are granted without restriction to airlines of member states. More recently in 1996, fourteen governments within the Caribbean Community concluded an agreement to provide a more liberal exchange of traffic rights between member countries. It is thought by some that, eventually, the entire system of bilaterally agreed freedoms of the air may be replaced by some form of multilateral agreement, or at least a series of plurilateral agree-ments, under which traffic rights are increasingly traded on a regional rather than national basis. But the growth in global alliances, and the multinational ownership of privatized airlines, are likely in the end to prove to be more important developments than whether countries or regions will allow external airlines to carry traffic on routes previously reserved for national airlines. All this may take some time to change things. And nationalism in civil aviation will die hard. In the meantime the airlines likely to gain most from further liberalization of international routes will be those best placed to develop hub and spokes networks designed to capture sixth freedom traffic.

4.3 Accidents of geography

The countries whose airlines have relatively good opportunities for sixth freedom traffic are those in Europe, the Middle East and in the Far East. Relatively few opportunities are afforded to airlines based in Australasia, in Southern Africa or in North and South America. An airline's sixth freedom opportunities depend to a very large extent upon the geograph-ical position of its hub in relation to major flows of air traffic. This explains why opportunities are much greater in certain parts of the Northern Hemisphere than they generally are in the Southern Hemisphere.

Airlines in Europe for whom sixth freedom traffic is an important part of total traffic include KLM, SAS, Sabena, Swissair, Austrian and TAP Air Portugal. These airlines operate out of small countries and consequently have comparatively little 'home grown' demand in terms of origin and destination traffic; but they are able to feed in traffic from other countries in close proximity that generate and attract large volumes of air traffic. Major sixth freedom carriers based in the Middle East are Egyptair, Gulf Air, Royal Jordanian, Syrian, etc. All these airlines have the advantages of bases sited midway along the 'silk road' between Europe and the East. In the Far East, the rapid rates of growth achieved by Garuda, Korean Airlines, Malaysian (MAS), Philippine Airlines, Thai International and, most prominently, Singapore International Airlines (SIA) are due mainly to their participation in sixth freedom markets, especially for travel to and from Australia. For the Australian airline Qantas, for South African Airways and for airlines in South America, long haul sixth freedom opportunities are very limited indeed. There are also relatively few opportunities in North America, although US carriers do of course have the advantage of high levels of cabotage traffic.

The advantages afforded by geography to some countries but not to others leads to situations in which the benefits derived from a bilateral agreement are noticeably imbalanced. If one country consistently gains more in terms of market share, then there is the danger of the other party to the agreement renouncing the pact, or at least demanding an *ex post facto* review, with the objective of redressing the balance. But the exploitation of geographical advantages to carry fifth and sixth freedom traffic inevitably involves relations with third countries elsewhere; and it may be difficult for the home state to offer the grantor state additional rights of any real value, without at the same time jeopardizing the operations of its own carriers. In this event the home state might bring to the negotiating table some non-aviation *quid pro quo*, or some agreement might be reached on the payments of royalties. Non-aviation *quid pro quos* are not usually documented in formal treaties but are covered by confidential 'memoranda of understanding'. It is often suggested that the Dutch Government has made frequent use of this negotiating technique, on one occasion threatening to withold contributions to NATO until the United States granted specific concessions to KLM. Trade incentives have also been employed in the negotiations. For example, on one occasion the Malaysian Government insisted upon increased frequencies to/from London for MAS, in return for promising to purchase defence equipment from British manufacturers.

Where route traffic royalties are used as an alternative way of finding a balancing benefit, the form in which they are paid can vary. In some cases, the airline of the grantor state receives a certain percentage of the revenues (or net revenues); and in other cases the payment is set at a fixed amount per passenger, sometimes applying only when the number of passengers carried is in excess of a given number of 'free' passengers. The level at which royalties are charged also varies, both over time and from route to route. This is something influenced by the value that an aspiring fifth freedom carrier attaches to gaining access to the particular route involved.

To maximize its opportunities to carry connecting traffic, an airline needs a hub located along one of the main flows of traffic, ideally in a position suitable for routeings along both axes, north–south and east–west. This explains why many important hubs in the United States are to be found towards the centre of the country, and why some airports along the eastern or western seaboards have not for the most part emerged as major hubs, their suitability for domestic linkages being limited largely to those on the north–south axis.

The classic example in the United States is at Hartsfield Airport in Atlanta, where Delta Airlines operates what it can claim to be the busiest single-airline hub in the world, with some 600 daily departures. More than 20 000 Delta passengers change planes in Atlanta each day, giving rise to a joke amongst the American travelling public about a dying Southerner being told that, whether he was going to heaven or hell, he would have to change planes in Atlanta! Each of Delta's arriving and departing waves consists of over 50 aircraft, requiring all four runways to be used simultaneously for arrivals and then simultaneously for departures. Each pair of arriving and departing waves is known as a 'complex'. The scheduled duration of each complex – from the time the first aircraft lands to the time the last aircraft takes off – is no more than 90 minutes, and the minimum connecting time is a mere 35 minutes, a slick operation by any standard. Each complex in Atlanta generates a total of 2 500 possible city pair linkages. North–South linkages predominate, but there are a great many routeings via Atlanta on the east–west axis as well.

On the other side of the globe, at Changi Airport in Singapore, flight activity is concentrated very much in the evenings, the time when SIA's flights to and from Europe link up with its services to and from Australasia. Services from Europe arrive in the early evening, in time to enable passengers to transfer to flights to Australia and New Zealand taking off two or three hours later. Just as flights to Australasia are leaving, those from that part of the world start arriving, to connect with European services scheduled to depart in the hour before midnight. In all, the airline handles the arrival and departure of about a dozen Boeing 747 'Kangaroo route' flights in its evening complex, this not counting connections with other points in the Orient arriving and departing at roughly the same time. With spokes emanating from its hub in diamet-

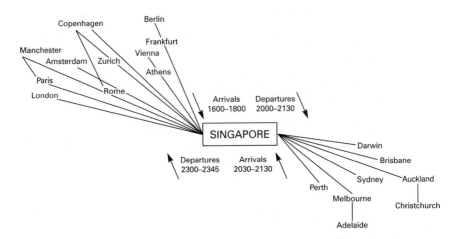

Figure 4.5 Connections through Singapore, May 1993 (*Source:* Adapted from *ABC World Airways Guide*)

rically opposite directions, SIA operates a classic example of an hourglass hub ideally suited for the carriage of sixth freedom traffic (Figure 4.5). This network shape also affords an advantage especially important in long haul operations, insofar as it makes it easier for the airline to slot services into appropriate time 'windows', allowing for differences across time zones. SIA services depart from passengers' origins early in the evenings and arrive at their final destinations early in the mornings, something that passengers generally find more convenient than arrivals and departures at midday or in the middle of the night. Schedule windows are important, not just because of the desirability of providing popular departure and arrival times, but also because of the need to meet curfews at spoke airports. SIA has been most successful in exploiting these advantages in the Europe–Australasia travel market and is now turning its attention to other markets such as the North Atlantic. Other Asian carriers have also built up connecting complexes based on hub and spokes scheduling: Thai International in Bangkok, Cathay Pacific in Hong Kong, MAS in Kuala Lumpur, Garuda in Jakarta, and Philippine Airlines (PAL) in Manila. For their participation in London–Australia sixth freedom traffic, PAL, MAS and Thai International pay royalties to the third/fourth freedom carriers, British Airways and Qantas. In Thai International's case the royalties are paid only in respect of passengers not spending at least a night in Thailand; and in PAL's agreement with BA, the level of royalties also depends on the value of interline traffic generated for BA's services (Doganis, 1991).

In the Middle East, Syrian Arab Airlines schedules connections

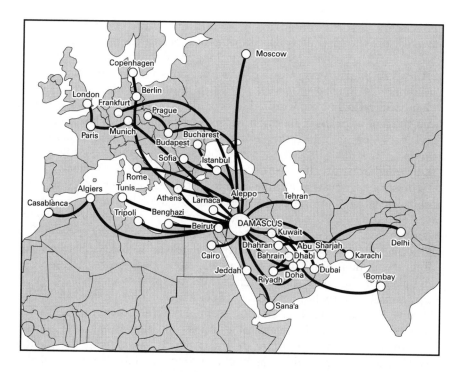

Figure 4.6 Network of Syrian Arab Airlines, May 1993 (*Source:* Adapted from *ABC World Airways Guide*)

through its hub at Damascus, linking cities in Europe and North Africa with points in the Gulf, Saudi Arabia and the Indian sub-continent (Figure 4.6). Similar services are operated by Royal Jordanian Airlines through Amman, Gulf Air through Bahrain, Emirates through Dubai and, when the political/military situation permits, Middle East Airlines through Beirut and Kuwait Airways through Kuwait City. These carriers often compete quite fiercely for sixth freedom traffic by offering through travel at some competitively priced low fares, in for example the UK–India market (Hanlon, 1986).

There are various kinds of hubs in Europe and liberalization is opening up many new opportunities for them. Most of the European services of TAP Air Portugal fly outbound in the morning and inbound in the evening, so that convenient connections are possible with the early morning arrivals and late evening departures of long haul services between Lisbon and South America and between Lisbon and points in Southern Africa. Iberia, the national airline of Spain, has a similar focus on Latin America, not only developing connections through Madrid, but also establishing hubs on the other side of the Atlantic. TAP's hub in

Lisbon and Iberia's in Madrid are both in the nature of hourglass hubs, located on the periphery of Europe but nevertheless in quite good positions to serve as gateways for long haul traffic. In Copenhagen, SAS's hub is also very much of the hourglass variety and also on the periphery of Europe, not well placed in relation to the main flows of long haul traffic but more suited to providing links between Scandinavia and the rest of Europe. Austrian Airlines also operates an hourglass hub and provides an interesting example of a predominantly short haul operator exploiting its geographical position to develop high volumes of sixth freedom traffic between West and East Europe via Vienna.

The strongest hubs in Europe tend to be those of airlines based in more central locations: Lufthansa in Frankfurt, Swissair in Zurich, and KLM in Amsterdam. British Airways in London is at a geographical disadvantage for Europe-to-Europe connections (save for city pairs like London–Oslo). Nor is it particularly well placed to offer links between domestic points. But it is in a relatively good position for UK–Europe and also for Europe–North America, although not so well placed as its continental competitors for Europe–Africa, Europe–Middle East, Europe–Far East, etc. London, Paris and Frankfurt all have the advantage of sheer scale, in terms of number of destinations and service frequencies. Clearly, the more destinations that are served the greater the chance of an intending passenger finding a suitable connection, and the odds shorten with every additional flight. In these respects, London ranks ahead of its continental competitors, but the lead it enjoys is diminished by the split of traffic between its two main airports. Heathrow is still the European airport with the greatest number of destinations, but Gatwick ranks alongside Rome as a relatively weak hub in the international context. There is less of an imbalance in Paris, which enjoys a more central location, but a traditional policy of route sectorization between Charles de Gaulle and Orly means that as individual airports both slip below Frankfurt in scale of departures and destinations. Liberalization of air services in the EU presents opportunities for airlines to overcome their geographical disadvantages by seeking hubs in other European countries. One of the first to do so was British Airways, with its investments in TAT and Deutsche BA. Any restrictions on cabotage, such as those limiting it to consecutive flights or to 50 per cent of the capacity operated on the primary international route, are likely to be less of a deterrent to airlines setting up a new hub. For the new hub can have a number of international routes feeding into a number of domestic sectors. In this way, an airline can establish 'mini hubs' in foreign countries. This is what Iberia is doing in Amsterdam, taking advantage of Amsterdam's central location. Flights from Madrid and Barcelona are routed via Amsterdam on their way to Copenhagen, Gothenburg, Helsinki and Stockholm and timed so that passengers can

Table 4.3 Some examples of fifth and seventh freedom hubs owned or controlled by foreign carriers (October 1998). *Source*: *Airline Business*

Hub	Airlines
Paris	British Airways/Air Liberté
	(BA owns domestic network)
Nice	Lufthansa/Air Littoral
	(Lufthansa could eventually own hub network)
Singapore	British Airways/Qantas
	(5th and 7th freedom hubs)
Stockholm	Finnair
	(5th and 7th freedom services intra-Europe)
Vancouver	American Airlines/CAIL
	(American control could increase)
Sharjah	Lufthansa Cargo/Hinduya
	(Europe-India cargo hub)
Subic Bay	Federal Express
	(5th and 7th freedom cargo hub)

make suitable connections between them in Amsterdam. It is likely that there are going to be many more mini hubs of this kind.

Greater access to fifth and seventh freedom rights, not just in Europe but across the world more generally, is also encouraging airlines to establish some fairly large hubs in foreign countries. Some examples are given in Table 4.3. Sometimes the hubs are set up in conjunction with a regional airline subsidiary (as in the cases of British Airways with Air Liberte in Paris and Lufthansa with Air Littoral in Nice); and sometimes they are a joint effort with an alliance partner (like British Airways/Qantas in Singapore and American/CAIL in Vancouver). Also there are a few fifth and seventh freedom cargo hubs (such as that jointly run by Lufthansa and Hinduya in Sharjah and the Federal Express operation at Subic Bay in the Philippines).

4.4 Europe compared with the United States

There are a number of reasons why, even with cabotage completely unrestricted, the experience of the United States will not be repeated on quite the same scale in Europe. One is airport congestion. If airport slots remain scarce, and if as a result it becomes increasingly difficult to co-ordinate flight schedules into waves of arrivals and departures, then the scope for developing effective hub and spokes systems will be that much

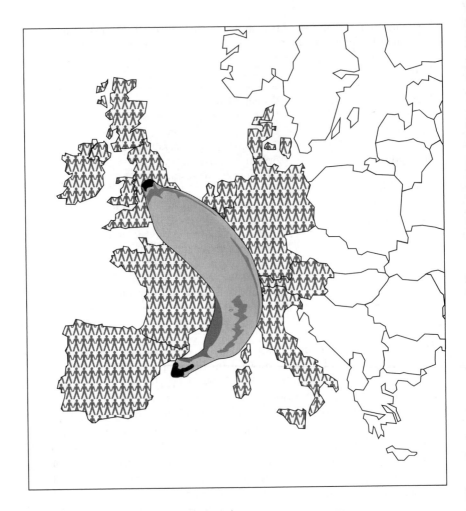

Figure 4.7   The European 'hot banana'

less. The problems of airport capacity are discussed later, and there are other reasons why US-style hubbing will not become so prominent in Europe, at least so far as intra-European services are concerned.

For one thing, some immutable geographic and demographic factors mean that the proportion of passengers who can readily travel on an indirect routeing via an intermediate airport is considerably smaller. Population density is very much lower in the United States, $26/km^2$ as compared with $164/km^2$ in the EU. At the same time the US population is much more widely dispersed geographically, leading to longer average journey lengths (approximately 1200 km as against circa 900 km in the EU). In terms of total passenger-kilometres flown, the US domes-

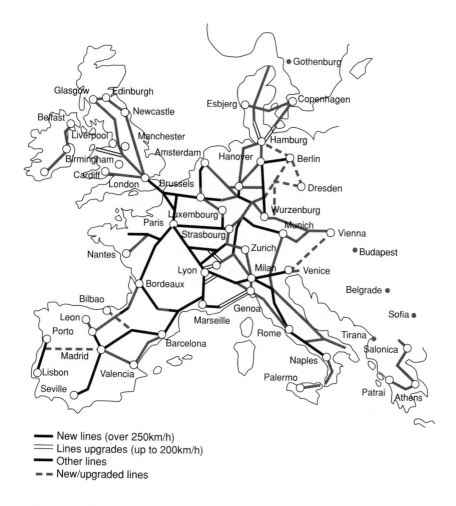

Figure 4.8 European high-speed rail network (*Source:* Community of European Railways)

tic market is more than five times greater than the intra-European market so that, despite the wider population dispersion, the density of traffic is still very much higher in the US than it is in Europe.

In Europe most of the important travel-generating centres are fairly close to one another – especially those business centres within the so-called 'hot banana' (Figure 4.7) running across from south-east England to northern Italy. As a result most routes are too short to be susceptible to competition from indirect flights. Also a much higher proportion of travellers than in the United States begin and end their journeys in a hub city. Hence, on many intra-European routes, cross-elasticities of demand between direct and indirect flights are always likely to be fairly low. At the same time, on many routes, cross-elasticities between air and surface transport are fairly high.

The shorter distances in Europe mean that road and rail are much closer substitutes. In particular there is much greater competition from high-speed trains in Europe (see Figure 4.8). There has already been evidence of significant diversion from air to rail, 25 years ago on the London–Glasgow route following electrification, and 15 years or so ago on the Paris–Lyon route where air lost more than two-thirds of its traffic following the introduction of TGV (*Train à Grande Vitesse*) services. There will clearly be some further modal substitution as a result of the Channel Tunnel. But perhaps of greater importance in the present context are the possibilities of rail services linking airports, replacing some short haul feeder services. It is for short haul journeys (including those to/from hub cities) that surface modes offer the most effective substitutes for air travel. Air transport is at a substantial disadvantage compared with rail on most short haul routes because of the difficulty of getting between the airport and major business/residental areas. Air transport's speed advantage is often offset by long access and egress times to, from and at airports. In Europe the development of high-speed trains has extended rail's competitiveness for distances up to 300 miles; and the chief of Lufthansa has predicted that it will not be long before many short haul services into Europe's major hubs are replaced by trains. For some years Lufthansa has been operating the airport express rail service between Frankfurt and Dusseldorf via the cities of Bonn and Cologne, and there are now plans to extend it. The TGV services pioneered by the French are now spreading throughout Germany, Italy, Sweden and Spain; and in the liberalized market they will provide some stiff competition for intra-European air services. The access/egress disadvantages of air services are diminished in the case of feeder links to hubs, when passengers are making onward connections. But nonetheless the progressive shortening of city-centre to city-centre journey times by rail, together with improved railheads at airports, is tilting the balance increasingly in favour of rail on many of the shorter routes. Further extensions to the high-speed rail network, including routes like London–Paris and London–Brussels (following the opening of the Channel Tunnel) and Paris–Frankfurt and Paris–Zurich, will further enhance rail's position in the short haul market.

All this may not be totally unwelcome to the airlines. For short haul services are not all that profitable in Europe. In the accounts of British Airways for instance, it is revealed that intra-European services in some years earn only a tiny surplus and in others actually sustain a loss, with virtually all the airline's operating surplus coming from operations outside Europe. It is on the long haul routes that airlines make money. Almost all major carriers in Europe have long haul networks, and another major geographic difference between European and US air transport is in the relative importance of traffic flows to/from points outside the region. International passenger-kilometres flown on routes to/from the United States amount to about 50 per cent of domestic passenger-kilometres, whereas the number of passenger-kilometres flown on routes between EU and non-EU countries is some three times the number flown on routes entirely within the EU (Poole, 1989). This difference is largely explained by the relatively self-contained US economy and by the significance of former colonial links for EU countries. To many EU airlines, the real value of short haul routes lies in their ability to feed high yield passengers onto their long haul networks. This is where the hub and spokes systems of the United States find their closest parallel in Europe and why hub location is so crucial. But geographical location is only one factor determining the relative success of a hub. Another important factor is flight scheduling, which is discussed in Chapter 5.

4.5 Regional services

Another difference between Europe and the United States is in the scale and importance of regional services, which have recently been expanding much faster than the airline industry as a whole. This expansion has been particularly noticeable in Europe, although regional services are still far more prominent in the United States, where they are a well-established part of the public transport scene, accepted and used by travellers more or less as airborne bus services.

Regional airlines in the United States today are the direct descendants of what in the regulated era used to be classed as 'commuter' airlines. Under regulation the US interstate industry developed on three levels. On the first level, ten trunk airlines became the major domestic carriers, principally serving high-density, long haul routes with jet aircraft. On the second level, local service airlines were licensed to expand services to small cities and to feed the trunk system. Just before deregulation eight of these airlines were still in existence. But their role had changed to include greater provision of longer-haul, higher-density jet service, turning them into 'mini trunks', each with a distinctly regional focus. Finally, on the third level, the commuters, which began service after the Second World War, were restricted to flying piston-engined and turbo-prop aircraft on short haul routes serving mainly small communities. Some services were operated under subsidy, under conditions that obliged airlines to provide adequate service, at specified minimum frequencies, to/from all points eligible for subsidy. There was no automatic freedom of exit and withdrawal from a route often entailed a

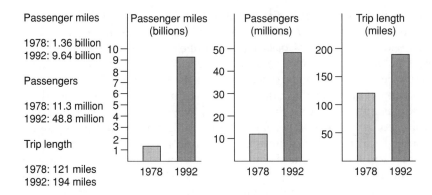

Figure 4.9 Regional airline traffic in the United States (*Source:* Regional Airline Association)

long administrative process and the provision of a replacement carrier. As a result, before deregulation many points were served with equipment which was far too large to be economic.

In liberalizing route entry and exit, deregulation effectively shifted the opportunity and responsibility of serving small communities to third-level carriers. At the time many small communities feared that deregulation would result in them losing airline service altogether. Their argument was that, with open price competition, airlines would find it less easy to cross-subsidize loss-making services on low-density routes. There had already been some evidence of airlines seeking to pull out of subsidized services, where the subsidies paid did not cover the higher costs of operating larger aircraft. And to begin with, it looked as if their fears were going to be realized. In the early years of deregulation many small towns and cities did indeed lose service, although it has never been entirely clear just how far this was due to deregulation and how far to the contemporaneous events of fuel price increases and economic recession. But in any event it was not long before a high proportion of the routes abandoned by first- and second-level carriers were taken over by the regionals. After deregulation regional airline traffic continued to grow apace, total passengers enplaned increasing more than four-fold, with an even greater increase in revenue passenger-miles, reflecting a 60 per cent increase in average trip length per passenger (Figure 4.9). But the number of carriers operating on regional routes has fallen (by around 40 per cent). The Airline Deregulation Act provided for subsidies to communities that would otherwise lose service, under a new Essential Air Service (EAS) subsidy programme. Under the new arrangements the US Department of Transportation determines the level of EAS subsidy required to ensure continued access and then requests competitive bids from airlines willing to operate the route. To be eligible for an EAS subsidy, a community must be located at least 70 miles by highway from the nearest medium or large hub airport, 55 miles from the nearest small hub airport or 45 miles from the nearest non-hub airport that enplanes 100 passengers or more per day; and no community can receive a subsidy exceeding $200 per passenger. The total amount paid out in subsidies has been reduced quite considerably over the past decade or so, from $121.7 million in 1981 to $34.8 million in 1992 (Regional Airline Association, 1993). Some political representatives have complained about the apparent deterioration in services to small communities in their constituencies that this seems to imply.

The effect on services to small communities is often presented as an adverse outcome of deregulation. One writer put it thus:

> While deregulation has a class of beneficiaries, consumers in small towns and rural communities are not amongst them...With the elimination of entry and exit regulation, airlines have been free to reduce their level of service to less lucrative communities and focus their energies and equipment on more profitable market opportunities. The result of airline deregulation is that many small communities have experienced a drastic reduction in air service.
>
> (Dempsey, 1990)

In the first two years of deregulation more than 100 communities lost service altogether, inducing a feature advertisement to be placed in the *Wall Street Journal* in 1980 exclaiming that 'Deregulation has shot down more planes than the Red Baron!' This resulted not so much from the reduction in subsidies, but more from the fact that, as carriers left thinly trafficked routes for denser markets elsewhere, regional airlines shifted their operations to take their place, exiting many routes previously ineligible for subsidy. But did this lead to the 'drastic reduction' in air service to small communities that writers like Dempsey claim? There are a number of aspects to consider here. Besides those communities that have lost scheduled service altogether, there are others which have experienced some reduction in the number of destinations served by direct flights or in the frequency of those flights. Also there are many more for whom destinations and frequencies have failed to increase at the same rate with secular increases in air services generally. The most relevant comparison is always with what might have been the case had regulation continued. But simply counting the number of flights may misrepresent some of the more important changes taking place, including the development of hub and spokes systems. Other things being equal, service to a hub is superior to service to a non-hub, because the former generates greater opportunities for connections; and a flight to a large hub is better still, especially if it arrives at the hub just prior to an outgoing bank of flights. What small communities tended to lose were flights to non-hubs, or to small hubs; what many of them gained was an increase in service to the larger hubs, often flights with vastly increased online connections. Taking all this into consideration it is highly possible for a small community to have come out of deregulation with a net gain in airline service. And some recent studies confirmed this. Butler and Houston (1990) for instance, in a study of 225 non-hub airports, found that even where the number of direct flights fell, this was swamped by a surge in possible connections, so that the average non-hub airport enjoyed a 55 per cent increase in airline service.

In the past few years the pattern of regional services in Europe has been undergoing radical change. It has for some time been the policy of the European Commission to promote air services to small communities in order to encourage regional economic growth. In one of its first steps towards liberalization the EC issued its Inter-Regional Air Services Directive in 1983. This was intended to give more or less automatic multilateral approval for airlines to provide international services on regional routes throughout the Community. But it was an agreement qualified in a number of important respects: the services could only be operated by aircraft up to 70 seats and only on routes of 400 km or over; routes to/from airports classified as Category 1 airports – which included 25 of the busiest airports in Europe – were excluded; and protection was granted for indirect or parallel services to nearly all airports (and also for a group of more than 20 specified airports in Denmark, Greece, Italy and Spain, which were made exempt). With all these limitations it was hardly surprising that the 1983 Directive did not result in any immediate upsurge in regional operations. The main reason for this was the exclusion of Category 1 airports. These serve the main travel-generating centres and are almost without exception important hubs for the major carriers. So if the hope was to stimulate regional services, it was a mistake to exclude these airports, particularly since US experience had shown that the biggest growth area in regional air transport was in feeder traffic to the hubs. As it was, only 10 new services were authorized under the 1983 Directive, and in 1985 the market for regional airlines, limited as it was to non-Category 1 airports, covered only 115 city pairs or just 2.6 per cent of passengers on international air services in Europe (Wheatcroft and Lipman, 1986). Restrictions in the 1983 Directive were about to be relaxed when they were overtaken by the more wide-ranging measures to liberalize route licensing and market access leading up to the third package of reforms that came into effect in January 1993. The intention of EC liberalization is that there should be almost total freedom for EU-licensed airlines to fly anywhere within the Community, including regional routes. The only significant restriction in the EC's proposals concerns routes with a low traffic volume. The EC has been concerned to see that some essential but uneconomic 'lifeline' services to national development regions, and also services between regional airports, survive in the single market. Accordingly it protects public service routes with fewer than 30 000 seats per annum by limiting access for a period of up to three years. Otherwise, regional airlines are now free to operate to as many Category 1 airports as they please, provided that is, they can acquire the necessary take-off and landing slots.

The capacity constraints at European airports constitute a major impediment to development of regional services. The response of governments and of the EC has been to consider means of reforming the present system of allocating take-off and landing slots, so as to reduce the barriers facing new entrants and encourage competition. As discussed later, this is a very difficult matter and finding a solution acceptable to all concerned is no small problem. One suggestion is that slots be auctioned, a possibility that would have very serious consequences for regional airlines: 'A regional airline operating a Saab 340 on a 300 km route would be in an impossible position against an airline operating a B747 across the Atlantic' (Wheatcroft and Lipman, 1990). What the EC has decided to do is to take all new and unused slots at congested airports, place them in a 'pool' and allocate anything up to 50 per cent of them to new-entrant airlines. The problem with this is that hardly any new slots are becoming available at congested airports and incumbent airlines are prepared to go to almost any lengths to keep the slots they already have, under the system of 'grandfather rights'.

Perhaps a regional airline's best prospects for gaining access to congested airports lie in going into partnership with a major airline. Two other powerful forces propelling regionals into partnership with majors are computer reservations systems and frequent flyer programmes. The potential anti-competitive effects of CRSs and FFPs are discussed in Chapter 3. Despite increasingly strict rules laid down by competition authorities on both sides of the Atlantic, they can still amount to formidable entry barriers. To avoid finding themselves on the wrong side of these barriers, regionals are often prepared to sacrifice their independence; and for the majors, linking up with regional airlines is one means of adding to or consolidating traffic feed.

The practice is widespread in the United States, where the majors have grouped the services of their regional partners under single brand names: American Eagle, United Express, Delta Connection, Northwest Airlink, US Airways Express, Continental Express and Transworld Express. The groups formed by the seven major carriers now carry over 90 per cent of all regional traffic in the United States.

Sometimes the regional airline is owned or part-owned by the parent in whose name it flies and sometimes it is not. Recent developments suggest that the US majors are becoming relatively less interested in owning or taking stakes in their regional partners and more interested in franchising them their brand image. One explanation for this concerns the lower pay and more flexible conditions accepted by staff employed by the regionals. For the same reason – and also because they are often facing fresh competition from low-cost operators offering no-frills point-to-point service – some airlines are setting up separate organizations or separate subsidiaries to handle operations on short haul regional routes. In the United States two such subsidiaries are United Shuttle and Continental Express; in Asia the regional subsidiary of SIA is known as Silk Air; and in Europe there is British Airways Regional, KLM CityHopper and Lufthansa CityLine. Other major airlines in Europe have either taken over domestic or regional airlines entirely (e.g. Air Inter by Air France; Linjeflyg by SAS; and Air UK by KLM) or have bought substantial equity stakes in them (e.g. Swissair's 40 per cent holding in Crossair; KLM's 80 per cent in Transavia; SAS's 40 per cent in Airlines of Britain (the parent company of British Midland); and so on). The main reason why major airlines are entering into various kinds of relationships with regionals is to gain market access, ensure traffic feed and extend their marketable networks at low cost.

4.6 Extending marketable networks

Where it is possible, one way of extending networks is to acquire the routes of other carriers. This was the main way in which the large US airlines which were previously restricted to domestic routes, American, Delta and United, were able to move into international operations, purchasing the route authorities of Pan American and TWA, the two traditional US flag carriers, when these airlines got into financial difficulties (Table 4.4). Elsewhere it is mostly not possible to do this, given constraints in bilateral agreements on the designation of airlines to international routes. But a large part of the economies of scope associated with network size can in fact be reaped without the airline necessarily operating all services on all routes itself. Many of the marketing benefits from large network size, in advertising, customer loyalty devices, computer reservations systems, etc., can be achieved by close co-operation with other carriers serving complementary routes. Growth in such co-operation is a major feature of liberalized air travel markets. Three particular kinds are especially important in this regard:

Table 4.4: International route sales between major US airlines (1985–92).
Source: US General Accounting Office

Buyer	Seller	Route(s)	Price[a] ($ million)
American	Eastern	Latin American system	471
American	TWA	3 US–London routes	445
Delta	Pan American	European routes	526
Delta	Pan American	New York–Mexico City	25
Northwest	America West	Honolulu–Nagaya	15
Northwest	Hawaiian	Pacific routes	9
USAir	TWA	2 US–London routes	50
United	Pan American	Pacific routes	716
United	Pan American	US–London routes	400
United	Pan American	Latin American system + Los Angeles–Mexico City	148

[a] In some cases the price includes the transfer of related facilities

- franchising,
- blocked spacing,
- code-sharing.

Franchising

This is the practice of one airline permitting another to use its name, aircraft livery, uniforms and brand image generally. One airline sells these privileges to another, often as part of an overall package in which the franchisor undertakes the franchisee's marketing and sales management as well. In return the franchisee pays royalty fees and often acts as a feeder carrier to the franchisor's main network.

A list of franchise agreements, current in December 1998, is given in Table 4.5. It is true to say that franchising is still rather in its infancy outside North America, where the branding of regional services under the colours of major airlines has been one of the most significant and lasting effects, not just in the United States but in Canada as well. British Airways was the pioneer of franchising in Europe. It has seven UK-based franchise operations (including Loganair, Manx Airlines and GB Airways) and two outside the UK (Sun-Air of Scandinavia and Comair of South Africa). Together the nine BA franchises, flying under the brand name British Airways Express, carry about 7 million passengers a year. Following BA's development of franchising several other European

Table 4.5 Franchise agreements, December 1998. *Sources:* compiled from *Airline Business* and various press reports

Franchisor	Brand name	Franchisee(s)
Air Canada	Air Canada Commuter	Air Alliance
		Air BC
		Air Nova
		Air Ontario
		NWT Air
Air Europa	Air Europa Express	Canarias Regional
Air France	Air France Express	Brit Air
		Jersey European
		Gill Aviation
		CityJet
Air New Zealand	Air New Zealand Link	Air Nelson
		Eagle Airways
		Mount Cook Airlines
Alaskan	Alaskan Commuter	Era Aviation
Alitalia	–	Azzura Air
American	American Eagle	Executive Air
		Flagship Airlines
		Simmons Airlines
		Wings West
Ansett Australia	–	Aeropelican Air Services
		Flight West
		Hazelton Airlines
		Impulse Airlines
		Kendell Airlines
		Skywest (of Australia)
British Airways	British Airways Express	British Regional[a]
		Brymon Airways
		Maersk Air
		GB Airways
		British Mediterranean
		CityFlyer Express
		Sun-Air
		Comair (of South Africa)
CAIL	Canadian Partner	Air Atlantic
		Calm Air
		Canadian Regional
Continental	Continental Express	Continental Express
Delta	Delta Connection	Comair (of USA)
		Business Express
		SkyWest (of USA)
		Atlantic Southwest
EasyJet	–	TEA Switzerland

Iberia	Iberia Regional	Air Nostrum
		Binter Canarias
		Binter Mediterraneo
		Regional Airlines
Lufthansa	Team Lufthansa	Air Dolomite
		Augsburg Airways
		Business Air
		Cimber Air
Northwest	Northwest Airlink	Business Express
		Express Airlines
		Mesaba Airlines
		Trans States Airlines
		Horizon Air
Qantas	Qantas Airlink	Eastern Australian Airlines
		Southern Australian Airlines
		National Jet System
		Sunstate Airlines
United	United Express	Air Wisconsin
		Atlantic Coast
		Great Lakes Aviation
		Gulfstream International
		Mesa Airlines
		SkyWest
		UFS
US Airways	US Airways Express	Allegheny
		CC Air
		Chautauqua Airlines
		Commutair
		Mesa Airlines
		Piedmont Airlines
		PSA Airlines
		Trans States Airlines

[a] Incorporates Loganair and Manx Airlines Europe.

airlines have begun to form similar agreements. Air France, Iberia and Lufthansa each have four franchises, while Alitalia, Air Europa and EasyJet each have one. But apart from Europe and North America the only other part of the world in which franchise operations take place is Australia and New Zealand.

A franchising agreement can be beneficial for both franchisor and franchisee. The benefits for the franchisor include: the spreading of its name more widely; the transfer of some high-cost, low-yield routes to franchisee carriers, which are often more suited to operating such services cost-effectively; and, most significant of all, increased traffic feed to its main network. The franchisee benefits from the value of the franchisor's brand; from being able to use the franchisor's marketing and distribution expertise; and from an increase in traffic over what it would otherwise be able to attract as an independent operator.

Generally speaking, franchising has been profitable for both parties. This has certainly been the case for the franchising arranged by British Airways (Civil Aviation Authority, 1998). But there are also the questions of what impact it has on passengers and how it affects the degree of competition on the routes affected. It is possible that passengers may benefit from the lower costs of franchise carriers, if these are passed on in reduced fares. Whether that will be the case may depend on whether the franchise increases the franchisee's market power relative to independent operators. Other possible benefits for passengers are that marginal routes are more likely to survive if they are operated under a strong brand name, that service of a particular standard is assured and that there may be improved linkages to connect with the franchisor's main network. On the other hand, franchising may cause confusion for passengers even though airlines are legally obliged to inform passengers which carrier is actually operating the flight; and another potential disadvantage for passengers will arise if franchising strengthens an airline's dominant position and results in the carrier charging excessive fares or engaging in predatory behaviour.

It is possible that franchising will become more widespread in the future. There may be no global air transport market in the same sense that there is for cars, computers, food and drink, etc. For instance, the production of air services on domestic routes in Japan is not of direct relevance to passenger demand on the North Atlantic. Under the present system of traffic rights, negotiated in terms of freedoms of the air and with restrictions on cabotage, each country or region tends to be an individual market, with generally rather limited competition on routes between these markets. In order to be thought of as a 'global' carrier, an airline will need to be perceived as a major supplier in foreign markets, on domestic routes in other countries and also on all major international routes, not just those to and from its home country. This is presently precluded by lack of traffic rights, but franchising possibly represents a way in which an airline can tap into foreign markets using its own brand name.

Franchising has been used to great effect in some other industries, turning certain businesses into truly global operations. Two prominent examples are the Coca-Cola company and McDonald's hamburger restaurants, instances that provide good illustrations of two main forms of franchising working successfully. Coca-Cola is an example of a 'product' or 'trademark' franchise. Here the franchisor supplies its brandname plus some essential ingredient, like the Coca-Cola syrup; and the franchisees put in something else, e.g. carbonated water and bottling, and then distribute the product to final consumers. The case of McDonald's is an example of a 'business format' franchise. In this the franchisor supplies its brandname plus a blueprint for running a particular type of business and assists by providing training, monitoring, quality control, marketing and advice generally, all to a much greater extent than is typically the case with a product franchise. Both have led to truly global products, ensuring that a coke is a coke is a coke, wherever you happen to be in the world, or that the McDonald's hamburger, and the way it is delivered to the consumer, is essentially the same whether it is bought in Tokyo, Toronto or Tottenham. By supplying a standard product, slightly adapted if desired to local taste, and relying on a well defined franchise concept for management control, McDonald's have actually been able to raise capital during its growth, rather than spending it, as some airlines have done, on mergers and acquisitions.

How far can the franchise concept be applied in airline operations? Both kinds of franchising are possible, but perhaps it is the business format kind that airlines are more likely to adopt. There is little doubt that the image projected by one airline can be more favourable in marketing terms than that projected by another; and that the brandname associated with one carrier is more saleable than that of another. Airline branding is a nebulous concept, but one that is becoming more and more crucial for success. On one definition, an airline's brand is the property it owns over and above the 'hard' and 'soft' values of the physical product in operating services (Simons, 1994). In this context hard values are the fundamental requirements for operating flights, in terms of aircraft, infrastructure, schedules, finance, managerial resources, sales outlets, etc., all the things an airline needs before it can even enter the market. Soft values on the other hand are the more tactile aspects of flying services, such as cabin staff, inflight catering, seat configuration, video systems, interior design and so on. And beyond these hard and soft values, brand values are those associated with the 'personality' of the airline, often deriving from its company or geographic heritage. Over time the relative importance of hard, soft and brand values has been changing. In the past the most important things distinguishing one airline from another were the hard values. For example, if one airline flew a new and improved aircraft type (e.g. a 'whisper' jet) whilst its competitors persevered with older aircraft, that gave it a distinct advantage in the eyes of passengers. But as flight equipment became more and more standardized amongst the major airlines, passengers began to take the hard values more or less for granted. The competitive struggle then switched to the soft values, with airlines attempting to out-do each other in inflight service and entertainment. But any competitive advantage

Figure 4.10 Advertisements taken out by Virgin Atlantic and British Midland. (*Source: The Times* and *Sunday Times*, December 1993)

Figure 4.10 (*continued*)

won in soft values tends to be relatively short lived, as other airlines respond swiftly to any innovation finding favour with passengers. Expenditure on soft values is also subject to diminishing marginal returns: ultimately there must be some limit to the number of video channels passengers can view or the number of glasses of champagne they can drink or the amount of cordon bleu cooking they can enjoy, even on a long haul flight!

The current focus on brand values is manifest in the various ways airlines market their services. In 1988 British Airways became the first airline to adopt a policy of branding individual classes of service; and now it has as many as seven main brands: Concorde, First, Club World, Club Europe, World Traveller, Euro Traveller and Super Shuttle. The choice of the 'Traveller' label to replace 'economy' class is particularly significant in this regard. The promotion of brands is also evident in recent airline advertisements. Two such advertisements, seeking to associate brands with the personalities of company chairman taken out by Virgin Atlantic and British Midland in conjunction with American Express are illustrated in Figure 4.10.

For many years certain airlines derived competitive advantages from their positions as national flag carriers. Flag carriers typically display their nationalities on the fuselages of their aircraft, and the airlines of advanced industrial nations often gained from this relative to airlines from developing countries. The airlines of some countries are often perceived by passengers as being in some sense safer or more reliable than those of others. But with the standardization of hard values this is changing somewhat. It may still be the case that many passengers prefer, other things being equal, to fly on airlines from certain countries, but increasingly the brand value of flag carrier is giving way to brand values based on emotional or attitudinal factors more generally. In most other markets consumers go for brands that are perceived in one way or another as 'best', regardless of where they are produced and regardless of whether the producer is British, French, German, American or Japanese. It is possible that the same will eventually emerge in markets for air travel, so that brand values based on the flag carrier concept may to some extent become passé. Also, those airlines whose nationalities are perceived as competitive disadvantages but which still possess valuable third, fourth and fifth freedom traffic rights, may see a lot of benefit in becoming franchisees to airlines with strong brandnames. The latter may also view the possibilities as attractive, insofar as it permits extension of their marketable networks without the requirement to finance heavy capital expenditure.

Block spacing

Under a block space agreement one airline allocates to another a number of seats on some of its flights, a kind of partial 'wet' lease. The other airline then sells these seats to the travelling public through its own marketing and distribution system. This kind of agreement is used where the airline to whom the seats are allocated is unable for one reason or another to serve the city airport in question.

Block spacing is no simple matter, however. First the size of each block has to be agreed, and then the booking policy has to be decided. For instance, will the block be expanded if one airline happens to receive more bookings than it has space for? And how will each airline allocate seats within its block between different categories to be shared between the carriers when passengers travel on either of the partners beyond the sector to which block space agreement applies? All these are details that need to be ironed out satisfactorily before an agreement is reached.

Block space agreements known to be in operation in December 1998 are listed in Table 4.6. Two airlines that favour this approach more than others are Swissair and Finnair. Swissair has block space agreements with twelve other airlines and Finnair with eleven; and other airlines with several agreements are CSA (six), Lot Polish (five) and SAS (four). The advantage to the airline selling a block of seats is an expected increase in revenue when the purchasing airline markets its service across its distribution network. The increase in passengers might enable the selling airline to increase its frequency of service and thus gain from the generally well-established S-shaped relationship between frequency and market share. The purchasing airline can gain by being able to sell tickets on relatively thin routes that would be costly to operate itself.

While not all that common so far, block space agreements are, like franchising, likely to increase in the years ahead, as more and more airlines seek to break out of conditions attaching to bilateral air service agreements negotiated by national governments. Another means of doing this, far more frequently used, is the practice of code-sharing.

Code-sharing

This is a commercial agreement between two airlines under which an airline operating a service allows another airline to offer that service to the travelling public under its own flight designator code, even although it does not operate the service. The practice is now becoming widespread across the world, although as yet not so pervasive as it is in the US regional industry, in which around 96 per cent of passengers flew on code-sharing airlines (Chambers, 1993). It is normal for franchising and block space agreements to be accompanied by an agreement on code-sharing also; and code-sharing agreements often include provisions for revenue or profit sharing, co-ordination of schedules, baggage handling, etc.

Each monthly issue of the *OAG World Airways Guide* contains a detailed listing of shared designator codes, from which it can be determined

Table 4.6 Block space agreements (December 1998). *Sources:* Compiled from *Airline Business* and various press reports

Partner airlines	Routes
Aer Lingus/Finnair	Dublin–Copenhagen/Stockholm/Helsinki
Aer Lingus/ Sabena	Dublin–Brussels
Aeroflot/Swissair	Geneva–Moscow, Zurich–Leningrad
Aerolines Argentinas/MAS	Buenos Aires–Kuala Lumpur/Jo'burg/Cape Town
AeroMexico/Swissair	Atlanta–Mexico City/Cancun
Air Canada/Finnair	Helsinki–Toronto[a]
Air China/Finnair	Helsinki–Beijing
Air China/SAS	Copenhagen–Beijing
Air China/Swissair	Zurich–Beijing
Air France/CSA	Paris–Prague
Air France/Malev	Paris–Budapest
Air-India/SAS	Copenhagen–Delhi
Air-India/Swissair	Zurich–Mumbai (Bombay)
Alitalia/Gulf Air	Rome–Abu Dhabi/Bahrain
Austrian Air/Finnair	Vienna–Helsinki/Stockholm
Austrian Air/Lot	Warsaw–Vienna
Balkan/Lot	Sofia–Warsaw
China Airlines/Japan Asia	Taipei–Tokyo
CSA/KLM	Prague–Amsterdam
CSA/Lot	Prague–Warsaw
CSA/Lufthansa	Prague–Munich
CSA/Malev	Prague–Budapest
CSA/Swissair	Prague–Geneva/Zurich
Delta/Finnair	Nine 3/4/5 freedom city pairs[b]
DHL/SAS	Copenhagen–Riga[c]
El Al/Finnair	Helsinki–Tel Aviv
Estonian/Finnair	Helsinki–Tallin
Finnair/Iberia	Helsinki–Barcelona, Madrid-[Hamburg]-Helsinki
Finnair/Lot	Helsinki–Warsaw
Finnair/Sabena	Brussels–Stockholm/Helsinki
Finnair/Swissair	Helsinki–Zurich
Garuda/Swissair	Zurich–Jakarta
Japan Airlines/SAS	Scandinavia–Japan[c]
Japan Airlines/South African Airways	Osaka/Kansai–Johannesburg
Lot/Swissair	Zurich–Krakow
Lot/Tarom	Warsaw–Bucharest
MAS/MEAL	Beirut–Dubai/Kuala Lumpur
Malev/Tarom	Budapest–Zurich
Martinair/Lan-Chile	Netherlands–South America[c]
Olympic/Saudia	Athens–Jeddah/Riyadh

Olympic/Vasp	Athens/Rio de Janeiro/San Paulo
Oman Air/Swissair	Muscat–Zurich
Swissair/Tarom	Zurich–Bucharest
Swissair/Ukraine International	Zurich–Kiev
Swissair/Vietnam Airlines	Zurich–Ho Chi Minh City
Thai Airways International/ Kuwait Airlines	Kuwait–Bangkok
Transbrasil-Varig	Domestic Brazalian routes
Virgin Atlantic-Continental	London–New York

ᵃ Peak summer season only.
ᵇ Helsinki–Frankfurt/Zurich/New York, Helsinki–San Francisco (peak summer season only), New York–Washington/Boston/Atlanta/Chicago/Miami.
ᶜ Freighter services.

which airlines are actually operating the relevant services. The *Guide* (in its April 1998 issue) shows that all flights under British Airways' designator codes BA6003-BA6038 are in fact flown by Finnair and codes BA7540-BA7599 by America West. It also shows that British Midland flies under the codes of American Airlines, Lufthansa, SAS and United Airlines. Lufthansa's LH code is used by as many as twenty-five different airlines, while the AF, SR and UA codes of Air France, Swissair and United are each carried by twenty different airlines. The KLM/Northwest alliance makes extensive use of code-sharing, both for through flights via KLM's hub in Amsterdam and Northwest's hubs in in the United States, and for non-stop services across the Atlantic. The same is true of the Star Alliance, centred around the services of Lufthansa and United. And reciprocal code-sharing is one of the things British Airways and American Airlines wish to introduce once its Oneworld alliance gains full regulatory approval. An extensive list of code-sharing agreements involving major airlines is given in Table 4.7.

Two particular instances illustrate how code-sharing is practised. British Midland code-shares on the through route Edinburgh–London Heathrow–Chicago with United Airlines. British Midland's designator code is BD and United's is UA. A morning flight from Edinburgh (dep. 08.45) is shown in the *OAG World Airways Guide* (April 1998 issue) as UA4833 to Heathrow (arr. 10.05) and as UA929 from Heathrow (dep. 11.00 to Chicago; arr. 13.20). British Midland operates the Edinburgh–Heathrow sector and markets point-to-point service on the route under its own code BD053; and United is able to 'hold out' a through service to/from Edinburgh as its own although it does not fly there.

In another example, Qantas operates a daily service between Sydney and Los Angeles under its code QF11 and has the codes QF3000–QF3008 assigned to connecting flights between Los Angeles and New York, Washington, Boston and Chicago which are operated by American

Table 4.7 Code-sharing agreements involving the largest airlines, December 1998[a]. *Sources:* Compiled from *OAG World Airways Guide, Airline Business* and various press reports

Air France (AF)

Aces Columbia
AeroMexico
Air Austral
Air France Express carriers
Air Mauritius
Air Seychelles
British Midland
Crossair
CSA Czech Airlines
Debonair
Delta
Eurowings
Flandre Air
Japan Airlines
Lot Polish
Malev
Maersk
Regional Airlines
Royal Air Maroc
Tunisair

All Nippon (NH)

Air Canada
Austrian
Lufthansa
United

American (AA)

Aero California
American Eagle carriers
Aspen Mountain Air
British Midland
CAIL
China Airlines
Iberia
Hawaiian
Gulf Air
Lot Polish
Qantas
Reno Air

SIA
South African Airways
Taca International
TAM

British Airways (BA)

Air Liberté
America West
British Airways Express carriers
British Asia Airways
CAIL
Commercial Airways
Deutsche BA
Eastern Australian
Finnair
Korean[b]
Lot Polish
Qantas

Continental (CO)

Air Canada
Air Micronesia
Alitalia
American West
China Airlines
Colgan Air
Continental Express
Continental Micronesia
CSA Czech
Eva Airways
Gulfstream International
Northwest
SkyWest
Transavia
Vasp
Virgin Atlantic

Delta (DL)

Aer Lingus
AeroMexico
Air France

Austrian
China Southern
Delta Connection carriers
Korean
Malev
Sabena
Swissair
TAP Air Portugal
TransBrasil
TWA

Japan Airlines (JL)

Air France
Air New Zealand
American
CAIL
Japan Air Charter
KLM
Qantas
South African Airways
Swissair
Thai Airways International
THY Turkish Airlines
Varig
Vietnam Airlines

KLM (KL)

Aer Lingus
Ansett Australia
Emirates
Eurowings
Kenya Airways
KLM Cityhopper
KLM Exel
KLM UK
Korean[b]
Japan Air System
Maersk
Nippon Cargo[b]
Northwest
Oman Air
Regional Airlines
Sun-Air

Lufthansa (LH)

Adria Airways
Air Atlantique
Air Baltic
Air Canada
Air Dolomite
Air Littoral
Air New Zealand
All Nippon
Augsburg Airways
Austrian
British Midland
Cimber Air
Crossair
CSA Czech
Lauda Air
Lot Polish
Luxair
Qatar Airlines
Rheintalflug
SAS
SIA
South African Airways
Team Lufthansa carriers
Thai Airways International
United
Varig
VLM

Northwest (NW)

Alaskan
America West
Continental
KLM
KLM UK
Northwest Airlink carriers
Pacific Island Aviation

Swissair (SR)

Aeromexico
AOM French Airlines
Azzura Air
Austrian
Crossair
CSA Czech

Table 4.7 *continued*

Delta	Lot Polish
Finnair	Lufthansa
Ladeco	Regional Airlines
Lauda Air	Spanair
Korean[b]	Skyways
Malaysia Airlines	South African Airways
Maersk	Thai Airways International
Malev	United
Sabena	Varig
Tatra Air	Wideroe's
Tyrolean	
Tap Air Portugal	**United (UA)**
THY Turkish	
Ukraine International	Aeromar Airlines
	AeroMexico
Qantas (QF)	ALM Antillean
	Aloha Airlines
Air Caledonie	Air BC
Air Niugini	Air Canada
Air Pacific	Air-India
Air Vanuatu	Air New Zealand
Air Zimbabwe	Air Nova
American	All Nippon
Asiana	Ansett Australia
Australian Airlink carriers	Ansett New Zealand
British Airways	British Midland
CAIL	Cayman Airlines
Emirates	Emirates
Japan Airlines	Kendall Airlines
Reno Air	Lufthansa
Solomon Airlines	Mexicana
Sunstate Airlines	SAS
UPS[b]	Saudia
Vietnam Airlines	Thai Airways International
	Trans States Airlines
SAS (SK)	United Express carriers
	Varig
Air Baltic	
Air Canada	**US Airways (US)**
British Midland	
Cimber Air	Deutsche BA
Falcon Air	US Airways Express carriers
Icelandair	

[a] The codes used are those of the airline in bold type, beneath which are listed the airlines actually operating the codeshared services.
[b] Freight services.

Airlines. In reciprocation American Airlines operates to Los Angeles under its own codes and assigns the codes AA6100–AA6118 to Qantas's connecting flights between Los Angeles and Sydney. In this way both airlines can market through services New York/Washington/Boston/Chicago–Sydney, with Qantas operating the transPacific sector and American Airlines the US domestic sectors.

The above examples can be referred to as 'complementary' code-sharing, where two carriers link up with each other to provide connecting services for an origin–destination city pair. Another kind is 'parallel' code-sharing, where two carriers operating on the same sector share codes. The main purpose of parallel code-sharing is to offer passengers a higher (co-ordinated) flight frequency than the carriers would be able to supply without code-sharing, in the hope that both would benefit from the L-shaped relationship between frequency and market share. For instance, Air Canada (whose designator code is AC) and Korean Airlines (designator code KE) code-share on the Vancouver–Seoul route, flight numbers of non-stop services (071 and 072 in the summer 1998 season) being prefixed by both carriers' codes, AC and KE.

Some alliances involve code-sharing of both kinds, as for example the KLM/Northwest alliance does. On the translantic sectors, KLM operates the Boeing 747 services and Northwest the Douglas DC10 flights, but both are entered in CRSs and in the *OAG World Airways Guide* under both carriers' codes. Beyond the hubs, KLM operates in Europe and Northwest on US domestic sectors, but both can market through services under their own codes.

Although it can be traced back 30 years or more code-sharing became a major marketing activity only relatively recently. The proliferation of code-sharing agreements reflects the growing emphasis on feeder traffic in hub and spokes networks. The contemporaneous development of sophisticated computer reservations systems has given some further impetus to code-sharing. This is especially so where the display algorithms give preference to online over interline services, whether the 'online' services are genuinely online or only made to appear so through code-sharing. For domestic travel within the United States all CRSs except Delta's DATAS II give preferential display treatment to online services; but for international travel this is not the case, because Codes of Conduct drawn up by the EC and ECAC specifically prevent such display preference. However it is still possible that international code-sharing has affected competition through CRS screen 'padding', when code-sharing airlines clutter the screen display with multiple entries of the same service, in this way pushing other airlines' service further down the screen, or onto the next screen page. Both the EC and ECAC Codes of Conduct limit this effect by permitting only two combinations of code-shared flights to be shown. Nevertheless permitting a code-shared flight to be displayed twice can penalize other, possibly better, travel options displayed only once. But the Civil Aviation Authority (1994) concluded that, in overall terms, the rise of international code-sharing in recent years was unlikely to have been caused by attempts to gain CRS advantages.

Where both carriers operate on the same route, the fact that they code-share could have a substantial impact in lessening competition between them, particularly if the agreement covers revenue or profit sharing as well. Code-sharing implies close co-ordination between the partners and it may be difficult to ensure that this does not lead to collusion in other areas, such as capacities and fares on other routes. On the other hand code-sharing may have some pro-competitive effects, insofar as it enables carriers to enter or develop routes that would not otherwise be viable to operate. This was for example the justification, put to the US Department of Transportation, by Northwest and KLM in defence of code-sharing on the Amsterdam–Detroit and Amsterdam–Minneapolis routes; and by Delta and Swissair in defence of Zurich and Cincinatti code-sharing (de Groot, 1994).

A number of studies have investigated the effects of code-sharing. One by the US General Accounting Office (1995) found that code-sharing often generates large gains for airline partners in terms of increased passenger numbers and enhanced revenues. But a paper by Hannegan and Mulvey (1995) shows that the gains achieved are largely zero-sum in that they come at the expense of competing airlines. The increased market shares achieved by the Northwest/KLM alliance (Table 4.8) can be attributed in large part to the code-sharing these airlines introduced in the first half of the 1990s.

Many factors other than code-sharing influence traffic development. An attempt to measure the net effects of code-sharing has been made by the International Civil Aviation Organization (1997a). The results of this study are summarized in Table 4.9. The ICAO study analyses traffic data for a sample of transatlantic city pairs over a period of ten years, to give an idea of the general pattern of traffic development. Using published information on airlines operating the services and on changes in market shares, comparisons were made of with/without code-sharing situations, due allowances being made for the effects of other factors on traffic growth and market shares. To the question of whether code-sharing resulted in strong increases in traffic, the evidence was mixed: the answer was negative in 45 per cent of cases and positive in 40 per cent (the remaining 15 per cent being cases in which it was too soon to tell). On the issue of the relationship between code-sharing and competition, the ICAO study suggested that in about three-quarters of the city pairs the competitive situation remained unchanged, but where it did change the effect was in the direction of reducing competition.

Table 4.8 Passenger traffic travelling Northwest/KLM between the United States and Europe/Middle East.[a] *Source:* Hannegan and Mulvey (1995)

	1991	*1992*	*1993*	*1994*
Total passengers on all carriers	1 488 160	1 688 570	1 744 090	1 810 780
Passengers on Northwest/KLM	17 510	23 260	52 510	60 630
Northwest/KLM market share (%)	1.2	1.4	3.0	3.3

[a] Routes between 34 US cities and 30 cities across Europe and the Middle East.

It should be noted that the ICAO results relate to parallel code-sharing in point-to-point city pairs, on direct non-stop routes between hubs. But, as explained in Chapter 3 (section 3.6), it is entirely possible for competition to fall on direct routes to/from hubs while at the same time increasing in through markets served via the hubs. And in another study, this time of complementary code-sharing on transPacific routes, it was found that code-sharing caused the leading airlines to behave more competitively and led to overall increases in traffic (Oum, Park and Zhang, 1996).

Other issues concern the effects on passengers. On the positive side passengers may benefit insofar as code-sharing facilitates the provision of higher service quality in terms of more convenient connections, single check-ins, baggage transfers, transferable bonuses in frequent flyer programmes and so on. It may also have the effect of reducing through fares. All this may increase the value of the joint product to the passenger. And code-sharing agreements do not necessarily imply exclusivity. It is at least possible to connect from a non-affiliated flight to one of the code-sharing flights; but where schedules, marketing, etc. are not co-ordinated in quite the same way, it is much less likely that the passenger will be able to find a convenient connection. Hence airlines participating in code-sharing agreements often argue that passengers derive substantial benefits from them. But an alternative view, expressed by the UK Civil Aviation Authority (1994) is that all these benefits could be provided by airline alliances without the need to code-share. And it has also been argued that code-sharing results in passengers being deceived or misled, when the airline identity at the boarding gate is not the same as that printed on the passenger's ticket.

Despite rules requiring the operator of the flight to be properly identified, it is clear that many passengers are still not being given full information on this. The rules apply only to CRSs and to things like the *OAG World Airways Guide* and there is no guarantee that correct information

Table 4.9 Effects of transatlantic code-sharing agreements on traffic development: agreements between European and US airlines in effect as of 31 December 1994. *Source:* International Civil Aviation Organization

Airlines	Route[e]	Context of traffic development[a]	Positive effect on traffic development[b]	Situation with code-sharing Change in competition[c]	Frequency of service[c]	Airline benefiting from change in market share[d]
Aeroflot/Delta	MOW–NYC	+	no	=	=	Delta
Alitalia/Continental	ROM–NYC	–	no	=	=	=
	MIL–NYC	–	(B)	=	=	=
	ROM–HOU	(A)	(B)	=	+	Alitalia
Alitalia/US Air	ROM–BOS	–	yes	–	–	Alitalia
Austrian/Delta	VIE–NYC	–	yes	–	–	Austrian
	VIE–WAS	(A)	(B)	=	+	Austrian
BA/US Air	LON–BWI	+	yes	=	=	BA
	LON–BOS	+	no	=	+	BA
	LON–CLT	=	yes	=	=	–
	LON–LAX	=	no	=	=	BA
	LON–NYC	+	yes	=	=	=
	LON–PHL	+	yes	–	–	BA
	LON–PIT	=	yes	=	=	=
SAS/Continental	CPH–NYC	–	no	–	–	SAS
	OSL–NYC	–	no	–	–	SAS
	STO–NYC	–	no	–	–	SAS
Malev/Delta	BUD–NYC	+	yes	–	–	Malev
Sabena/Delta	BRU–ALT	–	yes	=	=	Delta
	BRU–BOS	–	(B)	=	=	=
	BRU–CHI	=	(B)	=	=	=
	BRU–NYC	–	no	–	–	Sabena
Swissair/Delta	ZRH–ATL	+	no	=	=	=

Carrier	Route	[a]	[b]	[c]	[d]
	ZRH–CVG	(A)	yes	+	=
	ZRH–NYC	-	no	-	Swissair
	GVA–WAS	(A)	(B)	-	Swissair
TAP/Delta	LIS–NYC	=	no	=	Delta
KLM/Northwest	AMS–ATL	+	no	-	=
	AMS–BOS	+	yes	=	=
	AMS–CHI	=	no	=	=
	AMS–DTW	-	yes	+	=
	AMS–HOU	+	no	=	=
	AMS–LAX	+	no	=	=
	AMS–MSP	-	yes	+	Northwest
	AMS–NYP	+	no	-	KLM
	AMS–ORL	+	yes	=	=
	AMS–SFO	+	yes	=	=
	AMS–WAS	+	yes	=	=
Lufthansa/United	FRA–ATL	+	no	+	=
	FRA–CHI	+	no	+	=
	FRA–SFO	+	no	+	=
	FRA–WAS	+	yes	+	=

[a] An indication of how traffic was developing without code-sharing. The + sign denotes a growing trend, the - sign a decreasing trend and the = sign a standstill. (A) means the service was non-existent before the code-sharing agreement.

[b] Shows whether code-sharing has produced a positive effect on traffic development, i.e. a growth superior to the normal trend described in the previous column, or a reverse trend in the case of declining traffic. (B) means code-sharing agreement concluded too recently to allow sufficient perspective.

[c] - = decreasing; + = increasing; = no change.

[d] = signifies no change in market shares.

[e] Decoding as follows:

AMS	Amsterdam	LON	London
ATL	Atlanta	MIL	Milan
BOS	Boston	MOW	Moscow
BRU	Brussels	MSP	Minneapolis
BUD	Budapest	NYC	New York
BWI	Baltimore	ORL	Orlando
CHI	Chicago	OSL	Oslo
CLT	Charlotte	PHL	Philadelphia
CPH	Copenhagen	PIT	Pittsburgh
CVG	Cincinnati	ROM	Rome
DTW	Detroit	SFO	San Francisco
FRA	Frankfurt	STO	Stockholm
GVA	Geneva	VIE	Vienna
HOU	Houston	WAS	Washington
LAX	Los Angeles	ZRH	Zurich
LIS	Lisbon		

is passed on by the travel agent to the traveller. In two telephone surveys, one conducted by the US Department of Transportation and one by the UK Civil Aviation Authority sufficient information on the identity of the airline operating the flight was not given in a large number of cases (30 per cent in the US survey and as high as 60 per cent in the (preliminary) UK survey). Often the first time a passenger knows of a code-sharing arrangement is when he or she reports to the departure gate in the airport terminal (and in some cases perhaps even later than this). In particular business travellers not making their own reservations may be confronted with some unpleasant surprises! In this sort of situation passengers sometimes lodge complaints. The only real way of avoiding such complaints is to ensure greater disclosure at the time the passenger's booking is made. But so far as multisector journeys involving transfer connections at intermediate points are concerned, much of the purpose airlines have in code-sharing – and in franchising and block spacing as well – is to make interline connections appear so far as possible as online ones. Other things being equal, passengers prefer online to interline connections, in order to enjoy what is referred to as 'seamless' service right across their itineraries.

4.7 'Seamless' networks

In marketing joint services airlines have paid some attention to advertising their alliances. The text of a press advertisement placed by the former Delta/Swissair/SIA alliance read as follows:

> Global Excellence: A Seamless Travel Experience around the World with Three Excellent Airlines. For you, the co-operation of Delta Air Lines, Singapore Airlines and Swissair has pleasant consequences on a global scale. The timetables of all three airlines are co-ordinated to give you smooth access to more than 300 destinations worldwide. En route, there are 400 city ticket offices ready to serve you. And on a trip around the globe, you can benefit from specially attractive (around-the-world) fares. All these benefits add up to the perfect fit: Global Excellence and you.

Similarly, Northwest and KLM have made the following points in their publicity:

> The partners' synchronised timetables and once-only passenger and luggage check-in have created a seamless network of connecting flights...Hundreds of routes within North America have been opened up to UK travellers through feeder flights to KLM's home base at Amsterdam Schiphol Airport. The partners run joint venture services from there to 11

US gateway cities, of which three are major Northwest hubs offering dozens of onward connections.

The concept of a seamless network can be promoted when partner airlines adopt a common aircraft livery. This is what Northwest and KLM have decided to do in all their international operations, combining different features of their separate logos. And sometimes aircraft have been painted in the colours of both partner airlines, such as on the Alitalia/Continental code-shared service between Newark and Rome, on which the aircraft carried the Alitalia livery on one side of the fuselage and that of Continental on the other. But a common livery, or a common uniform for cabin staff, is unlikely to disguise a change of aircraft type, something that can cause some consternation to passengers preparing to board flights, as the author David Lodge (1984) knows:

> Inside the Rummidge Airport terminal...the flight to Heathrow is called, and Morris follows the ground hostess out onto the tarmac apron. He frowns at the sight of the plane they are to board. It is a long time since he has flown in a plane with *propellers*.

The emphasis appears in the original (and in this work of fiction 'Rummidge' seems to serve as a thin cloak of anonymity for Birmingham, from where at the time of the hero's fictional journey, flights to Heathrow were flown in non-pressurized Shorts 330 turbo-props).

Props are generally perceived as being less comfortable than jets. A passenger's inflight experience is clearly affected by noise, vibration and pressurization to a far greater extent in propeller aircraft. These physical discomforts can sometimes, for marketing reasons, limit the length of route over which props can be deployed, in some cases imposing more severe constraints on maximum flying times than the technical payload-range characteristics of the aircraft itself. Typical cramped-at-the-shoulders seating configurations add to the general discomfort, as do the arrangements for boarding and disembarking the aircraft. Manufacturers of the latest turbo-props are making efforts to render their machines compatible with standard (jetway) airbridges in use at major airports, in the hope that this will help to eradicate the distinction in passengers' minds between jets they hardly see and props which they often have to brave the elements to board. But perhaps even more important is passengers' perception of propeller aircraft as being 'old' and relatively less safe. For all these reasons passengers tend to prefer jets. But on short haul regional routes, and on feeder services to the hubs, props are very often cheaper for airlines to operate.

At the regional level the trade offs between jets and turbo-props can be described as follows: jets offer superior comfort, higher cruising speeds and greater productivity in terms of seat-miles per hour flown, whereas turbo-props offer better field performance and manoeuvrability, savings in fuel burn from greater propulsive efficiency and lower capital costs. The relative advantages of jets increase with sector distance. As a broad generalization, the break point occurs at a distance of around 250 miles. Below that turbo-props come out best in operating economics, their lower fuel costs outweighing jets' faster speeds. On the shorter routes there is often little appreciable difference in block (chocks off to chocks on) flight times, the higher performance of jets at cruising altitudes being, to varying degrees, offset by turbo-props' greater manoeuvrability at and near airports. For example, modern turbo-props, such as the ATR 42, Fokker 50 and British Aerospace ATP cruise at between 265 and 285 knots, considerably below the 425–450 knots offered by the British Aerospace 146, the new Canadair Regional Jet and the Fokker F28 and F100 aircraft. But the vast majority of regional routes are less than 250 miles. In an analysis of flight departures by jet and turbo-prop aircraft of less than 90 seats, across the Western world in 1988, it was found that over 80 per cent were operated on routes less than 250 miles, with only 7 per cent above 350 miles (Snow, 1990). In the USA the average distance per passenger travelled on regional airlines was 194 miles in 1992 (Regional Airline Association, 1993) while in Europe the mean sector distance flown by members of the European Regional Airlines Association in June 1991 was 225 miles (European Regional Airlines Association, 1991a). Sectors flown by the Swiss regional airline Crossair are typical, with 65 per cent of flights below 200 nautical miles. On sectors of this length the jets' higher speeds translate into a block-time advantage of just five to ten minutes. On longer routes jets retain more of their block time advantage, but the recent introduction of high speed turbo-props, like the Dornier 328 and Saab 2000, cut into their speed advantage here as well. At the same time the block fuel consumed by jets can be up to 50 per cent greater than that burnt by turbo-props of equivalent size on the same route. This is partly because the proportion of block fuel used by a jet during taxiing, take off, climb and descent rises to as much as 40 per cent on a 200 nautical mile sector.

On a great many routes turbo-props are more cost efficient and only marginally slower in terms of block time. They are also smaller, and in many cases more suited to the frequency sensitive business travel market served on regional routes than any of the jets currently in service. These factors should ensure that they have an important role to play for many years to come. But their relative lack of passenger appeal renders them vulnerable to competition from the new generation of regional jets soon to appear in the markets for 45 to 70 seater aircraft. Substitution in the reverse direction, from jets to turbo-props, did of course take place on deregulation in the USA, but in that case the jets that were redeployed

– to higher priorities on first and second level routes – were quite simply far too large to be in any sense economic on regional routes. Smaller jets will be far closer substitutes for turbo-props. And there are already indications of a return to jet service by some of the larger US regionals, as for example the sale of 10 British Aerospace 146 aircraft to Air Wisconsin bears witness.

It is likely that the choice between jets and turbo-props will be influenced by the hub-based major airlines to which regionals feed traffic. With competition in through travel markets becoming keener all the time, increasing attention is being paid to the seamless product concept. More and more, the larger carriers are demanding that regionals employ aircraft types that will minimize any perceptible differences in service quality in the eyes of the through passenger. Service quality is often of prime importance to passengers paying full business or first class fares, and while such passengers may be relatively few in number on any particular flight, the fares they pay form a disproportionately large part of total revenue yield, especially for the trunk route airline to which the passengers connect. When there is fierce competition between hubs, and when a passenger in planning an itinerary has an effective choice between two or more hubs, this can be a very important consideration. The contributory revenue from high yield passengers may compensate for the higher cost of operating jets and may be especially important in Europe, where many passengers on regional flights are using them as one leg on long haul intercontinental journeys. These points were apparently not lost on the Italian authorities when at one time they refused Crossair permission to upgrade to British Aerospace 146 'Jumbolina' aircraft on the regional route between Lugano and Venice, on the ground that the aircraft is 'too comfortable' (Crossair, 1991)!

Passengers may be concerned not just with the type of aircraft they are to fly in but also with the name and reputation of the airline operating the service. Large, well known, profitable or flag carrying airlines are often more acceptable to passengers than small, financially strapped and not very well known carriers from some remote or less developed regions of the world. Whether justified or not, passengers tend to associate airline names with varying degrees of safety, reliability and service quality. It was mainly recognition of this that led many airlines to fly under the banners of major carriers, such as American Eagle, Delta Connection, Northwest Airlink and United Express in the United States, a pattern is now emerging elsewhere in the world with British Airways Express, Team Lufthansa, Air New Zealand Link and so on. There is a lot in a name, at least so far as marketing is concerned. Just as McDonald's or Coca-Cola sell a universally known product through a usually unknown local operator, airlines may seek to market a brand, by standardizing and, where necessary, upgrading safety, reliability and service quality generally. To an airline parenting a brand this can be a useful way of transcending the limitations of air service agreements and generating additional feeder traffic. To airlines operating under another airline's brandname it can offer some escape from the competitive disadvantages they might be at on account of their relatively small size, their lack of presence in main markets and their image generally.

Bringing networks together so that they appear seamless to the travelling public is not always easy. Ensuring that passengers perceive no material difference in standards when changing from one airline to another within the overall brand may require extensive staff training. There is also the possibility that problems with one of the airlines flying the brand can have disproportionately damaging effects on the parent company and also perhaps on other brand carriers. One example of where such a problem might arise is where one of the airlines is beset by a number of fatal crashes in fairly quick succession.

5 Scheduling through hubs

5.1 Co-ordination of flight activity

Traditionally airline schedules were designed, either for the convenience of local point-to-point passengers, or to meet operational objectives such as maximizing aircraft/crew utilization, minimizing airport and station costs, etc. But the emphasis has now clearly changed. As markets become more competitive, more and more importance is attached to co-ordinating arrival and departure times to attract connecting traffic. An important part of this is to concentrate flight activity at the hub into a limited number of peaks, or waves, during the day. Services on the spokes are timed so that they connect at the hub, arrivals preceding departures in sufficient time to permit the transfer of baggage from inbound to outbound flights. Ideally a lot of inbound flights should arrive within a short a space of time and then depart again as soon as some minimum connecting time (MCT) has elapsed. To maximize the potential benefits the amplitude of each wave should be as great as possible. The fewer the number of waves across the operating day, the greater the number of possible connections. The theoretical maximum is achieved only if all flights are scheduled into just one large wave; and in theory, if all flights to or from a particular airport are timed so that a passenger could connect between any two, the maximum number of possible connections would equal the square of the number of flights. The objective here is to maximize the number of *useful* connections. Not all connections are useful ones, however. Some are entirely useless ones to return flights and some involve so much backtracking as to be of little use to passengers. Some are unattractive because they entail lengthy waits at the hub. But careful network planning can minimize the number of redundant connections and ensure that most of the scheduled linkages are indeed useful ones. In practice the number of waves an airline can schedule is subject to a number of important considerations concerning airport and airspace capacities, flight safety, aircraft/crew rostering, etc. High waves place severe peak load demands on airport capacity. The ideal kind of airport to operate as a high-capacity hub is one with a multi-runway airfield and just one large terminal building. Runway slots are often the most binding constraint, especially where there are restrictions limiting flexibility in their use. Peak load capacity can sometimes be marginally increased, for example if in the first phase of a wave all runways could be used for arrivals and in the second all used for departures. This is not always possible, however. Sometimes it is inhibited by environmental controls.

Other things being equal, concentration of flight activity at certain airports at certain times of day, increases the danger of collisions, both in the air and on the ground, as compared with spreading the same level of activity across a number of airports and across the day. To some extent there is a compensating factor here, insofar as connecting flights tend to reduce conflicting movements between arriving and departing aircraft. But most aviation accidents occur in landing/take-off or in climb/descent and, to the extent that hub and spoke operations reduce average sector lengths and encourage multisector routeings against direct non-stop flights, the development is not entirely conducive to flight safety. Flight safety records indicate that the risk to passengers on a non-stop flight is virtually independent of its length. On that basis, flying from A to B via C, which entails two flights, may be considered twice as dangerous as flying from A to B non-stop. However, it is by no means necessarily the case that hub and spokes systems, once fully developed, will result in a reduction in non-stop travel. Experience in the deregulated US domestic market has been that connecting passengers as a percentage of total passengers has increased only marginally since 1978 (Boeing Commercial Airplane Company, 1986). The proportion of passengers changing planes in hub and spokes networks is only fractionally greater than it was in linear networks before deregulation. What has changed with deregulation is the proportion of passengers changing airlines as well as planes: in deregulated markets online connections are now five or six times as numerous as interline connections, compared to the situation in regulated markets when they were both about the same. There is some evidence that non-stop point-to-point service, far from ubiquitous in the regulated era, has increased markedly in recent years. Much of this increase has no doubt been due to secular growth in US passenger demand, but an analysis of the years 1977 to 1989 (Barnett, Curtis et al., 1992) has shown that airline hubbing probably did not retard this development and perhaps accelerated it.

But there may be other reasons for concern about safety. One is the critical importance of punctuality. A late arrival at the hub has a multiplicative effect on delays, and from time to time there have been some suggestions that safety has been compromised in the interest of protecting schedules. There have been reports in the United States of 'near misses' and of maintenance checks and other procedures being rushed or simply overlooked in the rush to keep aircraft and crews in planned positions. In closely co-ordinated operations the pressure to maintain punctuality can be great. An initial delay can generate substantial widespread 'knock on' effects throughout the timetable. If in order to await a connection, a flight is held at the hub beyond its scheduled departure time, it is likely to be late again on its return to the hub leading to still further delays and missed connections. Late running may no longer be isolated to a particular flight but can be rapidly transmitted throughout the entire schedule. One of the drawbacks of hub and spokes networks is that inclement weather at the hub airport can delay or, in the worst eventuality, cause the cancellation of virtually all the airline's flights. Clearly, the prevalence of inclement weather is another important factor in hub location.

The problem of delays poses some difficult decisions. The principal dilemma lies between slightly delaying many passengers ready to board a flight departing the hub and severely delaying a few trying to connect to it. Some airlines take account of revenue yields from connecting passengers (i.e. first and business class exerting more influence than tourist or economy) and others consider the consequences of missed connections (the last service of the day being the one likely to be held the longest). At busy hubs delays can lead to difficulties in the allocation of runway and terminal slots, affecting other aircraft movements, and even where aircraft can absorb a delay, this may not be possible for its crew – especially the crew on the flight deck. When flight crews are approaching their duty-hours limit for the day, there is the additional complication and cost of finding fresh crew.

Despite all this there are airlines operating to demanding schedules that are consistently amongst the best in terms of on-time performance. In Europe for example, Swissair, SAS and KLM all operate to very tight schedules and yet all maintain excellent punctuality records. It is of course rather a case of having to be punctual if the highly complexed hub operations of these airlines are to succeed. Connections through European hubs are typically scheduled as shown in Figure 5.1.

Considerations of crew rostering sometimes place limits on the number of complexes per day. On short and medium haul operations there is little demand for services during the night (when in any case most airports have curfews). So most of an airline's fleet is necessarily left idle overnight, and traditionally aircraft return to the airline's home base, where maintenance and 'deep' cleaning are undertaken during the small hours. If the home base is being operated as a hub, this has an adverse effect on total connection opportunities, since the first flights out in the morning and the last returns in the evening are without feeder links. In effect one of the complexes is broken overnight. This could be avoided, if instead aircraft were to be stabled overnight at spoke airports. In the example illustrated in Figure 5.2, stabling at spoke airports

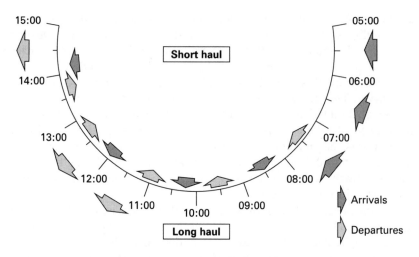

Figure 5.1 Typical connections scheduled at European hubs (Mondays to Fridays, up to 15:00 hours))

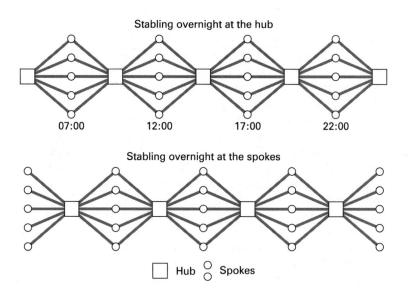

Figure 5.2 Effect of where stabling overnight takes place

increases possible connections by one third, with no change in the length of the operating day or in the number of flights. With stabling overnight at the hub, the airline can schedule only two connection complexes, whereas with stabling overnight on the spokes it can schedule three. Stabling on the spokes has been standard practice in US domestic networks for some time, but is still very much the exception in Europe. Stabling at the hub is far more common in Europe, partly because many long haul flights arrive at European hubs very early in the morning, to connect with short haul services starting out from the hub. But at the other end of the day there are not that many late-evening departures from European airports (apart from a few intercontinental services to Africa and South America), so that when the short haul aircraft return to the hub, they have little or nothing to connect with. Some European airlines, like KLM and Lufthansa, are beginning to stable away from the hub in their hinterland operations, in order to maximize connections in short haul markets. There are however certain diseconomies in this. It is more difficult and expensive to make standby provision at spoke airports, and some economies of scale in aircraft maintenance are sacrificed when the fleet is scattered overnight across the network. It is always possible to schedule maintenance by withdrawing aircraft from service in rotation, but emergency work may often require less 'flying spanners', mechanics and engineers travelling out from the hub, and this can push up maintenance costs quite appreciably. Stabling on the spokes might be less popular with crews. Unless crews are resident in spoke cities, extra lodging expenses will be incurred. These can amount to some not inconsiderable additions to costs, especially where the crew bringing in the aircraft on the last flight in the evening (perhaps landing as late as 23:00 hours) is unable to fly the first sector the following morning (taking off at 07:00 hours), so that two crews are required to night-stop in the spoke city. Stabling on the spokes can also be important to ensure the most appropriate schedules for the convenience of passengers. Passengers resident in spoke cities at both ends of a route through a hub can have vastly different requirements. More passengers in spoke City A may wish to travel to spoke City B than vice versa. For example, this may be the case, in some short haul business markets, where A is a small city and B a large one or where A is an outlying city in the airline's home country and B a capital city or major business centre in a country abroad. Differences in originating demand generate directional imbalances in passenger flows, the predominant flows being from A to B in the mornings and back from B to A in the evenings. Clearly, this can be an important consideration in deciding where to stable the aircraft overnight. To illustrate, British Airways schedules through services between cities in Scotland and cities on the continent via the new 'Eurohub' terminal in Birmingham. Aircraft are stabled in Aberdeen, Edinburgh and Glasgow, from where the first departures take place first thing in the morning, the final services of the day arriving back in Scotland in mid to late evening.

Another aspect of hub scheduling that can be very important for the convenience of passengers is the pairing of connections for round-trip journeys. To the extent that passengers' choice of transfer point is influenced by the ability to fly the same routeing on both outbound and return journeys, it is often not all that useful to have fast connections in one direction without matching ones in the reverse direction. This has been a particular problem for British Airways in London, sometimes putting the airline at a serious competitive disadvantage in markets for connecting traffic. For example, in summer 1986, fast (within 90 minutes) connections to/from BA transatlantic flights were available in just five Europe–North America city pair markets, a lot fewer than those to/from other airlines' transatlantic services. KLM for instance had over 50 paired connections.

5.2 Online and interline connections

Historically, BA's competitive position in through markets via London owed much to the advantage it derived from the sheer scale of flight activity at Heathrow, both in terms of service frequencies and in range of destinations served. London has always been an extremely important point on the international air services map. London's role as a leading political, commercial and cultural centre generates an enormous demand for air travel, and from this there developed a vast set of possibilities for connecting traffic. But hitherto London's success as a transfer point has been in terms of interline connections and, when the emphasis changed to online connections, its airports system was not ready to accommodate the change, rather like the system in New York.

In this respect BA's ability to compete for online connecting traffic has been hampered in ways similar to the problems that beset the former Pan American airline in the United States. Pan Am's main base was in New York which, like London, has been heavily congested for some time; and the operations of Pan Am in New York were split between two airports, just as BA's are split between Heathrow and Gatwick. Pan Am operated only a limited number of domestic routes and tended to rely on interline connections to supply feeder traffic from elsewhere in the United States. But with the demise of interline arrangements, other airlines increasingly preferred to feed their own hubs rather than supply interline passengers to carriers like Pan Am, a trend reinforced by computer reservations systems giving priority to online over interline connections. BA has always operated a large number of routes to/from London, but its flight schedules for connecting traffic have not always been well co-ordinated, partly because of the difficulty of securing appropriate slots (especially at Heathrow) and partly because of the ready availability of interline traffic.

Table 5.1: Traffic connecting through London[a] in 1984. (All values are percentages.) *Source*: Derived from Civil Aviation Authority (1984) London Area Airports Study

Delivering carrier	Receiving carrier			
	British Airways	*British Caledonian*	*Other airlines*	*Total for delivering carrier*
British Airways	27	–	15	42
British Caledonian	1	6	3	10
Other airlines	17	4	26	48
Total for receiving carrier	45	10	45	100

[a] Heathrow, Gatwick and Stansted
– Less than 1 per cent

The latter point is illustrated in Tables 5.1 and 5.2, which contain some results of a representative sample survey undertaken by the Civil Aviation Authority in 1984. The matrices here show distributions of connecting traffic by receiving and delivering carriers. Table 5.1 shows that just over a quarter of total connecting traffic was online to BA and 6 per cent online to British Caledonian, and that the now merged BA/BCAL was involved in just about half the connections either as delivering or as receiving carrier. These proportions were about double the

Table 5.2: Connections through Heathrow in 1984. (All values are percentages.) *Source*: Derived from Civil Aviation Authority (1984) London Area Airports Study

Delivering carrier	Receiving carrier					
	BA short haul	*BA long haul*	*Domestic UK[a]*	*Foreign short haul*	*Foreign long haul*	*Total for delivering carrier*
BA short haul	10	9	2	5	7	32
BA long haul	10	3	1	2	1	17
Domestic UK[a]	3	2	–	3	2	10
Foreign short haul	5	2	2	3	5	17
Foreign long haul	8	1	2	4	7	22
Total for receiving carrier	36	17	8	16	23	100

[a] Excluding BA domestic (included in BA short haul)
– Less than 1 per cent

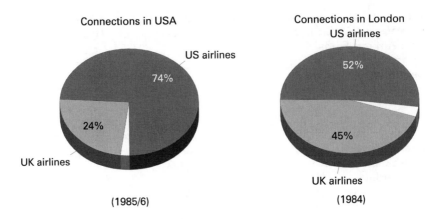

Figure 5.3   Connecting traffic London–USA routes (*Source:* Derived from the CAA's *London Area Airport Study,* 1984 and Office of Population Censuses and Surveys', *International Passenger Survey,* 1985–86)

proportions to be expected, if the numbers of connecting passengers simply mirrored the numbers of flights operated. So the British airlines did derive significant advantages from their hubs in London. But their position in London was not nearly so dominant as that enjoyed by some foreign airlines elsewhere. For example, KLM was involved in four out of every five connections in Amsterdam, compared with one in two for BA/BCAL. And roughly 60 per cent of Amsterdam's connecting traffic was online to KLM – more than twice the proportion of London transfers contributed by BA–BA transfers (27 per cent). A more detailed examination of transfers at Heathrow (Table 5.2) reveals some striking comparisons. It became apparent that BA fed more traffic to foreign carriers' long haul departures than it received in return for its own intercontinental flights – a rather unusual situation to occur at a home carrier's main base. Not only was the total number of connecting passengers received by foreign carriers' long haul services greater than the total received by BA's long haul flights, but the number fed from BA short haul to foreign long haul was almost three times as great as the corresponding number fed the other way, from foreign short haul to BA long haul. (The same imbalance was seen in traffic moving in the reverse direction.) Of course part of the explanation for this lies in the pattern of services supplied, the preponderance of BA on short hauls and the exceptionally wide range of foreign carriers on long hauls. But a relative dependence on interline transfers has often placed British airlines at something of a competitive disadvantage in some important markets, like the North Atlantic. It was clear that US airlines – at that time mainly Pan Am and

TWA, now replaced by American and United – received the lion's share of interline feed. And survey data relating to London–USA routes (Figure 5.3) shows how US airlines dominated when the transfers took place in the USA and how they even had the edge for traffic connecting in London. It was difficult for UK airlines to attract passengers transferring in the USA, not only because the gateway airport was often a major hub for a US airline, but also because computer reservations systems have given advantages to online over interline connections. The ability to share flight codes with domestic carriers in the USA reinforced these advantages. Overcoming the competitive disadvantages they faced in the US transfer market was clearly a prime motive behind the various alliances that European carriers formed with major airlines in the United States: BA with USAir, Lufthansa with United, KLM with Northwest, Air France with Continental, Delta with Swissair and so on. In London the US airlines possess 'combination rights' permitting them to market through USA–European services under single flight numbers and this has enabled them to achieve shares of London transfer traffic that are high in relation to the number of services operated.

It is now clear that the traditional concept of a hub simply as an airport with a large volume of flight activity undertaken by a large number of airlines is not so appropriate in deregulated markets as it was under regulation. This is because airports can now serve as effective hubs only for particular airlines. The US experience of interline connections being replaced by online connections is being repeated in international markets. Even at Heathrow, with all its problems of congestion, online connections as a proportion of total connections have increased quite dramatically in the last few years: BA–BA connections rose from 27 per cent of total connections in the 1984 CAA survey to 43 per cent in the 1991 CAA survey and are now thought to be in excess of 50 per cent. Except where carriers have joint marketing or code-sharing agreements, it is highly likely that interlining will decline still further. Passengers always tend to prefer single-airline service, both for convenience and for reliability. In the past restrictions on route entry often meant that airlines operating in different city pairs did not see each other as direct competitors and so they were more than willing to devise mutually satisfactory schedules to facilitate interlining. But now that these restrictions are being lifted, airlines are able to enter city pair markets previously closed to them and by routeing services through hubs can often provide online travel that is far superior to any interline alternative. For each airline the priority in scheduling is to complex flights at their own individual hubs. There may indeed be a strong motive for airlines to avoid timing services so that they connect with other airlines' services, because this could lead to a loss of through traffic. Also when airlines can enter through markets on their own, there is less incentive to offer joint interlinable fares.

Table 5.3 Interline connections through Manchester to/from Norwich (April 1998). *Source:* derived from *OAG World Airways Guide*

	Morning complex		Weekly frequency
Arrival			
0745	CB 201	Norwich	5
Departures			
0825	BA 6992	Gibraltar	1
0840	LX 881	Mulhouse	5
0845	JE 322	Isle of Man	7
0845	BA 1604	Paris	6
0850	LH 4627	Frankfurt	7
0850	BA 1705	Edinburgh	5
0850	BA 1615	Glasgow	6
0855	BA 7601	Belfast	6
0855	EI 203	Dublin	7
0900	BD 371	Aberdeen	5
0900	BA 8246	Billund	5
0905	BA 1640	Madrid	6
0910	LH 4553	Dusseldorf	6
0915	NG 9227	Vienna	5
0940	AC 843	Toronto	7
0955	SQ 327	Mumbai(Bombay)/Singapore	2
0955	BA 1720	Warsaw	2
1010	BA 7723	Knock	5
1015	BA 1654	Rome	4
1015	CX 290	Zurich/Hong Kong	2
1020	BA 7762	Jersey	5
1030	DL 139	New York/Philadelphia	7
1035	AA 55	Chicago	7
1040	SK 540	Copenhagen	6
1040	AY 934	Stockholm/Helsinki	1
1045	BA 7655	Londonderry	5
Arrivals			
0620	BA 1502	New York	7
0655	FR 5564	Dublin	1
0720	CX 271	Hong Kong	4
Departure			
0815	CB202	Norwich	5

	Evening complex		*Weekly frequency*
Arrival			
1715	CB 203	Norwich	5
Departures			
1755	BA 1610	Paris	6
1805	LH 4529	Frankfurt	7
1810	SK 542	Copenhagen	7
1815	AY 938/ BA 6008	Stockholm/Helsinki	6
1820	BA 8248	Billund	6
1825	BD 317	Aberdeen	5
1830	LH 5955	Munich	6
1845	BD 387	Edinburgh	6
1850	IB 3911	Madrid	7
1855	LX 887	Mulhouse/Zurich	6
1855	BD 397	Glasgow	6
1900	FR 557	Dublin	1
1900	LH 5937	Dusseldorf	6
1915	LH 5945	Hamburg	6
1915	NG 9229	Vienna	6
1920	BA 7609	Belfast	6
1925	BA 1622	Brussels	6
1940	JE 330	Isle of Man	7
1945	UK 3855	Geneva	3
2010	FR 559	Dublin	6
Arrivals			
1450	BA 1541	Madrid	6
1500	BA 1619	Brussels	5
1500	BA 7771/7773	Jersey	2
1500	BD 392	Glasgow	5
1550	AI 133	Mumbai (Bombay)	1
1555	BA 6993	Gibraltar	1
1605	BA 7914	Hanover	6
1625	BA 1869	Edinburgh	5
1630	BA 4887	Aberdeen	5
1640	BA 7765	Jersey	1
1655	LH 5690	Munich	6
1655	FR 556	Dublin	6
1655	BA 7786	Belfast	5
1700	BA 1687	Dusseldorf	6
Departure			
1740	CB 203	Norwich	5

Interline fares are now often more expensive than fares charged for online travel. For all these reasons online travel via hubs can be expected to grow at the expense of interline travel.

It is possible that interlining might survive at some places. Manchester Airport for example has made an interesting attempt to bring different airlines together to create a multi-airline hub. At Manchester there is a large diversity of airlines offering international scheduled services and the airport authority recognized that, if the airport was to achieve the 'critical mass' to sustain hub operations, with more routes and higher frequencies, it would have to embrace interlining (Muirhead, 1993). Otherwise it would tend to remain a spoke airport in the two-tier airport system polarizing in Europe. The view taken by Manchester was that, so long as Europe remained only semi-deregulated, interlining between carriers would still be an important factor. So the airport authority launched a marketing campaign, 'Manchester Connects', to publicize connections between international flights and regional services to cities like Belfast, Norwich and Cardiff. The connections are illustrated in Table 5.3.

At first sight they represent an impressive array of interline linkages. Norwich is a fairly large city, with a population of around 128 000, but it is not well served by direct flights. The only significant ones with onward connections are those to Paris and Amsterdam, operated by turbo prop aircraft taking 50 to 55 minutes. Similar turbo prop services to Manchester operated by Suckling Airways also take 55 minutes and these feed into morning and evening complexes to provide through passengers with a variety of connection possibilities. The airport authority was conscious of the desirability of providing good connections in both directions. But in this respect the schedules are not wholly successful. The morning flight from Norwich arrives in Manchester at 07:45, in good time to connect with flights leaving during the peak period for departures; but the aircraft turns round in half an hour and flies back to Norwich at 08:15, which is too early for connections to be made from all but just a few of the morning arrivals at Manchester. Also the Norwich-Manchester feeder links are operated twice daily, but only on weekdays. So a passenger from Norwich who wishes to make either the outbound or return journey at the weekend faces the prospect of surface travel on the Norwich to Manchester leg. And another problem with these schedules is that they are always vulnerable to hub airlines adjusting their service timings. If for instance Lufthansa were to advance its morning departure to Frankfurt by half an hour, or retard its arrival from Munich by 20 minutes, some important linkages will immediately be lost. The Manchester interline hub was clearly a well thought out marketing exercise, but the problem with it lies in coping with capricious alterations to flight schedules by a host of largely independent airlines, including the airlines supplying the feeder links. Indeed, the feeder links originally

Table 5.4 Minimum connecting times (MCTs) at selected airports, April 1998[a].
Source: OAG World Airways Guide

Amsterdam	0:40	short haul ↔ short haul
	0:50	otherwise
Atlanta	0:55	domestic ↔ domestic
	1:00	domestic → international
	1:30	international → domestic
	1:30	international ↔ international
Birmingham	0:30	domestic ↔ domestic
	0:45	otherwise
Chicago O'Hare	0:50	domestic ↔ domestic
	1:15	domestic → international
	1:30	international → domestic and
	1:30	international ↔ international
Copenhagen	0:30	domestic ↔ domestic
	0:45	otherwise
Frankfurt	0:45	
Hong Kong	1:00	
London Heathrow	0:45	within Terminals 1 and 4
	1:00	within Terminals 2 and 3
	1:00	Terminal 1 ↔ Terminal 4
	1:10	Terminal 1 → Terminal 2
	1:15	Terminal 1 ↔ Terminal 3
	1:15	Terminal 2 → Terminal 1
	1:15	Terminal 2 ↔ Terminal 3
	1:30	Terminal 2 ↔ Terminal 4
	1:30	Terminal 3 ↔ Terminal 4
London Gatwick	0:40	domestic ↔ domestic, South Terminal
	0:45	domestic → international, South Terminal
	0:45	within North Terminal
	0:55	international ↔ international, South Terminal
	1:15	South Terminal ↔ North Terminal
Mumbai (Bombay)	0:30	domestic ↔ domestic
	1:30	international ↔ international
	2:30	domestic → international
	4:00	international → domestic
Munich	0:35	
New York Kennedy	1:00	domestic ↔ domestic
	1:15	domestic → international
	1:45	international → domestic
	2:00	international ↔ international
New York La Guardia	0:45	domestic ↔ domestic
	1:00	otherwise
Paris Charles de Gaulle	0:45	within Terminal 2
	1:00	within Terminal 1
	1:15	between terminals
Paris Orly	0:50	domestic ↔ domestic

	1:00	otherwise
Rome	0:45	domestic ↔ domestic
	0:45	international ↔ international
	1:00	domestic ↔ international
San Francisco	0:50	domestic ↔ domestic
	1:00	domestic → international
	1:45	international → domestic
	1:45	international ↔ international
Vienna	0:30	
Zurich	0:40	

ᵃ There are numerous exceptions and variations by individual airlines.

featured in some of Manchester Airport's interlining publicity – and also used as an illustration in the first edition of this book – were those to and from Cardiff. But the airline operating these services, Air Kilroe, subsequently withdrew them when it decided to concentrate more exclusively on executive air charters. And so there are now no direct scheduled services between Manchester and Cardiff, and hence no interlining possibilities. Manchester has also lost some long haul services to which connections used to be possible. Qantas and South African Airways withdrew their Manchester services because the proportions of lucrative business passengers on these flights were rather low, 2.8 per cent and 3.9 per cent, respectively, as compared with 23 and 35 per cent from London Heathrow (House of Commons Environment, Transport and Regional Affairs Committee, 1998).

5.3 Quality of connections

Ian Botham, the former England test cricketer, in a television interview once declared Heathrow to be the 'best airport in the world', adding quickly as an after-thought, 'on the way in!' But as a UK resident Botham is unlikely ever to want to change planes there. Passengers making transfer connections might describe it in somewhat less complimentary terms.

One of the most important factors in the competition for connecting passengers is transfer quality, a factor embracing not just the interval of time required to change from one aircraft to another but also the simplicity and convenience of the connections process. Here single-airport, single-terminal systems operating some way below full capacity (e.g. Amsterdam) are at a distinct advantage. London however, is a multi-airport, multi-terminal system now heavily congested.

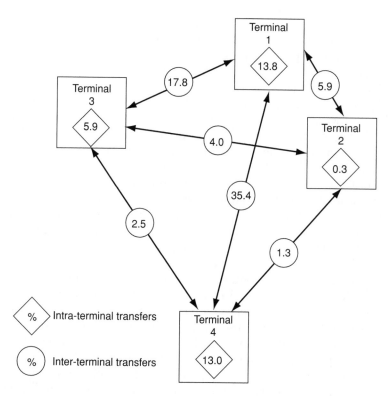

Figure 5.4 Intra- and inter-terminal transfers at London Heathrow (*Source:* Derived from 1996 CAA Survey)

Minimum connecting times (MCTs) for a selected number of airports are shown in Table 5.4. These refer to the minimum interval that must elapse between an arrival and a departure in order for a passenger to book a connection. Their length clearly depends on a number of factors. At busy congested airports (e.g. New York) the MCTs are longer than at places where the pressure on facilities is relatively less (e.g. at some of the smaller airports in the United States, where online connections can in some cases be made in as short a time as 10 minutes). Connections to/from long haul flights often require greater MCTs, because of longer loading and unloading times. Where the linkage is between domestic and international services, the requirement for passengers to pass through customs and immigration control also lengthens MCTs. Shorter MCTs apply where the transfer can be made entirely within the same airport terminal (e.g. in Amsterdam), especially if the terminal is a modern purpose-built facility (such as Birmingham's Eurohub and the new airport in Munich). Some of the longest MCTs occur where a domestic ↔ international connection involves an inter-terminal transfer (as at Chicago O'Hare, London Heathrow or, in an extreme case, Mumbai). At Heathrow 70 per cent of transfer passengers spend two hours or more making their connections, with 45 per cent of them taking over three hours.

A serious disadvantage at Heathrow is that ground facilities are divided between no less than four distinct terminals (and perhaps in the future five, if the proposed new terminal is built). What is more, unlike at some multi-terminal airports, the allocation of facilities is made with little attempt to minimize the number of inter-terminal transfers required. This situation is without a close parallel at any other major airport in the world and arises at Heathrow because of the traditional importance of interline connections and the sectorization of services between terminals in such a way that routes serving a similar geographical region leave from the same location. Generally passengers wish to connect between regions, not within them. There is for instance negligible demand for domestic ↔ domestic or Europe ↔ Europe transfers at Heathrow, and yet those are just those most likely to be accomplished within the same terminal building. This is illustrated in Figure 5.4, from which it can be seen that the proportion of Heathrow transfers involving a change of terminal is as high as two-thirds, and that just over 40 per cent of them require relatively difficult journeys, across one of the two main runways, between the central complex and Terminal 4. A possible alternative division between terminals is by airline, a system that operates well in other places where online connections predominate. Such an arrangement gives the locally based airline a useful advantage over competitors. For example, connections between the entire range of Air France's services can all be made within the same terminal at Charles de Gaulle airport in Paris.

And now, by concentrating all its own services and those of its partner airlines in the North Terminal, British Airways is seeking to do much the same thing at Gatwick – and with some considerable success. Gatwick's North Terminal is potentially capable of disembarking passengers from one service and embarking them upon another within 30 minutes, although the MCT is still (at the time of writing) scheduled at 45 minutes. And swifter connections between more highly co-ordinated arrivals and departures is already reflected in a dramatic increase in the number of transfer passengers handled by BA at Gatwick, up from 1.7 million (9 per cent of total passengers) in 1991 to 4.2 million in 1996 (17 per cent of total passengers). But it is not so easy for BA to achieve a similar result where the bulk of its transfer traffic connects, namely at Heathrow.

The relatively poor facilities for transfer passengers makes Heathrow vulnerable to competition from other airports in Europe. This has been recognized by the authorities – both British Airways and the British Airports Authority – who decided to invest £65 million in a new Flights Connection Centre. The purpose of this was to streamline the processing of transfer passengers, ease congestion in the terminals, simplify routes across the airport, provide dedicated lounges and enquiry desks, etc. At the same time improvements were made to the transfer baggage system, by adopting an airport-wide plan in place of arrangements under which all four terminals operated totally independent baggage handling.

Despite the problems at Heathrow, total transfer connections at the two main London airports have grown strongly. Between the years of the two latest CAA surveys, 1991 and 1996, international ↔ international connections doubled to 15 million passengers, while international ↔ domestic connections rose by 7 million. This compares with a growth of 29 per cent in non-connecting origin and destination traffic. In respect of international ↔ international connections a distinction can be drawn between 'airside' and 'landside' connections: passengers making airside connections do not pass through immigration control whereas passengers connecting landside do. At both Heathrow and Gatwick it has been airside connections that have been growing the faster. In 1991 only 8 per cent of total passengers at Heathrow were making airside connections, but by 1996 this proportion had risen to 14 per cent; and at Gatwick airside connections more than trebled over this period, from under 3 per cent of total passengers to over 9 per cent.

Passengers changing planes at Heathrow and Gatwick are travelling over a whole variety of different itineraries, and the major routeings they follow are identified in Table 5.5. The single most important routeing, especially for those passengers making airside connections, is between continental Europe and North America, which reflects the positions of both airports as gateways into Europe. This is reflected in the composition of passengers on board British Airways' transatlantic flights. See, for example, Figure 5.5, which shows that on one BA flight from Gatwick to Dallas no more than 30 per cent of passengers began their journeys in the UK. Due to the congestion in London increasing numbers of UK origin-and-destination passengers are making connections at continental European hubs. It is still the case that more connections are made by foreign origin-and-destination passengers connecting at a UK airport (Table 5.6) but the gap is narrowing rapidly. Direct international flights from regional airports are now much more of an alternative to services from London, the number having risen threefold over the last decade, from 68 349 flights in 1986 to 201 450 flights in 1997 (House of Commons Environment, Transport and Regional Affairs Committee, 1998). Most of the international services from regional airports are short hauls, Amsterdam now being served from seventeen regional airports in the UK, Dublin from sixteen and Paris from ten. These developments have meant

Table 5.5 Major routeings taken by transfer connecting passengers at London Gatwick and London Heathrow, 1996 (two-way flow in thousands of passengers and percentages of totals). *Source:* Civil Aviation Authority (1997)

(a) Gatwick

Airside

Europe	190 9.6 %				
Africa	115 5.8 %				
Asia/Oceania	58 2.9 %	0 0.0 %			
C&S America and Caribbean	164 8.3 %	1 0.0 %	1 0.1 %		
Middle and Near East	15 0.7 %	0 0.0 %	0 0.0 %	2 0.1 %	
North America	1 226 62.1 %	85 4.3 %	12 0.6 %	0 0.0 %	107 5.4 %	1975 100 %
	Europe	Africa	Asia/ Oceania	C&S America and Caribbean	Middle and Near East	Total

Landside

UK	23 1.1 %				
Europe	596 27.7 %	210 9.8 %			
Africa	91 4.2 %	43 2.0 %			
Asia/Ocenia	52 2.4 %	47 2.2 %	3 0.1 %		
C&S America and Caribbean	134 6.3 %	54 2.5 %	2 0.1 %	1 0.0 %	
Middle and Near East	31 1.5 %	12 0.6 %	0 0.0 %	0 0.0 %	0 0.0 %	
North America	482 22.4 %	279 13.0 %	52 2.4 %	11 0.5 %	0 0.0 %	24 1.1 %	2147 100 %
	UK	Europe	Africa	Asia/ Oceania	C&S America and Caribbean	Middle and Near East	Total

(b) Heathrow

Airside

Europe	288 3.8 %					
Africa	357 4.7 %					
Asia/Oceania	2 074 27.1 %	41 0.5 %				
C&S America and Caribbean	327 4.3 %	4 0.1 %	38 0.5 %			
Middle and Near East	152 2.0 %	2 0.0 %	21 0.3 %	8 0.1 %		
North America	3 310 43.2 %	194 2.5 %	411 5.4 %	0 0.0 %	434 5.7 %	7661 100 %
	Europe	Africa	Asia/ Oceania	C&S America and Caribbean	Middle and Near East	Total

Landside

UK	63 0.6 %					
Europe	2 518 24.2 %	895 8.6 %				
Africa	223 2.1 %	215 2.1 %				
Asia/Oceania	1 123 10.8 %	959 9.2 %	24 0.2 %			
C&S America and Caribbean	61 0.6 %	106 1.0 %	2 0.0 %	10 0.1 %		
Middle and Near East	344 3.3 %	171 1.6 %	0 0.0 %	0 0.0 %	11 0.1 %	
North America	1 398 13.4 %	1711 16.4 %	104 1.0 %	193 1.9 %	0 0.0 %	274 2.6 %
	UK	Europe	Africa	Asia/ Oceania	C&S America and Caribbean	Middle and Near East

North America row Total: 10402 / 100%

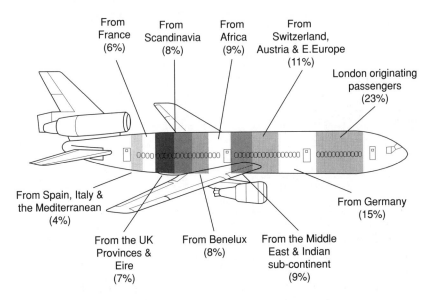

Figure 5.5 The importance of connecting passengers (example of Flight BA 193, London Gatwick–Dallas, 12 July 1996)

that only 55 per cent of passengers on international scheduled air services whose journeys originate or terminate in the regions actually travel via London airports, compared with 69 per cent in 1987 (and charter traffic is even better served from regional airports, only 14 per cent travelling via London). Nonetheless it is unrealistic to expect all regional demand to be met locally by services from regional airports, since they have a much smaller passenger base than the London airports, which in turn means that on many routes demand is insufficient to support a regular service, or at least a service at high enough a frequency to attract business travellers. For example, around 3 million passengers a year travel by surface transport from the West Midlands to board international flights at London airports rather than flying out of Birmingham International Airport. Although the pattern of services is changing in favour of direct flights from regional airports, it may be a very long time before regional airports can cater for the whole range of local passengers' demand.

5.4 Costs and benefits of hubs

Is airline hubbing a good thing? There is little doubt that it is good for the competitive position of the individual airline. But is it good overall? Does it produce any positive net benefits, when all the effects on the

Table 5.6 Balance in international ↔ international connections made by passengers using UK airports, 1994-95/1996[a]. *Source:* House of Commons Environment, Transport and Regional Affairs Committee (1998)

Airport	Estimated number of passenger connections[b]	
	out of the UK	over the UK
Belfast International	9 000	0
Bristol	32 000	0
Cardiff	32 000	0
Humberside	34 000	0
Teeside	18 000	0
Newcastle	79 000	1 000
Norwich	36 000	0
Southampton	14 000	0
Aberdeen	84 000	0
Birmingham	232 000	18 000
Edinburgh	145 000	0
Glasgow	193 000	2 000
London City	13 000	3 000
Gatwick	286 000	1 607 000
Heathrow	3 895 000	6 413 000
Luton	2 000	4 000
Manchester	632 000	40 000
Stansted	60 000	33 000
Total	5 796 000	8 121 000

[a] Data for Belfast, Bristol, Cardiff, Humberside, Teeside, Newcastle, Norwich and Southampton taken from the Civil Aviation Authority's Origin and Destination Survey for 1994–95. Data for Aberdeen, Birmingham, Edinburgh, Glasgow, London City, Gatwick, Heathrow, Luton, Manchester and Stansted is taken from the CAA's O and D Survey for 1996.
[b] Not including passengers travelling from a UK airport to a foreign hub and then transferring to a domestic flight in that country. (On routes to the USA such passengers can often form the majority of the on-board total.)

industry as a whole are taken into account? This is an important issue for public policy: to decide whether government authorities should do anything to prevent or discourage airlines from establishing and building up hubs or whether they should actively encourage hubbing.

This broad question is examined by considering the effects of hubs on:

- **airline costs**: does routeing via hubs have the effect of increasing or reducing the unit costs of operating services?
- **airports**: how do hubs affect the operation of airport facilities?

- **passengers**: what is the net effect of hubs on passenger benefits, when some passengers enjoy gains whilst others lose?

5.5 Effects on airline operating costs

To begin with, what effect does hubbing have on airline operating costs? Compared with direct flights, hubbing involves additional passenger handling, places greater peak-load pressure on the hub airport, and may have the effect of reducing the average sector distance flown. Passengers routed via a hub are involved in two boardings and disembarkations; and their baggage has to be transferred from one aircraft to another. The concentration of flight activity means that this has to be accomplished within a short interval of time which in turn means that extra staff and more sophisticated handling equipment are needed to cope with sharp surges in the flow of traffic. To a certain extent some of these costs are a burden, not just on the airline, but on the airport authority as well. But if hubbing reduces sector lengths, then the cost penalties from this fall on the airline alone, given that such a high proportion of its direct operating cost is incurred in take-off, landing, climb and descent. All these points are prima facie indications of a positive relationship between hubbing and unit cost – but that is far too simplistic a view.

One of the main determinants of unit cost is route traffic density. In this context density can be measured as the ratio of traffic to network size, for example passenger-miles divided by unduplicated route mileage, or passenger-miles divided by the number of cities served. It is well known that there are some significant economies in route traffic density (Bailey, Graham and Kaplan, 1985). These economies arise because greater density enables the airline to use larger, more efficient aircraft with lower costs per seat-mile and/or to operate at higher service frequencies and consequently at higher seat-load factors, which lead to lower costs per passenger-mile. An increase in density may also permit more intensive utilization of aircraft and crews, operating more flight hours per day. For all these reasons unit cost falls as traffic density in the airline's network rises, and hubbing has a major effect in increasing density.

Hubbing increases density by enabling the airline to consolidate traffic from many different origin–destination markets onto a much smaller number of links in the network. It makes it possible for the airline to carry, on a single spoke, passengers with the same origin but different destinations or, the other way around, passengers with different origins but the same destination. In this way hubbing reduces the number of round-trips necessary to transport a given number of passengers over a given set of itineraries. Total passenger-miles flown may or may not increase (depending on the extent to which passengers fly 'dog-legs'), but the main effects in reducing unit cost come from a reduction in sectors flown, an increase in aircraft size and/or a rise in service frequency and load factor. But to what extent does hubbing reduce unit cost in this way ?

Some empirical studies have been made using US data. Caves, Christensen and Tretheway (1984) provide some empirical evidence on the magnitude of economies of density. They estimated a statistical cost function for airlines that included both network size (cities served) and output (revenue passenger-miles) and found that, holding network size constant, total costs increase less rapidly than output, with the associated elasticity equal to 0.8. McShane and Windle (1989) found that for each 1 per cent increase in hubbing, unit cost fell by 0.11 per cent which, when related to airline output, implies that US airlines saved some $2 billion as a result of expanding their hub and spokes networks. And support for the hypothesis that hubbing reduces unit cost came also in another study (Brueckner, Dyer and Spiller, 1992), where it was found that mergers leading to a concentrated hub (between TWA and Ozark at St Louis and between Northwest and Republic at Minneapolis) generated significant gains in efficiency by creating larger networks. There have been other studies (e.g. Hansen and Kanafani, 1989) in which a more agnostic view was taken. The matter is quite complex. The indications that hubbing has some effect in reducing unit cost of airline operations are fairly convincing, but the evidence is not yet entirely conclusive.

5.6 Effects on airports

Airport economics

Hubbing is not entirely without its diseconomies, although these are largely external to the airline. In generating large volumes of transfer passengers, and requiring them to be handled swiftly, the hub airline contributes adversely to the peak-load capacity problem at the airport, not only on the runways but on the aprons and in the terminals as well. Its demand for facilities at the hub, such as baggage transfer equipment, can be very peaked indeed. Flight complexing leads to some severe peaking in arrivals and departures and this is necessary to ensure a large number of usable connections. But at the same time it can reduce efficiency in the utilization of airport facilities which might only be maximized when demand is spread evenly across the operating day. In this regard there can be a conflict between the interests of hub airlines and profit-motivated airport authorities. In many ways the economics of transfer traffic are not so attractive to airport operators as those of origin–destination traffic. In some cases fierce competition for 'footloose' transfer traffic, traffic that can choose between a number of different hubs, has induced some airports – like Amsterdam, Dublin and airports in Spain and Italy – to waive their passenger charges for connecting traffic. Income from aeronautical activities is often not so great as the revenue airports earn from their non-aeronautical commercial activities. But here too connecting traffic may often not be all that remunerative to the airport on a per-passenger basis. While at the hub transfer passengers do provide something of a captive market for retailers, but good connections mean less opportunity to spend money in airport shops. When passengers have barely half an hour to change planes, they have little time to patronize restaurants or the duty-free shop. Nor of course do they require car hire, parking and other things on which the airport earns income from concessions. Also there are no 'meeters and greeters' to provide an additional source of revenue, as there often are for travellers beginning or ending their journeys at the airport. For all these reasons privately owned airports subject to capacity constraints may, other things being equal, prefer to cater for origin–destination traffic, rather than connecting passengers.

For airports with spare capacity and for airports in public ownership, it may be a different matter. In the United States, airports are mainly owned by city and county authorities; and they actually vie with one another to become hubs. A clear motive is the huge potential for traffic growth, not just growth in transfer traffic, but in local origin–destination passengers as well. Demand from the latter can be greatly stimulated by the high level of service operated at a hub. Dennis (1993) illustrates this by comparing the 1977–91 growth of six medium-sized US airports, between three that developed as hubs and three that remained as non-hubs: the three hub airports (Salt Lake City, Minneapolis and St Louis) saw their traffic levels treble, while traffic at the three non-hub airports (Kansas City, New Orleans and Cleveland) tended to stagnate. The faster growth at a hub does have to be accommodated however, which often means that the airport authority has to invest in additional runway and terminal capacity, especially when peaks in traffic flows are exaggerated through flight complexing. But the growth in peak-load traffic will not generate the same proportionate increase in surface access and egress requirements, when a large part of the increased traffic is merely travelling through the airport to connect from one flight to another.

Scheduling through hubs can create peaks, not just at the hubs themselves, but also at spoke airports.   When aircraft are stabled overnight on the spokes, services to various hubs all start from the spoke airport in the early morning and return there in the late evening. So there are at least two localized peaks at the spoke airport, a departures peak at around 07:00 and an arrivals peak after about 22:00. And there can be a number of other peaks during the day, depending upon how many round-trip repeat cycles are made and on the distribution of route lengths from the spoke to various different hubs. If flying times between a given spoke and a number of different hubs are broadly similar, aircraft will be arriving and departing the spoke in waves just as they do at the hubs. But even if the flying times to the different hubs vary quite a lot, there can still be some peak problems at the spoke, if synchronization of activity at the hubs requires some variation in turn-around times at the spokes, i.e. lengthening those for the shorter flights. This can add to peak-load pressure on gate availability at the spoke. Given that virtually all traffic at spoke airports is origin–destination traffic, any accentuation of peaks in flight activity carries over to peaks in demand for surface access and egress facilities. The extent of this peak-load problem clearly depends on the level of traffic at the spoke. At some of the larger spoke airports in the United States, e.g. Norfolk, Virginia and Orange County, California, there can often be some very sharp peaks indeed.

Development benefits

The fundamental reason why local authorities are so keen to see their airports develop as hubs is the boost this gives to the local economy, both the direct impact on incomes from increased employment and the indirect multiplier effects from increased spending generally in the local area. In addition hubs play a role in attracting tourism, conferences and, most important of all, new industrial and commercial businesses, all of which can give further fresh impetus to the local economy. Various surveys of factors affecting industrial location have found that the presence of a comprehensive network of air services disproportionately strengthens the attractiveness of a particular city or region. Examples abound of firms' locational decisions being tipped in favour of one city rather than another because of its airport's function as a hub. Sony's decision to locate a large components factory in Pittsburgh mainly rested on the expansion of USAir's hub there. In 1991 United Parcels Service decided to move its headquarters from Connecticut (because of high housing and staff costs in that locality) and the final shortlist of alternative locations included Kansas City, Dallas and Atlanta. Kansas City was eliminated because of its comparatively low level of air services; and UPS eventually plumped for Atlanta, having calculated that the company would save the equivalent of over two man years of travel time on the 18 000 air journeys made by its headquarters staff each year by locating in Atlanta as compared with Dallas. Since 1976, the year in which Atlanta received its first transatlantic service, over 1000 foreign-based firms have located enterprises in the Atlanta metropolitan region. Another place where hub development has led to a dramatic increase in the number of firms locating there is Nashville. In 1991 Nashville attracted Caterpillar's finance division, a medical technology manufacturer, the brokerage headquarters of a British insurance company employing over 1000 people, the US headquarters of Bridgestone/Firestone Inc., the Canadian group Northern Telecom, the administrative centre of the National Federation of Small Businesses, and so on. Over 3000 new jobs were created from corporate relocations in one year alone (Small, 1993). The kind of businesses for which air service is an important locational consideration are: those whose operations are widely dispersed geographically, e.g. a large multinational organization; those whose highly specialized and technology- or knowledge-based activities require a diverse network of suppliers, clients and associates; and those manufacturing low-bulk, high-value products incorporating a high degree of added value. The highly skilled and highly paid employment generated by businesses like these enhance the multiplier effects on the local economy, when high disposable incomes are spent on locally produced goods and services, and when similar kinds of businesses are attracted in a kind of ripple effect.

None of this is lost on 'city fathers' and other local government officials. The economic development benefits flowing from hubs are such as to justify public investment in airports and expenditure on various inducements to airlines – in the form of tax breaks, low-cost loans and subsidies. Indeed there have been several notable instances of local authorities in the United States affording domestic airlines much the same thing as countries have supplied to national carriers as state aids. In the recent recession several hub cities have taken steps to support their incumbent hub airlines with financial packages that the press have come to label 'hubsidies'. For instance, in December 1991, an alliance between the State of Minnesota and the Minneapolis–St Paul city authorities put together a package of grant aid and loan guarantees for Northwest worth a total of $838m, in exchange for promises from the airline that it would maintain service levels and thereby safeguard local employment (*The Economist*, 1992). In 1992 a similar arrangement between the State of Arizona and the city of Phoenix raised $70m to keep its hub airline America West from bankruptcy. And now there are reports that American Airlines is being courted by the State of North Carolina regarding its hub at Raleigh–Durham, a conurbation which used to be heavily dependent upon the steel industry and which without its aviation-related employment would once again become a depressed area. The hub at Raleigh–Durham has never made much money for American, but its closure would have very serious repercussions on the overall level of economic activity in the area.

The importance local authorities place on hubs is reflected in some of the investments they make. Pittsburgh spent $870m on a new terminal complex to strengthen its role as a principal hub for USAir. In April 1993 Nashville agreed to buy USAir's Charlotte–London route licence for $5m, so that it could be transferred to Nashville and then operated by American. But the most ambitious investment was made by Denver, where an entirely new airport is being built on a greenfield site of 53 square miles, consisting of five runways and 80 gates with expansion potential for 12 runways and 260 gates. The total cost of this project is estimated at $2.7 billion, expenditure justified on economic development grounds to the electorate of the State of Colorado, where as much as 10 per cent of total employment has been attributed to Denver's original Stapleton Airport. Investments like this show a lot of faith in the power of hubs to generate external effects on incomes and employment. But the strategy is not without risks. Airport facilities cannot move in the same way as airlines can. And there have already been cases of cities losing their hubs, e.g. Dayton, Ohio. Nonetheless the attractions of hubs appear to be very great, at least to publicly owned airports – and not just within the United States. In Paris, the French have for a long time been developing plans to turn Charles de Gaulle Airport into a 'golden hub', with proposals for five runways, new terminals and improved surface access, to raise the airport's capacity to 100 million passengers a year early next century, dwarfing London Heathrow's current throughput of around 40 million.

The comparative lack of any similar plans in Britain led *The Times* (1 Dec. 1989) to comment that the 'contrast between French dynamism and British pettifogging in the field of transport planning is glaring'. This may seem a somewhat harsh criticism, given the formidable enviromental problems to be overcome if there is to be any significant expansion at Heathrow or, for that matter, at Gatwick. The French were able to select a greenfield site for Charles de Gaulle in 1964, in a tract of featureless and empty agricultural land, which gave room for almost any development that might be needed. Similar greenfield sites in South East England have proved very difficult to find, the main possibilities for entirely new airports being off-shore locations somewhere in the Thames Estuary. But one large airport can offer a much wider range of hubbing services than two or three airports of the same total capacity. This would indicate the further development of Heathrow. Without this there is a risk of the United Kingdom being set at an increasing disadvantage in competition with other European countries for the activities of multinational companies and international organizations. In particular, there could even be a serious challenge to London's position as a leading

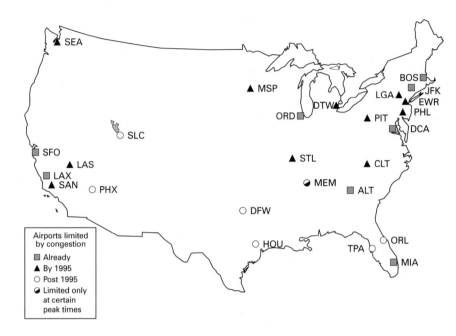

Figure 5.6   Congestion at airports in the United States (*Source:* SRI International)

centre for financial services. The external benefits from expansion of Heathrow are clear enough, but so too are the external costs, since it would mean increasing air traffic in one of the most environmentally damaging locations in the country. The question is whether the external benefits exceed the external costs; and also whether the total net benefit to the economy (the net difference between positive and negative externalities plus any net revenue from the increase in air traffic) is greater or less than the net benefit that could be gained by devoting the same amount of resources elsewhere.

Capacity shortages

Finding suitable sites for additional airport capacity presents some very great difficulties. There is often little prospect of any immediate relief from new construction. The timescale for planning and building new runway and terminal capacity is long, typically 10 years. In the meantime congestion is a serious and growing problem. There are already many airports around the world, approximately 130 of them, that are subject to scheduling constraints of one kind or another, and the number might rise sharply in the years ahead. Under a medium scenario

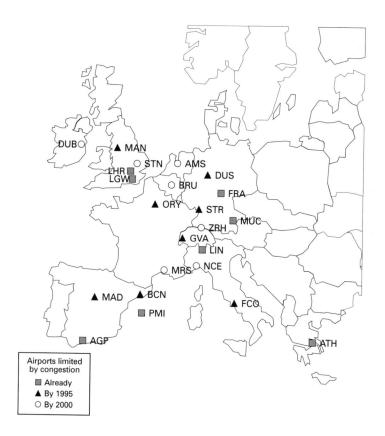

Figure 5.7 Congestion at airports in Europe (*Source:* Airbus Industrie)

of future growth in traffic, a group of 26 of the largest airports in the United States (Figure 5.6) and 24 in Europe (Figure 5.7) will be capacity constrained by the year 2000; and if as a result of increasing liberalization, the demand for services to and from busy hubs grows faster, the number could go over 30 in both cases. Of major airports elsewhere in the world, there are 15 that are capacity constrained in the Middle East and Africa, 14 in Asia and ten in Australasia. Some indication of the scale of activity at the busiest airports is given in Table 5.7.

The pressures on airport capacities are increasing all the time. With the increased emphasis on hubbing in liberalized air travel markets even more importance is attached to the S-shaped relationship between service frequency and market share. In order to maintain or increase their frequencies in more competitive markets, many airlines have been reducing the size of aircraft they fly. It used to be thought that the problem of airport capacity shortages might be ameliorated to some

Table 5.7 The top 50 airports (ranked by passenger numbers) January–June 1998. *Source: Airline Business*

	Airport (code)	Passengers[a] (millions)	Freight (tonnes thousands)	Aircraft movements (thousands)
1	Atlanta (ATL)	36.1	443.5	414.4
2	Chicago (ORD)	34.8	702.8	436.0
3	Los Angeles (LAX)	29.5	887.9	389.7
4	London (LHR)	28.8	638.8	217.9
5	Dallas (DFW)	28.2	389.7	420.2
6	Tokyo (HND)	23.6	314.8	114.7
7	Frankfurt (FRA)	20.0	707.5	202.1
8	San Francisco (SFO)	19.3	375.7	210.5
9	Paris (CDG)	18.1	488.9	203.0
10	Houston (IAH)	18.0	155.1	257.5
11	Denver (DEN)	17.9	218.9	236.5
12	Miami (MIA)	17.3	895 4	271.4
13	Phoenix (PHX)	16.2	179.4	264.0
14	Detroit (DTW)	16.0	145.9	271.1
15	Amsterdam (AMS)	16.0	610.2	184.1
16	New York (EWR)	15.5	541.5	224.9
17	Las Vegas (LAS)	15.0	–	225.1
18	New York (JFK)	14.9	800.2	172.3
19	Minneapolis (MSP)	14.3	195.2	243.2
20	St Louis (STL)	14.2	67.1	248.5
21	Orlando (MCO)	14.2	125.5	182.4
22	Seoul (SEL)	14.0	799.7	105.4
23	Hong Kong (HKG)	13.4	825.7	86.7
24	London (LGW)	13.1	142.0	115.1
25	Toronto (YYZ)	12.9	178.0	208.9
26	Boston (BOS)	12.7	219.4	240.7
27	Bangkok (BKK)	12.6	354.2	90.0
28	Rome (FCO)	12.2	139.9	125.4
29	Paris (ORY)	12.1	108.5	119.8
30	Madrid (MAD)	12.1	132.6	129.6
31	Seattle (SEA)	11.9	204.7	192.2
32	Philadelphia (PHL)	11.8	270.0	228.6
33	Tokyo (NRT)	11.7	789.7	–
34	Honolulu (HNL)	11.6	237.1	164.9
35	Singapore (SIN)	11.5	628.4	89.0
36	Charlotte (CLT)	11.3	87.3	217.5
37	New York (LGA)	11.1	35.7	175.5
38	Sydney (SYD)	10.3	250.8	138.3
39	Cincinnati (CVG)	10.2	181.1	216.6
40	Pittsburgh (PIT)	10.0	80.9	223.1
41	Salt Lake City (SLC)	9.9	92.0	177.3

42	Osaka (KIX)	9.3	358.5	59.3
43	Mexico City (MEX)	9.0	–	133.4
44	Munich (MUC)	9.0	58.6	128.3
45	Zurich (ZRH)	9.0	234.3	139.2
46	Brussels (BRU)	8.5	286.1	146.1
47	Stockholm (ARN)	8.0	71.5	134.2
48	Beijing (PEK)	7.9	154.7	–
49	Washington (DCA)	7.9	173.0	177.9
50	Sao Paulo (GRU)	7.9	183.9	90.6

a Passenger numbers include both those originating or terminating their journeys at the airport in question and those making transfer connections there. In these statistics each transfer passenger is counted twice, once on arrival and once on departure.
– Not available.

extent by an upsizing over time in aircraft types flown. But the increased emphasis on high frequencies (and also the introduction of smaller twin-engined long range aircraft) has meant that aircraft size has stopped growing, and there has been something of a reversal in trend, from upsizing in the 1960s and 1970s to downsizing in the 1980s and early 1990s. Changes over time in the average size of aircraft flown by members of the Association of European Airlines are shown in Figure 5.7. The average number of seats in aircraft operated by AEA members increased rapidly from 106 in 1973 to a peak of 139 in 1982, thereafter going into a gentle decline, so that by 1992 it had fallen to 133 (Doganis,

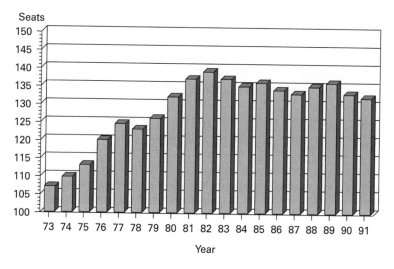

Figure 5.8 Average aircraft size, 1973–91 (*Source:* Doganis, 1992)

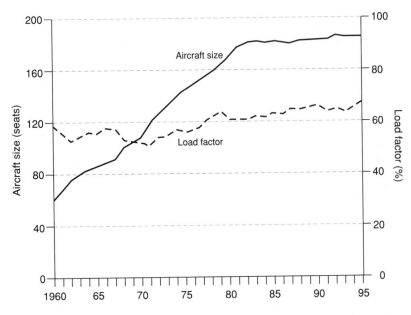

Figure 5.9 Average aircraft size and load factor (passenger aircraft on scheduled service)

1994). The same point is illustrated, for the world as a whole, in Figure 5.9. From 1960 to 1980 average aircraft size just about tripled from 60 to 180 seats, but since then it has remained fairly constant. Average load factors have been more or less constant too, although a slight upward trend is discernible (from load factors a little below 60 per cent to load factors a little above). Some comparisons between frequency and aircraft size at the main US and European hubs (Table 5.8) show very clearly the effect that the increased emphasis on frequency competition has had on the average number of seats per flight departure over the past decade or so.

To meet increased traffic demand some airport expansion is taking place. There are a few new airports being built, notably those in Denver, Sydney, Hong Kong and Osaka, but mostly the extra capacity is being provided by expansion of existing airports. In Europe, where some of the most serious capacity constraints apply, new runways are planned for Amsterdam, Paris Charles de Gaulle, Athens, Helsinki, Madrid, Manchester, Oslo, Rotterdam and Stockholm; but those cases apart, the plans are generally for more terminal and gate capacity. The UK Government set up the RUCATSE (Runway Capacity to Serve the South East) Working Group to investigate various possible ways of expanding airport capacity in the London area (Department of Transport, 1993). The

Table 5.8 Departures and seats per departure at main US and European hubs, July 1985 and July 1997. *Source: Airline Business*

Hub	Carrier	Departures per week			Seats per departure		
		1985	1997	% change	1985	1997	% change
Washington Dulles	United	103	1722	1572	200	67	-67
London Gatwick	BA	86	1163	1252	116	125	8
Los Angeles	United	520	1990	283	203	113	-44
Minneapolis	Northwest	940	3400	262	159	111	-30
Amsterdam	KLM	426	1416	232	178	129	-27
Brussels	Sabena	330	948	187	118	103	-13
San Francisco	United	894	2392	168	156	131	-16
Munich	Lufthansa	471	1206	156	128	105	-18
Vienna	Austrian	219	494	126	126	125	-1
Chicago O'Hare	American	1543	3327	117	165	117	-29
Dallas–Fort Worth	American	2584	5394	109	142	115	-19
Frankfurt	Lufthansa	936	1913	104	163	165	2
Zurich	Swissair	543	1109	104	148	130	-12
Atlanta	Delta	3219	5543	72	136	139	2
Chicago O'Hare	United	2263	3738	65	168	131	-22
London Heathrow	BA	1125	1642	46	178	212	19

RUCATSE Group was not asked to recommend one particular option but to set out the broad scale of the benefits and to assess the environmental and other implications. It considered the possibilities of adding an additional runway at Heathrow and/or Gatwick (Figure 5.10) but found the environmental costs to be rather high: a third runway at Heathrow would require the demolition of no less than 3000 houses together with the removal of some commercial property; and a second runway at Gatwick would have a major impact upon the historic village of Charlwood which would find itself sandwiched between the old and new runways. The RUCATSE Group considered the development of a new airport on land reclaimed from the Thames estuary. The so-called 'Marinair' concept involved an airfield as an artificial site about 32 km east of Tilbury and 8 km north of the Kent coast, with the main terminal constructed near Tilbury and linked to the airfield by rail, partly in tunnel and partly on viaduct (and with a tunnel/viaduct link to the Kent coast primarily for staff and supplies). Amongst the disadvantages that the RUCATSE Group saw in this proposal is the difficulty of attracting airlines and passengers away from other airports (as the example of Stansted has shown). The Group argued that pressure on existing airports might have to be intense before many airlines would mount services from a new airport at such a distance from central London; and it estimated that there might be little natural demand for a site like Marinair until around the year 2015. In its overall conclusion the RUCATSE Group suggested that the London and the South East area could manage with existing runway capacity for another 20 years, and that the need for additional runway capacity could be postponed further by providing extra terminal capacity, by making better use of existing runways and by diverting traffic to other UK airports. There is now a public inquiry into a proposal to build a fifth terminal at Heathrow (British Airports Authority, 1994); and a number of suggestions have been put forward for increasing runway capacity.

The Chartered Institute of Transport (1994) has argued that adding 'close-parallel' runways running 200 metres from the existing pair at Heathrow could have the overall effect of increasing total capacity by 50 per cent, from 80 to 120 aircraft movements an hour. If take-offs and landings were to be dovetailed, this would offer much greater scope for hub operations at Heathrow. Two close-parallel runways would be equivalent to building a third fully operated runway (as illustrated in Figure 5.10) but without any increase in the total land area occupied by the airport and without requiring the demolition of residential property. Although noise levels would increase with the increase in movements, Heathrow's total noise 'footprint' (the total area of land affected by noise) would remain the same, since the development of close-parallel runways could be carried out entirely within the existing airfield perime-

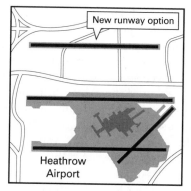
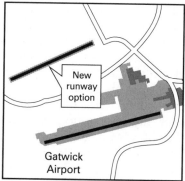

Figure 5.10 Possible new runways for Heathrow and Gatwick (*Source:* Adapted from the Department of Transport RUCATSE report, 1993)

ter. Close-parallel runway systems are already in use in Atlanta, Los Angeles and Miami, and there are advanced plans for similar developments in Manchester and Paris. They are a well proven method of increasing airport capacity and, if introduced at Heathrow, could do much to enhance the airport's competitive position *vis-à-vis* other major hubs in north west Europe. It is sometimes assumed that failing to do anything about the capacity constraints at Heathrow will simply lead to a redistribution of traffic to other airports in the South East, such as Gatwick, Stansted or Luton. But it is just as likely, if not more likely, that the diverted traffic will go to continental hubs such as Amsterdam, Paris and, to the extent that capacity constraints there permit it, Frankfurt. This is particularly likely in the case of through traffic connecting at the hubs.

Another suggestion for easing airport congestion has been put forward by the European Regional Airlines Association (1991b). The ERA argues that some additional capacity could be released through the adoption of revised operating procedures similar to those operated successfully at some US airports. The point being made here is that current take-off and landing procedures at European airports have been established for a considerable period of time and take no account of technological advance in the performance of regional aircraft (British Aerospace, 1991). In particular, European airports have so far taken little advantage of capabilities in modern aircraft for steep-angle approaches. At first this may sound a little dangerous. But experience in the United States has demonstrated that, with little expenditure on existing facilities, a new technique for regional aircraft could do much to alleviate the pressure on runway slots and improve access to busy hub airports, all in an entirely safe manner. Since the late 1970s a separate access landing system (SALS) has been in successful operation at busy airports like Washington National, Philadelphia and New York Kennedy. The SALS concept combines the manoeuvrability and steep-angle approach of the new generation of regional aircraft with a three dimensional area navigation system, to provide regional aircraft with a direct routeing through congested airspace separate from that of other aircraft. A regional aircraft can be taken out of the main traffic flow and given separate access to a landing on the stub of the runway, stopping short of any intersecting runway in use by other aircraft. This has a number of advantages. First, it reduces the load on air traffic control (ATC) since the approach path is flown automatically, on a pre-programmed route. Second, it improves the efficiency of the traffic flow. By removing smaller and slower regional aircraft, it reduces the need for large separations between aircraft of different sizes that would otherwise be needed to avoid vortex turbulence. The airlines benefit from savings in fuel burn and from fewer delays resulting in improved aircraft utilization. The latter is not an insignificant advantage. For delays can be a serious problem in regional operations as the managing director of Brymon Airways has explained:

> Our average flight time is just over the hour. If we suffer a 45 minute ATC delay the effect is clearly more pronounced than would be evident on, say, a transatlantic flight of seven or eight hours... In the past three months we have lost 800 flying hours to ATC delays. If that rate continues we could lose over 3000 hours during the year – equivalent to one aircraft's annual utilisation.
>
> (Naylor, 1991)

Many of the larger and more congested European airports, such as Athens, offer good opportunities for application of the SALS concept, but airport and ATC authorities understandably need to be convinced. To this end the European Regional Airlines Association (ERA) produced a proposal for Frankfurt airport, the experimental application of which is illustrated in Figure 5.11. There may be a case for investigating the general introduction of SALS in Europe. For not only could it help in relieving airport congestion, it could also provide regional operations with access to a greater number of slots at the hubs, something that is also becoming important to major airlines seeking to extend their marketable networks through partnerships with regional airlines feeding them traffic.

Slot allocation

Pressure on existing airport capacities has led to slots being rationed. Take-off and landing slots are typically rationed in one of two ways, by 'traffic distribution rules' or by scheduling committees. Under the

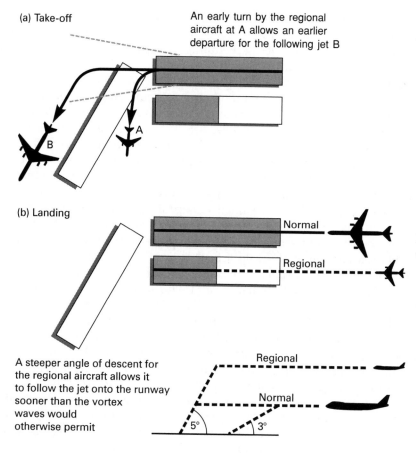

(a) Take-off

An early turn by the regional aircraft at A allows an earlier departure for the following jet B

B

A

(b) Landing

Normal

Regional

A steeper angle of descent for the regional aircraft allows it to follow the jet onto the runway sooner than the vortex waves would otherwise permit

Regional

Normal

5°   3°

Figure 5.11 Experimental procedures for regional aircraft at Frankfurt airport)

former, government authorities prevent certain types of air traffic (e.g. freight, general aviation) from using the busiest airports in peak periods, except on a highly restrictive 'prior permission' basis; and in scheduling committees, airlines bargain with each other for use of particular slots, with existing users having first entitlement, under a system of 'grandfather' rights, subject to a 'use it or lose it' rule (whereby if an airline was allocated the slot last year but used it less than a certain proportion (usually 80 per cent) of the time, the slot would be allocated to some other airline this year). Methods used to allocate airport slots form one of the most controversial topics in the whole field of air transport economics. Scheduling committees command wide support amongst airlines but have attracted criticism from competition authorities (e.g. Monopolies and Mergers Commission, 1990).

The way in which scheduling committees work is as follows. Each airline submits its application for slots about six months before the start of each travel season. The scheduling committee allocates the slots according to grandfather rights, the 'use it or lose it' rule and various operational criteria such as giving priority to regular year-round services and precedence to rescheduling to accommodate larger aircraft, rescheduling due to differences in daylight saving time, etc. Because of capacity constraints, not all airlines receive all the slots they ask for at the required times and, once the scheduling committee's allocation is announced, a process of trading takes place and airlines start swapping slots in order to improve their respective positions, with the committee acting as a kind of broker and only authorizing slot trades once it has checked there is sufficient terminal and apron capacity. This is the procedure that applies at most capacity constrained airports across the world, but in the United States there are four airports where slots for domestic flights can be bought and sold for money, rather than merely swapped for other slots. The airports in question are Chicago O'Hare, New York Kennedy, New York La Guardia and Washington National. At these heavily congested airports slots regularly fetch some high prices, anything up to $3 million depending on the time of day. It has been argued that monetarized slot trading is preferable to swapping for the following reasons: it makes trading more likely; it enables new airlines to enter the market without having to have existing slots to swap; it facilitates the leasing of slots; it should give airlines a legal title to slots and so permit mortgages to be taken out on them; it allows airlines in difficulties to sell out in whole or in part; and it offers airlines the option of selling or leasing out a slot rather than deliberately running loss-making services so as to avoid application of the 'use it or lose it' rule (Jones, Viehoff and Marks, 1993). All this has proved possible at the four US airports where monetarized buy-and-sell trading takes place at present. The experience there has been somewhat mixed and there are clearly some major difficulties to be overcome in operating a free buy-and-sell market in airport slots. One is the problem of airlines acquiring matching slots. In order to operate a working timetable an airline does of course need both a landing and a take-off slot, both at the airport in question and at an airport at the other end of the route. The complexities involved in bidding for combinations of slots render any simple auctions rather difficult to conduct. For, in a free market, slot prices can vary quite a lot, not just by time of day but also from airport to airport. Nevertheless US experience suggests that a dynamic and fluid market can operate, and some airlines, like British Airways, are known to favour the introduction of a similar market in Europe (Starkie, 1994). Other airlines may go further. Richard Branson, the Chairman of Virgin Atlantic, has called for grandfather rights to be 'exterminated', as he put it. But that is certainly unlikely to find favour with incumbent airlines and unlikely to gain international acceptance.

Monetarized slot trading at the four US airports mentioned above has been taking place for more than ten years. So, what can be learnt from it? For one thing slot trading should not in itself be expected to reduce the dominance of established airlines, perhaps the reverse. A study by the US General Accounting Office (1996) found that the established airlines' share of slots rose sharply in all four cases: between 1986 and 1996, American and United's share at Chicago O'Hare rose from 66 to 87 per cent; at Washington National the percentage held by American, Delta and USAir went up from 25 to 43; the same three airlines saw their combined share rise from 27 to 64 per cent at New York La Guardia; and combined share of American, United and TWA at New York Kennedy increased from 43 per cent in 1986 to 75 per cent in 1996. Some concern has been expressed about all this. Are substantial increases in slot holdings reinforcing the established airlines' dominance? In particular, is there anything to suggest that the established airlines have been buying up as many slots as possible in order to deter or drive out competitors? The possibility of established airlines doing something like this has been discussed by McGowan and Seabright (1989) who took the view that it is more likely for established airlines to direct any entry deterring or predatory behaviour to the services they operate rather than to the hoarding of slots. This may be a reasonable point in general terms but, as Starkie (1998) has argued, it is less convincing where the share of slots held by dominant airlines is already very high, as at Chicago O'Hare where over 85 per cent of slots is in the hands of American and United. When slot holdings are as high as this, the number of additional slots needed to forestall entry or pursue a predatory strategy could be rather small. However, if the established airlines acquire extra slots mainly to prevent them being used by competitors this might be reflected in lower slot utilization rates for the established airlines. But there is no evidence of this. For example, Kleit and Kobayashi (1996) examined the situation at O'Hare and found that American and United actually had higher slot utilization rates than their competitors (in respect of both the slots for which they had grandfather rights and slots they had leased).

In order to make room for new entrants to compete effectively – at peak periods and on roughly equal terms as regards frequency – slots might have to be confiscated from existing holders. But confiscation might cause a lot of dislocation and would very likely be strongly resisted by existing slot holders, some of whom might decide to close some of their services down rather than move them elsewhere. In February 1993 the European Commission introduced a regulation on slot allocation (Commission of the European Committee, 1993a), under which new entrants are offered up to 50 per cent of slots becoming available at congested airports, out of a pool containing new and unused slots. But the trouble is not all that many slots are in fact becoming available and incumbent airlines go to any lengths to hold on to those they have got. The UK Civil Aviation Authority (1993b) has argued that the EC regulation should be changed so that *all* newly created or unused slots are earmarked for new competitors and also that they be concentrated in such a way that effective 'third forces' can be established on as many routes as possible. In a review of how this appeared to work at Heathrow and Gatwick in summer 1994 and winter 1994/5 (Civil Aviation Authority, 1995) it was found that the regulation had little effect in encouraging competition from new entrants. This was partly because many of the slots allocated under the regulation were at different times of day to those requested by the new entrants: more than two-thirds of them were either before 07:00 or after 21:00, and many of these were simply returned to the slot co-ordinator. Another reason has been the limitation placed on the definition of a 'new entrant', this applying only to the airlines holding no more than 3 per cent of slots at the particular airport. As a result some established small and medium sized airlines remained ineligible, including for example British Midland at Heathrow despite its having been a most effective competitor on the routes for which it has been able to obtain sufficient usable slots. The regulation also excluded airlines such as Air UK, CityFlyer Express and Jersey European from additional slots at Gatwick. Recognizing these points the CAA propose a revised definition of a new entrant and has come up with some detailed recommendations designed to ensure that as many of the newly created or unused slots go to airlines most capable of mounting effective competition to hub airlines at congested airports.

The reason why so much attention is being given to slot allocation is that airport capacity constraints can confer on hub airlines some considerable market power. Once an airline is established at a particular hub, it often becomes very difficult for another airline to challenge it there, especially at peak times during the inbound and outbound waves in the hub airline's flight complexes. It is for this reason that the term 'fortress hub' has been used to describe an airport dominated by a single carrier. And when an airport is dominated there is always concern for the effects this might have on passengers.

5.7 Effects on passengers

The success of a hub and spokes system depends crucially on the airline's ability to control its traffic flows (and revenue yields) via the connecting bank of flights at the hub. Quite simply, hubbing will not work effectively without a major element of concentration.

Table 5.9 Market shares of enplanements at highly concentrated US hubs, 1978 and 1993. *Source:* Button *et al.* (1998)

Hub	1978		1993	
	Carrier	Market share (%)	Carrier	Market share (%)
Atlanta	Delta	49.7	Delta	83.5
Charlotte	Eastern	74.8	USAir	94.6
Cincinnati	Delta	35.1	Delta	89.8
Dayton	TWA	35.3	USAir	40.5
Denver	United	32.0	United	51.8
Detroit	American	21.7	Northwest	74.8
Greensboro	Eastern	64.5	USAir	44.9
Memphis	Delta	42.2	Northwest	76.3
Minneapolis	Northwest	31.7	Northwest	80.6
Nashville	American	28.5	American	69.8
Pittsburgh	Allegheny	46.7	USAir	88.9
Raleigh-Durham	Eastern	74.2	American	80.4
St Louis	TWA	39.4	TWA	60.4
Salt Lake City	Western	39.6	Delta	71.4
Syracuse	Allegheny	40.5	USAir	49.5

The problem with concentration at hubs is that it tends to create a number of local monopolies, conferring upon the hub-based airline the ability to raise fares on routes to and from the hub itself. For passengers whose origin or destination is the hub city, there is often little competition. But the dominance of the hub-based carrier is often overstated, especially when comparisons of concentration are drawn in terms of enplanement data. The latter refers to the number of passengers boarding aircraft; and the hub-based carrier's share of total enplanements does of course include all connecting passengers. The dominant airline's share of total enplanements at its hub – in many cases between 60 and 90 per cent (see Table 5.9) – is often very much greater than its share of local originating/terminating traffic. Jensen (1990) cites the example of American Airlines at Raleigh–Durham in 1988: American's share of total enplanements was 69 per cent, but when connecting passengers are removed from the comparison, its share of originating/terminating traffic was just 39 per cent. Shares of total enplanements can be very misleading as indicators of the intensity of competition. The hub-based airline's share can go up simply when it adds new services (or spokes) to its existing schedules, or just because other carriers decide to withdraw from the airport in order to redeploy aircraft over their own hubs. In the United States, hub and spokes networks have evolved to the point where one airline will generally fly to another airline's hub only from its own hub.

Despite these qualifications, there is no doubt that hub airlines enjoy considerable market power on local routes to/from the hub and, as shown in Table 5.9, the impetus given to hubbing by deregulation has greatly increased this market power. It has been argued that they have been using this power to charge average fares on routes to/from the hub that are significantly higher than average fares on other routes. A number of econometric studies (Borenstein, 1989; US General Accounting Office, 1990; US Department of Transportation, 1990; and Berry, 1990) have all found significant positive correlations between the premium charged on fares to/from the hub (over average fares for routes of similar distance elsewhere) and the degree to which local markets are concentrated. Borenstein (1992) has illustrated this by comparing the extent of 'hubness' (represented by the percentage of passengers changing planes at the hub) with both the Hirschman–Herfindahl Index (HHI) of concentration and fares premia, in local markets to/from the hub. For the 30 largest US airports these comparisons are shown in Table 5.10. In this sample the zero-order correlation coefficient between the measure of hubness and the HHI is 0.74 and that between the HHI and the fares premium much weaker at 0.44. But once allowance is made for other factors, such as the mix of business and non-business passengers in route traffic, the partial correlation between fares premiums and the HHI was found to be very much higher.

It is not only from airport capacity constraints that hub airlines derive market power. There are other factors involved as well. An airline with a large presence in a given city gains some important customer loyalty advantages from frequent flyer programmes (FFPs) and travel agency commission overrides (TACOs). Borenstein (1989) found FFPs and TACOs to be highly significant factors in explaining why dominant airlines can charge higher fares to/from the hub than other airlines serving the same route. The effects of FFPs and TACOs are especially important on business routes; and they increase market power by increasing the costs of switching from one airline to another, lowering cross-elasticities of demand and reducing incentives for competitive price cutting. US experience has shown that airlines are following FFP and TACO strategies in areas where they have large market shares, such as on routes to/from dominated hubs.

Critics of US deregulation (e.g. Dempsey and Goetz, 1992) have stressed the adverse effects upon competition of increased market concentration to/from congested hubs. But at the same time it is clear that the development of hub and spokes networks induced by deregulation has enabled more airlines to provide through connecting services in city pair markets that could not be served non-stop on a financially viable basis.

Table 5.10 Hubbing, concentration and premium fares (30 largest US airports, second quarter of 1990). *Source*: Borenstein (1992)

Airport	Percentage changing planes	Hirschman–Herfindahl Index	Average percentage premium	Rank by size
Charlotte	75.7	5790	18.8	20
Atlanta	69.0	3470	17.2	3
Memphis	67.7	3550	27.4	29
Dallas	65.8	3860	20.5	2
Pittsburgh	62.1	5290	15.9	16
Salt Lake City	61.3	4300	19.1	28
St Louis	56.2	3540	–4.0	13
Chicago O'Hare	55.7	2700	14.8	1
Denver	54.1	2720	15.3	7
Minneapolis/St Paul	51.0	4180	31.5	15
Houston International	49.5	4230	15.6	19
New York Kennedy	47.3	2020	2.9	6
Detroit	43.6	2960	–0.7	11
Baltimore	40.5	2990	9.1	26
Phoenix	33.1	2050	–28.4	9
Miami	31.0	1710	–14.3	14
Seattle	27.3	1450	–8.7	24
San Francisco	25.3	1450	–1.5	5
Los Angeles	25.2	1100	–5.3	4
Philadelphia	24.9	2170	11.2	22
Honolulu	22.4	1990	–20.8	17
Newark	19.6	2920	11.5	12
Las Vegas	18.9	1770	–27.8	23
Houston Hobby	17.5	4810	–23.4	30
Orlando	16.8	1800	–15.6	21
Boston	13.8	1200	9.0	10
Washington DC National	11.1	1250	10.7	18
Tampa	11.0	1810	–12.4	27
San Diego	6.0	1380	–18.1	25
New York La Guardia	6.2	1180	9.5	8

So while competition *at* hubs has been falling, that *between* hubs has been rising. Later evidence (Belobaba and Van Acker, 1994) suggests that deregulation has had a positive effect in the top 100 (origin–destination) city pair markets, about 70 per cent of which experienced an overall decrease in concentration between 1979 and 1991. Also, while reduced competition has led to higher fares on routes to/from hubs, increased competition between hubs has resulted in lower fares in through connecting markets.

One illustration is provided in the case of fares and service levels on routes to/from Akron, Ohio. Before deregulation Akron received only a few flights, mostly those operated by the old commuter airlines; but now, following deregulation, Akron is connected to no less than six or seven major hubs and, although each spoke from these hubs tends to be operated as a point-to-point monopoly, passengers boarding in Akron and travelling beyond the hubs are presented with an enormous choice of alternative routeings. Airlines can exert monopoly market power on local routes between Akron and each of the different hubs; but in markets for through journeys between Akron and the rest of the United States, competition is fierce and fares have fallen substantially in real terms.

So, where hubbing results in increased market power on local routes to/from hubs and at the same time leads to greater competition in through markets via the hubs, how should the net result be weighed? Some through passengers may gain whilst other passengers on local routes lose; but do the pro-competitive effects outweigh the anti-competitive ones overall? There are reasons to believe that in many instances they do.

Many routes to/from hubs on which the anticompetitive effects of market power are likely to be most marked are relatively short hauls, whereas many of the through markets most likely to benefit from greater competition are relatively long hauls. If scheduling through hubs causes fares in through (long haul) markets to fall and fares in local (short haul) markets to rise, this can result in the structure of fares by distance reflecting more closely the manner in which average costs vary by route length. Cost per seat-mile bears a pronounced L-shaped relationship with route length, the cost per seat-mile on a flight of 300 miles often being around twice what it is on a flight of 1500 miles, for example. Fares per passenger-mile also taper with distance, but not in anything like as sharp a manner as cost per seat-mile does. Consequently price–cost margins are often much wider on longer hauls than on short hauls. Hence, to the extent that hubbing reduces margins on long hauls, there could be some significant consumer gains to offset losses suffered on short hauls. Clearly the net balance will depend in particular cases on the relative volumes of traffic carried on long and short haul routes. It will also depend on price elasticities of demand. It is for short haul journeys that surface modes offer the most effective substitutes for air travel – especially rail travel in continental Europe, for example – so that there are at least some limits to the exploitation of market power in short haul markets. For this reason cross-price elasticities of demand are likely to be higher on short hauls, other things being equal. But at the same time aggregate own-price elasticities are likely to be higher on long hauls, given that business travellers, whose demand is known to be relatively price inelastic, tend to make up a larger proportion of total passengers on short hauls than on long hauls. So across the airline's entire network demand might rise overall. Also, if it is legitimate to consider the distribution of gains and losses in this context, the net balance between pro- and anti-competitive effects is likely to be 'progressive' in its impact. Most of the passengers gaining from the more competitive fares for through journeys will be those travelling on holiday or to visit friends and relatives. These are passengers who pay their own fares and who tend, other things being equal, to have lower average incomes than business travellers flying on short services to/from hub cities.

Given that hubbing can generate procompetitive as well as anticompetitive effects, given that losses to some short haul passengers might be offset, or more than offset, by gains to passengers making long haul journeys, and given that hubbing may result in some significant density economies, there is no case *per se* for government authorities to deter airlines from forming and operating hubs. In many cases the positive effects may exceed the negative ones. But there may still be reasons for the authorities to be concerned about hubs. There may be some concern over the impact of hubs on the economics of direct flights and some concern about the environmental diseconomies associated with busy hub airports.

5.8 The future of hubbing

The success of some airlines that do not operate hub and spokes networks but concentrate on supplying low-cost, low-fare, 'no frills' service on direct point-to-point services has led some people to question the overall efficiency of hubs. In the United States the only major airline not operating a 'traditional' hub and spokes network is Southwest Airlines, an airline which has made healthy profits in a period when other hub-based majors have sustained heavy losses. Southwest's unit costs are often as much as 50 to 70 per cent below those of many of the majors. Because it has less need to synchronize flights or bank them into complexes, Southwest achieves much higher utilization rates, of both aircraft and crews. Its strategy is to specialize in very high density short haul markets served at high frequencies. It operates an average of between six and seven daily departures on each of its 100-plus routes. With such high frequencies it attains some very high market shares: it is the dominant airline in over 90 of its top 100 city pair markets and enjoys a market share of 67 per cent or more in over 50 of these markets. In many markets competition from Southwest has persuaded airlines previously operating to withdraw, leaving Southwest with a number of monopolies or near monopolies (e.g. at Albuquerque in New Mexico, where seven of Southwest's twelve routes are monopolies). Less than 20 per cent of Southwest's traffic comes from passengers making transfer connections and the airline offers no interline arrangements.

In contrast to Southwest's success in point-to-point markets, other US airlines have experienced some disappointment with some of their hub operations. USAir has closed down its hubs at Dayton and Syracuse; American has abandoned its San José operation; and United has withdrawn from its north–south hub at Washington Dulles. There has also been some significant scaling down in activity at other hubs: by USAir in Baltimore, by Delta in Dallas, by American in Nashville and by Northwest in Memphis. But before concluding that this has been entirely, or even mainly, the result of competition from Southwest and other low cost operators, a number of important points should be noted. In the post-deregulation frenzy of hub building, probably too many hubs were established; and the closure or scaling down of some of them was a downsizing adjustment, in response to competition between hubs as well as competition from point-to-point carriers. The relative geographic concentration of US hubs and the ensuing competition for traffic has probably been the most significant reason for the lack of profitability of most of the smaller hubs. American's hub at Raleigh-Durham has been losing money as has Northwest's at Memphis; and both hubs compete, not only with each other, but also with Atlanta, Nashville, Charlotte and to a lesser extent, Cincinnati. Geographic concentration is particularly marked in the case of USAir, all of whose hubs are situated in the north east part of the country, so that routeings via Pittsburgh, Charlotte, Philadelphia and Baltimore are often in close competition with each other. Delta's hubs in contrast are much more widely spread across the country, at Salt Lake City, Dallas, Atlanta and Cincinnati. At Dallas Delta faces competition not just from Southwest operating from a different airport but also at the same airport from American.

Some of the factors responsible for the success of Southwest are in any case not directly related to the difference between hub and spokes and point-to-point networks. Much of Southwest's cost saving comes from higher density seating configurations in its single-class aircraft, lower commissions paid to travel agents, a boarding system that does not require reservations and the fact that its services are not listed in any of the computer reservations systems, thus avoiding CRS fees, which can often be quite high. Southwest (and also the other low-cost airlines) tend to operate from less expensive downtown airports in major cities, such as Dallas Love Field, Houston Hobby and Chicago Midway, airports which are popular with business travellers but which had been abandoned by the major carriers.

It is not easy to apply that concept in Europe. For cheap downtown airports simply do not exist in Europe, and low-cost airlines are often forced to use more distant airports, such as Stansted or Luton outside London, Pontoise Cormeilles outside Paris and Malpensa outside Milan. And the idea of extending the 'Southwest concept' to Europe has always had to face the facts that surface modes are more competitive on short haul routes than they are in the United States and that major European airlines offer business travellers flying short sectors more 'frills' than the US majors do. It is true that there are now some good examples of low-cost airlines in Europe: Ryanair, EasyJet, Debonair and the British Airways subsidiary Go. Ryanair did indeed set itself out to replicate Southwest Airlines in Europe (O'Leary, 1994) and it appears to have made a success of its entry, in particular to the UK–Ireland market. But in this case successful operation of point-to-point routes owes at least something to the unusually high proportion of ethnic demand in the particular city pair markets served and also to the fact that the only surface competition comes from a sea crossing. Nonetheless Ryanair has been able to broaden its operations and now flies to 33 destinations in 10 countries from its base in Dublin and its hub at Stansted. It has also been able to make profits from these operations, in every year since 1991 (Gill, 1998). EasyJet has also been expanding rapidly, not only on inter-national routes but also on domestic sectors (e.g. Luton–Edinburgh) where it competes as much against rail transport as it does against other airlines. Debonair also plans a major expansion, from its pioneering hub at Pontoise Cormeilles, and the expansion includes an extensive 'airbridge' operation for pilgrims travelling to the religious sanctuary of Lourdes from ten European cities. And Go, which was launched in May 1998 is tripling the size of its fleet of Boeing 737 aircraft and at the same time doubling its workforce, in preparation for increased services to Germany, France, Scandinavia, Italy and the Iberian peninsular. It is clear that competition amongst low-cost no-frills airlines is intensifying dramatically, but how far can they expect to compete against the major hub airlines?

Low-cost operators do pose a threat to hub airlines and limit their ability to earn monopoly rents on high-density routes to/from certain hubs. But they are unlikely to seriously undermine the fundamental advantages of hub and spokes networks that derive from economies of scope.

On the other hand hub airlines can often find themselves in a position to undermine the economics of point-to-point flights. When rival airlines seek to compete with a hub airline by meeting passengers' normal preference for direct non-stop flights, the hub airline might respond by (temporarily) undercutting fares in the affected markets, possibly financing reductions in revenues in the more competitive city pairs by higher revenues from elsewhere on the network. An airline operating a strong hub can often exercise fairly close control over tariffs. In a price sensitive market A–B (Figure 5.12) it might be fairly easy to divert traffic via an intermediate hub X by discounting fares, something that might be done without affecting the primary justification traffic and without dilut-

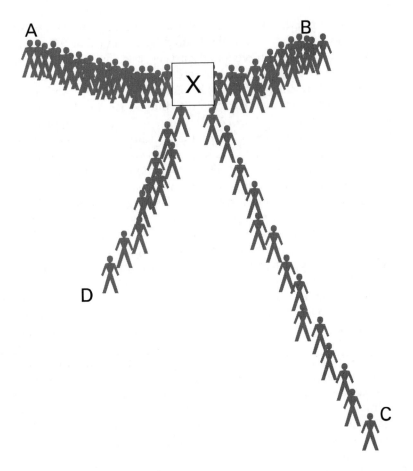

Figure 5.12   Controlling sales through a hub

ing revenues in the local A–X and X–B markets. An airline based at X and operating to both A and B need not impair its revenue yields in the A–X and X–B markets by reducing its fare for A–X–B travel in order to undercut a carrier that flies A–B direct. A hub airline relates costs to revenues across its network as a whole. Revenues might be maximized by reducing fares where its competitive position is relatively weak (in connecting markets) and raising them where it is relatively strong (on routes to/from the hub).

The main problem for the hub airline is to control the amount of capacity to be sold at discounts. Some close monitoring of sales is needed to ensure that the most lucrative traffic is carried, and it is here that CRSs perform a valuable secondary function in the management of revenue yields. In hub and spokes systems it is inevitable that some flights load more heavily than others and some passengers may have to be turned away because the flight on one sector of their required journey is full. For instance, spokes A–X and X–B may load rather heavily; and so selling one A–B ticket may be at the expense of selling two tickets A–C and B–D. The airline may therefore seek to control ticket sales for A–B, A–X and X–B. The hub airline may find it profitable to leave empty seats on some spokes in order to accommodate extra passengers on others. At the same time it may be commercially attractive to offer deep discounts for through journeys on the lightly loaded spokes. The stronger the airline's position at the hub, the more scope it will have for discriminating in this way. The ability to exercise price discrimination carries with it the ability to engage in predatory pricing. The same point applies to another competitive weapon, service frequency; and the twin weapons of pricing and frequency provide powerful means by which airlines can defend their hubs against point-to-point operators who do not have the same network strength to draw upon. This is clearly something the government authorities should guard against. The issues involved are discussed further in Chapter 6.

Government authorities may also be concerned about the environmental diseconomies of hubs. If the objective is to minimize these, then the concept of 'wayports' may be worthy of further consideration. Wayports are basically airports constructed in remote, sparsely populated areas, with almost no origin and destination traffic, and dedicated more or less exclusively to handling transfer traffic; a kind of 'hub in the desert'. Wayports could be relatively cheap to build, costing around a third to a half the cost of a new airport in a metropolitan area. There might be little if any demolition involved, land would be much cheaper and the airport would require much less in the way of landside facilities such as check-in desks, car parks, surface transport links and so on. Wayports could be developed at some presently underused sites: a military airfield due for closure perhaps, or possibly a civil airport whose role has diminished due to some other change (e.g. three possibilities in Europe might be Shannon, Prestwick and Porto, all of which were once used as refuelling stops for transatlantic flights but which are now left with considerable spare capacity). Compared with airports close to densely populated residential areas, wayports would be somewhat safer locations for highly complexed hub operations.

However, creating a wayport at some remote location would raise a number of questions: who would staff the facility? and which airlines would want to operate there? The local population might not be sufficient to run a large airport in an isolated community (e.g. in the interior of Nebraska, where it has been suggested a wayport could be sited in order to relieve congestion in Chicago). Also, there may be few airlines interested in serving connecting traffic on its own, since much of the scope and route traffic density economies airlines reap from hub operations derive from combining connecting traffic with local origin–destination traffic. On the other hand competition authorities should welcome wayports, insofar as multi-runway hubs away from major cities need not be dominated by individual airlines and could at least in principle cater for the flight complexes of several different carriers at different times of the operating day. At wayports there should be ample access for new entrants and also for feeder carriers.

Wayports might entail some huge financial risks but, as a means of relieving pressures on airports serving metropolitan areas, perhaps they should not be dismissed out of hand. They would be long-term investments to meet the ever increasing problem of airport capacities. But there would always be the danger of some of them turning out to be 'white elephants'. In the end the fundamental issue might be who is to finance and plan them: central government, local authorities, the airlines themselves, or some combination of all three.

Hubbing is not really expected to become a prominent feature in markets where distances are relatively short, as in Western Europe. It is much more suited to intercontinental travel, which is in any case the fastest growing segment of the total market for air travel. Hubbing is a more effective strategy in long haul markets, because the time cost of a stopover en route at the hub can be relatively small compared to total travel time. But the creation of fully fledged hub and spokes networks at the international level is going to require some significant restructuring of the industry. In particular, the constraints imposed by intergovernmental air service agreements will need to be relaxed or circumvented through alliances, code-sharing, blocked spacing, franchising and so on.

6 Pricing and predatory behaviour

6.1 Variations in fare levels

Anyone who has bought an airline ticket will know it is possible to pay any one of a large number of different prices to fly a given route. Fares vary with time of travel, whether peak or off-peak; with class of travel, whether first, business or economy; with the length of stay at the destination, whether it exceeds a certain number of days or weeks, or whether it includes a Saturday night; with where and when the ticket is purchased and paid for; and with a whole host of other factors such as the size of the travelling group and the ages of any children involved. The multiplicity of fare categories is often so great that for scheduled service by a particular airline on a particular route – across the North Atlantic, for instance – there can be as many as 50 to 60 separate fares published in airline tariff manuals. The variation between fares can be such that it is possible for two passengers sitting next to each other on the same flight, and enjoying exactly the same quality of inflight service, to find that one is paying very much more than the other, in some extreme cases even more than double.

There is also extensive variation across routes. There are often marked differences in fare levels from route to route, even when the distance flown is roughly the same. Fare levels taper with distance, so that the fare per kilometre is often much lower on a long route than it is on a short one. But even allowing for this, in comparisons of routes of the same or similar length, some considerable differences remain. There are some wide differences by region (see Table 6.1). European fare levels have for a long time been significantly higher, on a per-kilometre basis across different distance bands, than the levels of comparable fares in North America. Similarly, on routes between Europe and the Asia/Pacific region fare levels have long been appreciably lower than corresponding levels on routes between Europe and Africa. There are some big differences within regions too. Within Europe, when comparisons are drawn between cities in terms of the lowest available levels of business or standard economy fares, a clear distinction emerges between certain 'high-fare' and certain 'low-fare' cities. (Figure 6.1) Frankfurt,

Table 6.1 Average economy class normal fares by route group and distance (scheduled services) 1993. *Source:* International Civil Aviation Organisation

Route group	US cents per passenger-kilometre at varying distances (km)						
	250	500	1000	2000	4000	8000	16 000
North–Central America	64.0	43.9	30.1	20.7	14.2		
Central America	45.3	32.2	22.8	16.2			
North America	59.5	40.4	27.4	18.6	12.7		
North–South America		25.4	22.0	19.0	16.4	14.2	
South America	27.8	23.6	20.0	17.0	14.5		
Europe	76.3	56.3	41.5	30.6	22.5		
Middle East	44.5	32.6	23.9	17.5			
Africa	31.7	27.0	23.1	19.7	16.8		
Europe–Middle East		38.1	32.3	27.4	23.3		
Europe–Africa		32.1	28.0	24.4	21.2	18.5	
North Atlantic					21.5	16.9	
South Atlantic					17.2	17.2	
Asia/Pacific	26.4	23.7	21.2	18.9	17.0	15.2	
Europe–Asia/Pacific			15.9	16.0	16.1	16.2	16.2
North–Mid Pacific						13.2	10.4
South Pacific					20.9	17.6	14.8
World	52.6	41.1	32.1	25.1	19.7	15.4	12.0

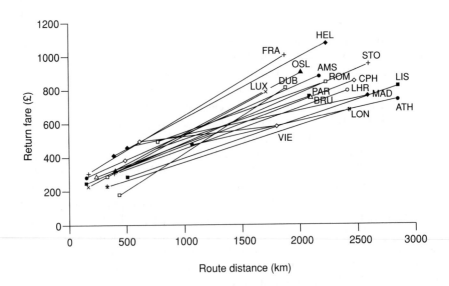

Figure 6.1 Fully flexible fares on European routes, December 1997 (*Source:* Civil Aviation Authority)

Table 6.2 Return fares on selected routes (at 1993 price levels). *Source:*
International Civil Aviation Organization (1994) and *ABC World Airways Guide*

Route	Miles		1951	1971	1993
London–Paris	210	Normal economy	204	182	318
(UK pounds)		Lowest fare	160	127	106
New York–London	3 475	Normal economy	4 165	1 612	2 084
(US dollars)		Lowest fare	3 085	970	397
Sydney–London	11 250	Normal economy	13 622	7 667	6 609
(Australian dollars)		Lowest fare	13 622	7 667	2 099

Amsterdam and the Scandinavian cities of Helsinki, Oslo and Stockholm tend to be high-fare cities, from where the per-kilometre levels on routes to other cities in Europe can be as much as 50 to 60 per cent above the levels from low-fare cities like Athens, London, Lisbon and Madrid.

There is no doubt that air travel has been getting cheaper over time. Reductions in fares on three selected routes, of greatly different distances, are shown in Table 6.2 in which the fares are expressed in the currencies of the countries of origin and are adjusted to remove the effects of general price inflation. In the earlier period, from 1951 to 1971, the range of fares on scheduled services was much more limited than it is today, and for that period the declines observed in normal economy fares are a good indicator of how the travelling public has benefited from cheaper air travel. In the more recent period there has been a proliferation of different types of fares, presenting the public with a wide range of options, including cheaper tickets subject to various advance purchase and time of travel restrictions. On the Sydney–London route for example, the number of fare types increased from just two (first and economy) in 1971 to eight in 1993 (and that excludes group fares, charter fares and preferential fares such as those for students). Between 1971 and 1993 normal economy fares have sometimes increased, as on the London–Paris and New York–London routes, but the lowest fares have, in many cases, become very much cheaper and increasingly accessible to the travelling public.

Some quite dramatic comparisons can be drawn when the variation in fares for individual routes is combined with variation in fares across routes. And such comparisons appear at regular intervals in the press. In one (Betts, 1993) the cheapest economy-class return for London–New York is set against the business-class return for London–Rome, the latter being found to be more than double the former, leading the journalist to question why it is more than twice as expensive to fly from London to Rome (1445 km) than to New York (5565 km). A comparison like this is not exactly on a like-with-like basis. The economy fare to New York is only available on certain flights in off-peak periods, is valid for travel only on the airline that sells the tickets, has to be booked sometime in advance, is subject to minimum limits on how long the passenger must stay before making the return journey, and does not permit stopovers nor any changes in reservations. The business fare to Rome on the other hand is fully flexible, available on demand for all flights, offers interline facilities, has no restrictions on length of stay, permits any number of stopovers and affords the passenger complete freedom to alter reservations. There is also a vast difference in route lengths, with a significant tapering in fares per kilometre. Nonetheless the gap in fare levels – nine pence per kilometre for the Rome fare as against just over two pence per kilometre for the New York fare – is so wide as to suggest that airlines are able to discriminate against business-class passengers on the London–Rome route and in favour of some economy-class passengers on the London–New York route, charging in accordance with what passengers in each of two markets will bear.

But before considering this further, it may be helpful to clarify exactly what is meant by discriminatory pricing.

6.2 Price discrimination

Doctors in private practice sometimes charge rich patients more than poor patients. Cinemas charge lower admission prices for children. Publishers of academic journals sometimes charge higher subscription rates to libraries and institutions than to individuals. And British universities levy higher tuition fees to students from non-EU countries than they do on home students. All these are instances of price discrimination, some being purer examples of it than others.

In economic theory price discrimination is held to be taking place when a producer charges different prices for different units of the same commodity, for reasons not associated with differences in the costs of supply. It occurs where price differentials do not directly correspond to differentials in cost. Price differentials often do correspond to differentials in cost. Differentials between peak and off-peak prices for instance are not in this sense discriminatory, insofar as they merely reflect the additional capacity costs incurred in catering for peak demand. Nor are such things as discounts for quantity purchases, to the extent that they reflect economies reaped by selling in bulk. Discrimination is being exercised whenever prices differ more than costs or, in what amounts to the same thing, whenever costs differ more than prices. The charging of uniform prices where costs differ significantly is just as much discriminatory as charging differential prices where costs are the same. It is only by comparing price–cost margins that one can assess whether prices for different customers are discriminatory. When price–cost margins vary, some customers are being discriminated against. More commonly customers paying higher prices are the ones discriminated against. But this is not always the case. It all depends on the size of the price differential relative to the size of the cost differential. Sometimes the discrimination is against customers paying lower prices, when the price differential is less than the cost differential.

In most cases of discrimination the greater influence is exerted, not by cost differentials, but by differences in demand elasticity. On the 'inverse elasticity rule', optimal pricing requires the firm to charge more where elasticity is low and less where it is high. If demand is inelastic, with price elasticity lying between zero and –1, a rise in price would increase the firm's total revenue; conversely, if demand is elastic, with price elasticity less than –1, a fall in price would increase total revenue. It is customary to refer to a price elasticity between zero and –1 as 'low' price elasticity and to a price elasticity less than –1 as 'high' price elasticity; and the effects of price changes under high and low price elasticities are illustrated in Figure 6.2. If from an initial situation (point A) in which price is P_1 and quantity Q_1, price is reduced to P_2, quantity will increase to Q_{2H} (point B_H) under high price elasticity but only to Q_{2L} (point B_L) under low price elasticity. The impact on the firm's revenue will be favourable in the case of high price elasticity because the additional revenue from the Q_{2H}-Q_1 increment in quantity (area Q_1CBHQ_{2H}) will be greater than the loss on existing quantity caused by the P_1-P_2 reduction in price (area P_1ACP_2). The opposite will be the case with low price elasticity, the additional revenue from the Q_{2L}-Q_1 increment in quantity (area $Q_1CB_LQ_{2L}$) being less than the loss in revenue on existing quantity.

It is explained in many economics textbooks how a firm seeking to maximize profits sets price (P) at the point at which the marginal revenue (MR) earned from the last unit sold is equal to the marginal cost (MC) incurred in producing that unit. It is further shown that MR is a function of price-elasticity of demand (E_p) via the relation:

$$MR = P \, (1+1/E_p)$$

when

$$E_p = \frac{dQ}{dP} \cdot \frac{P}{Q} < 0$$

where Q denotes the number of units sold.

Thus maximum profit requires that:

$$MC = P + P/E_p$$

or

$$(P - MC)/P = -1/E_p$$

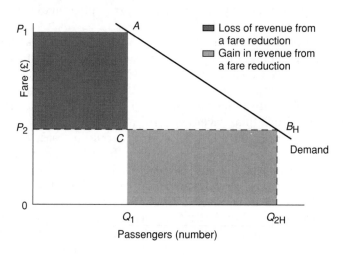

(a) High price elasticity

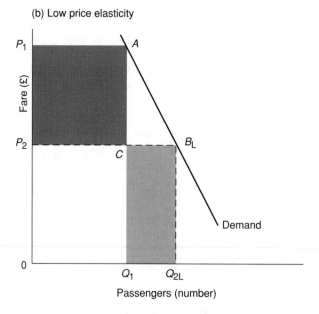

(b) Low price elasticity

Figure 6.2   Pricing under high and low price elasticities of demand

Table 6.3 Profit maximizing markups of price over marginal cost at varying price elasticities of demand

Price elasticity E_p	Profit maximizing markup (%) $\dfrac{P-MC}{P}\,100$
−0.25	400
−0.5	200
−1	100
−1.25	80
−1.5	67
−2	50
−2.5	40
−5	20

The expression on the left-hand side is the (proportionate) price–cost margin, and profit maximization requires this margin to be higher where demand is inelastic and lower where it is elastic. This is shown in Table 6.3. If the price elasticity is −0.25, which implies that a 10 per cent increase (decrease) in price leads to a 2.5 per cent reduction (rise) in sales quantity, the profit-maximizing markup is as high as 400 per cent; and if the price elasticity is −5, which means that a 10 per cent increase (decrease) in price leads to a 50 per cent reduction (rise) in sales quantity, the profit-maximizing markup is only 20 per cent.

To vary the price–cost margin a firm must be able to distinguish between customers by magnitude of E_p, to inhibit those whose demand is relatively inelastic buying at prices intended for those whose demand is relatively elastic, and to prevent customers charged low prices reselling to those who would otherwise be charged high prices. These requirements mean it is much easier to exercise discrimination in service industries, like air transport, than in markets for manufactured goods.

6.3 How airlines do it: yield management

Airlines prevent customers re-selling to each other by making tickets non-transferable. The customer's name is entered on the ticket and, for international travel, proof of identity in the form of a passport needs to be provided at check-in. Thus the process of arbitrage, which would be normal in markets for goods, cannot take place in the market for air travel. It is not possible for some customers to buy cheap tickets sometime in advance with the intention of selling them to other customers with a more inelastic demand closer to the time of departure.

From their market research, airlines know that high-income travellers, business travellers and those travelling for urgent personal reasons (e.g. to attend a funeral) have relatively price-inelastic demand. At the same time the airlines are aware that holidaymakers, those visiting friends and relations, students on vacation, etc. are all very sensitive in their demand to the fares charged. The price-inelastic travellers tend not to be able to book very far in advance, need fast and ready access to a seat on the flight or flights of their choice, want the flexibility to alter reservations at short notice, are generally subject to strict limitations on the time they can stay away at their destinations, and in some cases place a high value on the status or prestige afforded by travelling in relative luxury. The price-elastic travellers on the other hand are prepared to subordinate any preferences they might have so far as booking, seat access, reservations, length of stay and status are concerned to the benefit of being able to travel at lower fares. Differences between elastic and inelastic travellers in these respects are often rather wide and present airlines with good opportunities to segment the overall market by reason for travel and to use this as the basis for price discrimination.

Discriminatory pricing is clearly evident in the structure of fares for individual routes, as illustrated in Figure 6.3 by British Airways' London–New York fares. There is an enormous range, from the normal supersonic return at one extreme down to the cheapest advance-purchase excursion (APEX) fare at the other extreme, a twenty-fold difference. There is of course a large differential in operating cost between Concorde and Boeing 747 aircraft, the cost per seat-mile being very much higher on supersonic services, on account of Concorde's lower seating capacity, greater fuel consumption, smaller fleet size and so on. This cost differential may justify at least some part of the fare differentials – certainly perhaps the 30 per cent surcharge on the First class subsonic fare that the normal supersonic fare attracts. And there are clearly some cost differentials between the various classes of subsonic travel, between First, 'Club' (BA's brand name for business class) and 'Traveller' (BA's name for economy class). But it is doubtful that if cost differences can on their own explain, for example, the 350 per cent fare differential between Club and the most expensive fare for Traveller class. Passengers travelling Club class have seats of greater width and pitch and receive a higher standard of catering than their counterparts further back in the aircraft; and so on a fully allocated cost basis seats in Club class are clearly more expensive to provide than seats in Traveller class, due allowance being made for all the differences in capacity costs. Also, the average load factor is often lower in First and Club, so that the cost differential widens when considered on a per-passenger basis. Airlines generally plan for an average load factor of around 60 per cent in Club or Business class as against 85 to 90 per cent

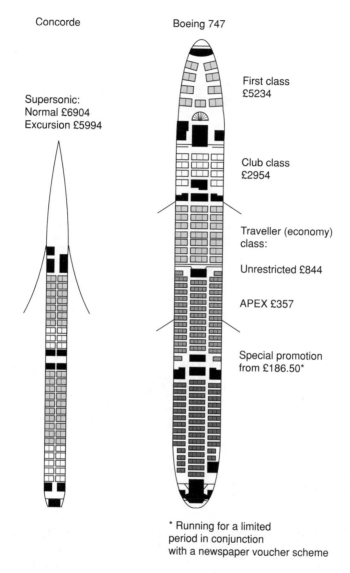

Concorde

Boeing 747

Supersonic:
Normal £6904
Excursion £5994

First class
£5234

Club class
£2954

Traveller (economy)
class:

Unrestricted £844

APEX £357

Special promotion
from £186.50*

* Running for a limited
period in conjunction
with a newspaper voucher scheme

Figure 6.3 London–New York return fares, November 1998, for British Airways Services

in Traveller or economy class. Club class passengers can be regarded as paying for seats on demand, right down to a few hours before take-off. For that kind of service they are, as it were, also paying for the empty seats around them. Nonetheless the fare differentials are so huge – £2280 per passenger between First and Club, and £2110 per passenger between

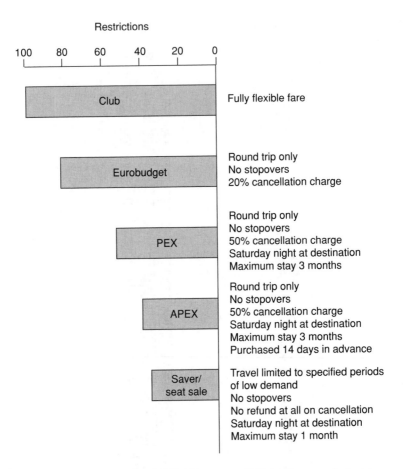

Restrictions

Figure 6.4 Structure of fares on UK–EU routes, British Airways, Autumn 1998 (*Source:* Civil Aviation Authority)

Club and the most expensive Traveller fare – that they can hardly be wholly justified by corresponding differentials in cost. The point applies more forcefully to fare differentials within Traveller class. Apart from some surcharges and discounts applying to fares for travel at peak and off-peak times, there is little prima facie reason in terms of airline costs to explain why passengers buying APEX tickets can fly for much less than half the full Traveller class fare. By far the greater part of the variation in Traveller class fares is due to discriminatory pricing. Discriminatory pricing is also evident in the structure of fares on routes between the UK and other EU countries (Figure 6.4). On these routes there is no longer any First class accommodation, but Club class passengers still travel in a separate cabin from passengers travelling on cheaper

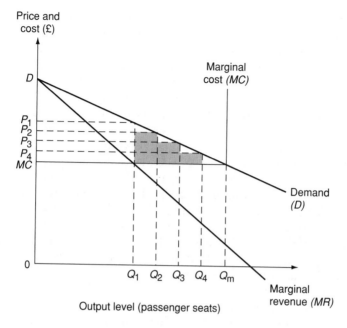

Figure 6.5 Price discrimination and consumer surplus

tickets. British Airways sells its 'Eurobudget' fare at an average discount of 16 per cent off the Club class fare; and the average discounts for the other fare types are: PEX 44 per cent, APEX 57 per cent and saver 62 per cent. Once again, there are some cost differences between fare types – some related to the progressively tighter restrictions passengers have to accept – but the main cause of variation in the fare structure is discrimination based on differences in willingness to pay.

Willingness to pay varies between passengers because of differences in 'consumer surplus'. In economic theory consumer surplus refers to the difference between what a passenger is prepared to pay for the service (rather than not be able to use it at all) and what he or she actually does pay when the fare is set by the airline. In a conventional price-and-cost against output diagram (Figure 6.5) points along the demand curve show what passengers are prepared to pay, and their consumer surplus is represented by the area between the demand schedule DD' and the appropriate price line. The airline may set its fully flexible fare for economy or traveller class to maximize profits at P_1, i.e. where $MC = MR$. At this price the number of seats sold is Q_1, leaving $Q_m - Q_1$ seats unsold. If the MC of an extra passenger is constant up to the full capacity of the flight Q_m (at which point it rises vertically reflecting the additional costs incurred in putting on a second flight) then the airline may seek to sell the remaining seats and increase its load factor by reducing fares selectively, selling some at P_2, some at P_3 and so on. Different passengers enter the market at different fare levels. Those who are able to book a long way in advance, but have a relatively low willingness to pay, may be charged P_4; and if the airline has any seats remaining on the day of departure, it may sell these off as standby tickets (i.e. at MC). By discriminating between passengers the objective of the airline is to expropriate as much as possible of what would otherwise be passenger consumer surplus if all seats were sold at MC (the shaded areas in Figure 6.5). The purpose of restricting the availability of the cheaper fares is to inhibit passengers trading down from more expensive fares, or to limit what in airline parlance is called 'revenue dilution'. From experience airlines know approximately how many seats to assign to passengers paying different fares and can vary the number of seats sold at each fare from flight to flight, and even on the same flight at different points in time up to departure. They also know how passengers purchasing different categories of fares tend to make their bookings, in particular how far in advance they book, as illustrated in Figure 6.6. Passengers buying business class accommodation often make their reservations only a few days in advance, whereas those travelling on advance purchase excursions and the lowest economy tickets are often able (or required) to book some weeks in advance. In some ways it would be

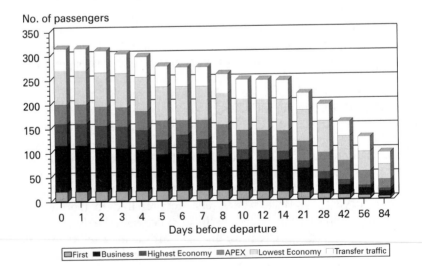

Figure 6.6 Distribution of passenger bookings over time and by fare category, representing typical pattern for a long haul flight in a wide-bodied aircraft (*Source:* British Airways)

easier for airlines to discriminate if it were the other way round, with the higher fare passengers booking first. But the use of sophisticated computer reservations systems, with finely tuned algorithms in 'yield management' programs, has greatly increased the facility for airlines to forecast the most revenue enhancing seat allocation. And some airlines do this for each and every flight they operate.

6.4 Is discrimination desirable?

Is it desirable for airlines to exercise discrimination and charge according to willingness to pay? The answer to this might vary with whose interest is being considered, whether it is that of the airline, that of passengers with elastic demand who would not have travelled unless the fares structure discriminated in their favour, or that of passengers with inelastic demand who find themselves discriminated against. The airline must gain from discriminatory pricing. Otherwise it would not engage in it (except by mistake). Indeed, whenever it is possible, price discrimination is a necessary condition for the airline to maximize its profits. But compared with uniform pricing, discrimination is clearly seen as undesirable by passengers for whom price is raised and desirable by passengers for whom price is reduced.

Is it fair?

To the general public discriminatory pricing can sometimes appear rather unfair. But not always. Discounts for the young or for the old are generally approved of, even where price–cost margins are very low or perhaps even negative. Children's fares are often offered at discounts, when the child occupies a seat and receives the same (if not more) attention from cabin staff as adult passengers do. (And a further point is that children do not of course make inflight purchases of duty-free tobacco, alcohol and perfume, on all of which the airline may make a small profit.) On most scheduled services the discount for which children between the ages of two and twelve are eligible is 50 per cent of the applicable fare, whether business, full economy or excursion. Infants under two and not occupying separate seats are charged 10 per cent. To a certain extent these are discounts for quantity purchases, in that children mostly travel in the company of their parents. But to a more significant extent they reflect the greater elasticity in family demand. Even so public opinion is rarely if ever against lower fares for children.

Similarly, public opinion is not so much offended if the discrimination is 'progressive' in its effects, in the sense of impacting adversely upon the relatively rich and tending to benefit passengers less well off. In the air travel context this is often not so great an issue as it is when discrimination is practised by other modes. For air travellers all tend to come from the higher income groups anyway (see Figure 2.8). There is some variation by income within the population of air travellers: income levels vary with country of residence; the average incomes of international passengers are higher than those of passengers flying domestic routes; and business travellers tend to have higher incomes than leisure travellers. To the extent that demand elasticities vary in much the same way, i.e. lower in rich countries, on international routes and for business travellers, discriminatory air fares do indeed have something of a progressive impact.

Business fares

Business travellers often complain about the degree to which airlines discriminate against them. There is some justification for business travellers paying higher fares, when they get almost instant access to seats, have greater flexibility in making and changing reservations and enjoy higher standards of comfort and inflight service. But business travellers sometimes argue that the additional amounts they have to pay for these privileges are excessive. Why, they ask, should people who have to travel in the course of work have to pay so much more than people going away on holiday, simply because their travel requirements preclude them meeting the length-of-stay and advance-booking eligibility criteria for the lower fares? A business class fare can often be some multiple of an APEX fare and this, they argue, is inequitable. But differences between fare categories can appear somewhat wider than differences in their real burden on different groups of travellers. To begin with, business fares are mostly paid, not by the travellers themselves, but by their companies, for whom expenditure on air travel is a pre-tax item, whereas excursion fares are usually paid personally by holiday travellers out of post-tax incomes. This of course is a general point that applies to all kinds of expenditure by firms and individuals. But the fact that air travel is a pre-tax expense for many companies was one of the reasons why airlines originally identified businessmen as a market segment capable of bearing higher fares; and comparisons of the impact of different fares upon different kinds of traveller might well take the tax effect into account. If for instance this is done by deflating business fares at the appropriate marginal rate of tax on company profits, the difference between business and excursion fares narrows quite considerably. For example, if UK corporation tax at 33 per cent is applied to Club fares on UK–EU routes, the average discount from the Club level at which APEX tickets are sold appears as 36 per cent rather than the 57 per cent shown in Figure 6.4. The importance of the tax factor obviously varies from

Table 6.4 Class of travel for company executives. All values are percentages. *Source: The Times* (1994)

	Board directors	Senior managers	Middle/junior managers
Short haul flights			
First	12	1	–
Business	40	3	14
Economy	42	62	77
Varies	6	7	9
Long haul flights			
First	19	3	1
Business	49	46	26
Economy	17	34	53
Varies	15	17	20

company to company. Some companies do not make sufficient profits to be liable to company tax anyway, especially when they have substantial allowances to set against their tax liability. Also the significance of differences in direct taxation is declining over time, as governments pursue policies of shifting the burden of financing public expenditure from direct to indirect forms of taxation, i.e. from company and income tax to value-added tax, excise duties, etc. Rates of company and income tax have fallen quite appreciably over recent years and this could partly explain why sales of first and business class fares have been so slow to recover from the economic recession and why more and more companies are requiring their business travellers to trade down to economy class.

Business travel tends to be concentrated rather heavily among executives employed by large multinational companies and it is known that most of these organizations adopt fairly specific policies on things like class of travel, fare types, etc. (see Table 6.4). Among the more important factors are the seniority of the traveller and the length of the journey. Considerations of comfort and the need to be fresh enough to be able to conduct business at the destination mean that more of the executives qualify for first or business class as the distance to be flown increases. And passengers occasionally have other, sometimes more compelling, reasons for choosing first or business class. (Kenneth Galbraith, Emeritus Professor of Economics at Harvard University is a prime example: at 6 foot 8 inches tall, and in his eighties, Galbraith insists on travelling first or business when going on lecture tours, explaining that he finds it difficult to squeeze into economy class accommodation!) The greater importance of comfort and fatigue factors on long journeys has some effect in lower price elasticities of demand on the longer routes. This is reflected in wider differentials between fares on the longer routes, as shown in the BA tariff: while a Club class ticket costs about twice as much as an APEX ticket on UK–Europe routes (Figure 6.4) on routes across the Atlantic it costs more than eight times as much (Figure 6.3). But the ability of airlines to exploit low price elasticities of demand has been curbed recently by many companies tightening up on their travel policies, in a new era of cost-conscious austerity. A few years ago a survey by the Civil Aviation Authority (1988) indicated that, in the matter of travel policies, UK companies divided into two broad groups: those for whom price was a relatively minor consideration, with quality of service being the paramount consideration; and those for whom price was a more significant factor. Recent indications are that the number of companies in the second group is growing rapidly. To cite just a few examples: GKN has eliminated all entitlements to first (and Concorde) service; IBM has adopted an economy-only ruling for transatlantic flights to the US East Coast, even for the chief executive; and ICI is now starting to implement a policy of buying discounted economy class fares for the outward leg of an executive's journey, only permitting the purchase of fully flexible fares, business or economy, for the return journey. Studies by ICI showed that 80 per cent of changes to their executives' reservations, if a trip has to be extended or cut short, occur on the return leg. ICI's top executives still travel business class on long haul flights, but the company's other representatives travel out a day early and take a day off to recuperate, and the company finds this cheaper than booking them business class. More and more companies are doing something similar, all looking for ways of reducing the size of their travel budgets, not simply as a result of the harsher economic climate they face generally, but also perhaps because of the declining significance of the tax 'cushion'.

When might all passengers gain?

The question of whether price discrimination is fair or unfair involves making value judgements. Do the gains to those charged less outweigh the losses suffered by those charged more? There is no unambivalent way of resolving that issue on economic analysis alone. It is possible however to envisage circumstances under which, at least in theory, everyone gains from discriminatory pricing.

One special situation in which all passengers gain when the airline practises price discrimination is where demand is too weak to permit profitable operation of the service under uniform pricing. The added revenue gained through price discrimination may be sufficient to make the difference in whether or not a service is supplied at all. If without discrimination nobody is given the opportunity of using the service, then all passengers must gain when discriminatory fares are charged, including the passengers paying the higher fares, since they can exercise a choice which would not be open to them if the airline could only charge uniform prices. This kind of situation might occasionally arise on thinly trafficked routes to remote areas.

It has been argued that this can be a more general effect; that where discrimination results in seats being sold in an elastic market in which none would be sold by an airline charging a uniform fare, all passengers benefit from lower fares. One line of reasoning used to support this proposition is that the price to passengers paying the higher business or full economy fares would have to be even higher, if more seats in the aircraft were left unoccupied rather than filled by passengers stimulated to travel by the lower excursion fares. This was essentially the view expressed some years ago by British Airways (1977) when it defended its fares structure on European routes against some criticism from the Airline Users Committee (1976), arguing as follows:

> The economics of scheduled airline operation have been greatly improved by the traffic expansion lower fares have generated . . . Paradoxical though it may seem, promotional fares are helping to hold normal fares down.

It is worth considering this argument in some detail. On any given flight the cost per passenger is lower, the lower the proportion of unoccupied seats. This may be so, but why would so many seats be left unoccupied in the first place? The proportion of unoccupied seats, the reciprocal of the load factor, is a measure of the degree to which capacity is in excess of demand. To reduce this proportion, to raise the load factor, there are basically two courses of action open to the airline: either it can reduce capacity or it can attract more passengers by reducing fares. Reducing capacity can take one of two forms, a reduction in service frequency or a downsizing in the type of aircraft operated. Both of these things have their disadvantages: under competitive conditions a cut in frequency could seriously damage an airline's market share, and a smaller aircraft has a higher cost per seat mile. So the alternative of promoting passenger demand through lower fares aimed specifically at the more elastic segments of the market can have some cost justification here. It permits the operation of a larger aircraft and/or a higher frequency of service than would be warranted for the carriage of the less elastic passengers alone. Take for example an airline currently operating a particular route with a Boeing B737 which is considering upsizing its aircraft type to an Airbus A320. The A320 has 150 seats compared to 110 in the B737. Clearly it would cost more per hour to fly the A320, but because of the A320's greater capacity, cost per seat-mile would fall by about 17 per cent or so (Doganis, 1991). Passenger demand currently justifies four B737 flights a day but, at the same load factors, only three if the A320 is flown. Service frequency can be a very important factor in attracting the first/business/ full economy passengers, for whom schedule convenience can often be a more significant factor in choice of airline than the level of the fare. So replacing the B737 by the A320 and operating one less flight a day could threaten the loss of some high-yield traffic. But if the airline stimulates total demand by introducing a wider range of low fares for price elastic excursion passengers, this may still make it possible to take advantage of the A320's reduction in cost per seat-mile without sacrificing daily frequency. But an increase in excursion passengers would reduce the average fare paid and would raise the load factor at which the airline would break even on the service. If the breakeven load factor rises above the actual load factor, the airline would lose money on the service. In that event the airline would need to find some way of increasing revenue, the burden of which would likely bear more heavily on the first/business/ full economy passengers, since any significant increases in fares charged to the more elastic excursion passengers would price many of them off the aircraft. If the demand of first/business/full economy passengers is less elastic with respect to fares than it is with respect to service frequency, the airline could choose to increase the fares these passengers pay rather than reduce the A320 frequency.

Hence the argument that business/full economy class passengers gain from the carriage of excursion passengers at discounted fares is a difficult one to sustain as a general principle. There is certainly a lot in the suggestion that discounted fares used to fill up aircraft already committed to a service improve the economics of scheduled operation. But whether they serve to hold down business/full economy fares in the long run is doubtful and this is something that would need to be demonstrated.

6.5 Discrimination and competition

To many people the most important consideration in deciding whether discrimination is good or bad is what it does to the level or intensity of competition. Does it help or hinder competition? Are its effects pro- or anti-competitive?

In its effects upon competition discrimination is something of a two-edged sword. It fosters competition by making it easier for firms to experiment in their pricing. Firms are less reluctant to change prices, if the changes do not have to be implemented across the board in each and every market served but can be applied selectively in a restricted number of test markets. Discrimination can also undermine pricing discipline in oligopolistic situations, removing price rigidity and causing firms to lose confidence in any form of collusive pricing. In order to utilize capacity more fully, some firms may offer secret concessions to selected customers

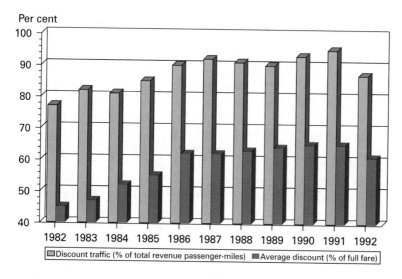

Figure 6.7 Discount traffic on US domestic routes (*Source:* Air Transport Association, 1993)

usually through an intermediary (such as, in the airline context, a travel agent or consolidator). Sooner or later other firms find out and match or undercut the concessions. As the concessions spread, published prices become increasingly unrealistic, so that eventually they are formally reduced, benefiting all customers, not just the favoured few. It is possible to argue that the practice of airlines channelling sales of heavily discounted fares through unofficial travel agencies – often referred to pejoratively as 'bucket shops' – have in these respects had some positive effects on the intensity of competition. The same is also borne out by experience of deregulation in the United States, but this shows that, if one reverses the question – what effect does the intensity of competition have on the prevalence of discriminatory pricing? – the relationship is very much a two-way simultaneous one. In the regulated era up to 1978, discriminatory air fares were effectively banned on US domestic routes (Civil Aeronautics Board, 1973); but since then there has been a veritable explosion in the number of passengers travelling on discounted fares, and the size of the discounts has increased sharply too (Figure 6.7).

The other side to the discrimination–competition relationship is where dominant firms with high market shares seek to weaken their competitors, by focusing price cuts on markets in which they face relatively fierce competition, whilst maintaining, or perhaps even increasing, prices in other markets in which they enjoy a greater degree of market power. This was what Laker Airways claimed IATA airlines on North

Atlantic routes were doing in the late 1970s and early 1980s. In a price war for excursion passengers the IATA airlines made deep cuts to the levels of their APEX and other promotional fares, but only on routes on which Laker Airways operated its Skytrain service. According to Virgin Atlantic Airways much the same kind of thing is happening again now. In Europe the operators of non-scheduled services often used to complain that scheduled airlines cross-subsidized low fares on routes on which they competed with charters (e.g. to the Iberian peninsula) by higher fares on routes where there was no charter competition (e.g. to Scandinavia).

Discrimination between markets based on the existence of competitive alternatives is also evident when direct and indirect operators serve the same city pair over different routes. When for instance hub airlines compete with point-to-point operators they often seek to match, or undercut, each other's fares, even when there are wide differences in their respective operating costs. In the deregulated US domestic market it was not unknown for discrimination between markets based on the existence of competitors to be carried to the extent that a hub airline would charge less for a journey beyond the hub than for one terminating there. (For example, passengers flying from Washington to Cleveland via Detroit sometimes paid less than passengers only flying the Washington–Detroit sector.) But despite the cost disparity, if direct and indirect operators did not seek to match each other's fares, effective competition would be impaired The same phenomenon is often present in international markets, when sixth freedom airlines compete against the services of third and fourth freedom airlines. In a bilaterally constrained situation, a sixth freedom operator can only compete with third/fourth freedom airlines, for the same traffic from the same catchment area to the same destination, by carrying passengers via an intermediate stop en route. To overcome the marketing disadvantage of the additional journey time, the sixth freedom operator may have to discount its through fares heavily in order to attract traffic. The sixth freedom operator may still find this worth doing, if the additional traffic enhances the profitability of the two sectors involved. Under these circumstances competition might well be diminished if the sixth freedom operator were to be denied the right to undercut the fares of third/fourth freedom airlines, even if its costs are higher. In any case it is by no means always the case that the sixth freedom operator's cost are higher. In some situations they might even be lower, especially if the carriage of through traffic leads to significant density economies.

In one sense, what Laker, Virgin Atlantic and the charter operators have complained about is no less than one would expect from the inverse elasticity rule. The most fundamental determinant of elasticity magnitude is the availability of close substitutes. Where airlines face competition, passengers have close substitutes; where passengers have close substitutes, their price elasticity – or more especially their cross-price elasticity – is high; and where elasticity is high, airlines will set fares at relatively low mark-ups over cost. Nothing in this seems any different from the normal process of competition. Firms in other industries do exactly the same. But the complaints of Laker, Virgin Atlantic et al. went somewhat further in suggesting that what the IATA airlines were doing amounted to predatory pricing.

6.6 Predatory pricing

Broadly defined, predatory behaviour is conduct by a dominant firm designed to eliminate, restrict or deter competition. In relation to pricing it has often been described as the practice of temporarily selling at prices below cost, with the intention of driving a competitor from the market, so that in the future prices can be raised and higher profits made.

Is it rational?

It has sometimes been argued that predatory pricing is not a rational policy for a dominant firm to pursue, and that therefore it is unlikely to occur. On this view predatory price cutting may not be all that sensible because it is typically more expensive for the predator than for the prey. By cutting prices to a level below cost and forcing its victim (or victims) to do the same, the predator forces everyone into a loss-making situation. So if the predator's market share is, say, four times that of its victim its losses from this may also be four times as great. But the predator expects to reap gains from the exercise once its victim has disappeared from the scene. And whether or not predation is economically worthwhile from the predator's point of view depends on the net present value (NPV) of the exercise.

Mathematically this can be expressed in the following way. Where the predator suffers losses of Λ_p in each period in which it is engaged in a price war with its competitor, but gains extra profits of π_p as a result of killing its rival off, if it takes t periods to drive the rival from the market, then at an interest rate of r representing the predator's opportunity cost of capital funds:

$$\text{NPV (predation)} = -\Lambda_p - \Lambda_p (1 + r)^{-1} - \Lambda_p (1 + r)^{-2}$$
$$- \ldots\ldots -\Lambda_p (1 + r)^{-t} + \pi_p (1 + r)^{-t + 1}$$
$$+ \pi_p (1 + r)^{-t + 2} + \pi_p (1 + r)^{-t + 3} + \ldots\ldots$$

If the NPV is positive, predation is economically worthwhile and therefore rational, even although the Λ_p losses suffered by the predator are of much greater magnitude than the losses suffered by the prey. Predation is only irrational if the NPV is negative. In other words it is only irrational if, in present value terms, the firm's losses outweigh its gains.

It may take rather a long time (t periods) for the predatory scheme to work and in the meantime the Λ_p losses may mount up to some considerable sums. Hence it has been suggested that a cheaper route to the π_p gains may be through purchasing the rival firm, although a tightening in government merger controls may effectively rule that out.

Where the competition authorities are prepared to sanction a takeover (e.g. to protect jobs) this may be a more profitable course for the dominant firm to adopt. For driving out a competitor by predatory pricing does not ensure the removal of capacity from the industry, given that the assets of the firm driven off can be sold and used by another firm to enter the market. In the airline context, assets most likely to be transferred to a new entrant include aircraft, aircrew, managerial expertise and, most crucially of all in some cases, take-off and landing slots at congested hub airports. The π_p gains following the exit of the prey are expected to come through the predator being able to increase its price–cost margin. But the scope for this may well be less, when the demise of one competitor is simply followed by the emergence of another.

It may be that the objectives of the dominant firm are better served by outright purchase or merger than by predatory pricing. But this alone does not make predation an irrational policy. Predation can produce some important strategic benefits for the predator. It may for instance serve the purpose of 'softening up' the rival firm causing it to revise downwards its expectations of future profits, making it willing to sell out at a lower price. Predation is of course only one means of preventing or limiting competition; and a dominant firm may use it only when it is less costly than some other means of raising entry barriers. The scope for raising entry barriers, including those related to predation, may be enhanced by takeovers or mergers, if this increases the market power of the remaining firms.

How can it be detected?

Predatory pricing is notoriously difficult to prove and this makes it difficult to police. It is very difficult to distinguish between a reduction in price with predatory intent (made in order to force out a competitor) and one which represents competition 'on its merits' (rendered possible by savings in cost or by revenue-enhancing yield management).

In an influential paper Areeda and Turner (1975) proposed a test based on cost. The Areeda–Turner test, which has been embraced by the US courts in a number of antitrust cases, holds that a price is predatory if it is set below a firm's short-run marginal cost (MC). But what exactly is the firm's short-run MC? Formally, MC is the addition to total cost resulting from the last unit of output. It refers to those elements of cost that can be avoided or escaped if the last unit is not produced. This very much depends on the time frame considered. So how short is the 'short run' in this respect? In the very short run, MC may be negligible or close to zero, especially in a service industry like air transport.

Airline output is an instantly perishable commodity which cannot be stored if demand is less than supply. Once the aircraft door is closed, a seat which may have been on the market at a fare of several hundred pounds suddenly becomes worthless. Empty seats represent a waste of resources. The additional costs incurred in carrying an extra passenger on a flight that is going to be flown anyway may amount to little more than an airport passenger's charge, the cost of any food or drink consumed in flight plus a fractional increase in fuel burn due to the extra weight on board. In those circumstances it would pay the airline to get whatever it can from the sale of the seat rather than fly it empty. There is often excess capacity in times of economic recession. Thus it is no accident that these are just the times when complaints of airlines pricing below cost tend to be most frequent (e.g. in the early 1980s and then again in the early 1990s). But many of the low fares sold during these times are designed to attract passengers to otherwise unoccupied seats. Whilst low they are usually above – well above – the revelant short-run MC.

There are always problems in determining MC, both in defining the marginal unit and in identifying the costs that can be attributed to it; but these problems are particularly difficult in air transport. The most fundamental problem is that the marginal unit of demand (a passenger journey) is not the same as the smallest unit by which supply can be varied at the margin (in most circumstances, an aircraft journey). Except where seats are sold in blocks (e.g. on a part-charter basis to tour operators and travel agencies) it is the marginal unit of demand which has to be used as the pricing unit, but it is the marginal unit of supply to which the costs relate.

Recognizing this kind of difficulty Areeda and Turner suggested the use of average variable cost (AVC) as a proxy for short-run MC; and they argued that a price ≥AVC should be regarded as competition on its merits, but that a price <AVC should be condemned as predatory. They qualified this basic rule by allowing prices <AVC in periods of weak demand or excess capacity. Areeda and Turner would not therefore regard as predatory temporary reductions during times of economic recession, nor standby fares and other fares sold on a space-available basis, like some of those sold through bucket shops. They would also sanction promotional

fares <AVC sold by firms without market power. This could mean that a new entrant could charge <AVC without being accused of predatory pricing, but if an established carrier with a certain degree of market power were to do so, that would be classed as predation.

How then is AVC to be measured? Variable costs are those that would be escaped if a flight or series of flights (i.e. a service) were to be discontinued. This includes all costs specific to individual flights: fuel, crew expenses, passenger service costs, airport and en route charges, aircraft handling costs, travel agency commissions, some allocation of engineering and maintenance costs, and so on. Items such as these are escapable more or less immediately once flight activity is scaled down. But over a longer term, many other costs became escapable too, if the withdrawal of the flights is permanent and aircraft can be disposed of, staff numbers cut, sales offices shut, etc. Given that airlines do not have to make infrastructure investments in navigation facilities, runways or terminals, the air transport industry is one in which the ratio of fixed to variable costs is fairly low and 'as much as 90 per cent of total costs can be varied in the medium term by discontinuing all operations or by a partial withdrawal of certain operations' (Doganis, 1991).

Nothwithstanding the problems involved in dealing with temporal dimensions in cost escapability, it is relatively easy to assess the AVC of a particular service. A far more difficult problem is how to allocate this between the various different categories of fares, first, business, full economy, APEX, etc. A great many of the costs incurred in operating a flight are incurred jointly on behalf of all fare categories. It is possible for these joint costs to be allocated to categories in accordance with space requirements (i.e. seating densities) and load factors. But if the Areeda–Turner test is to be applied to particular fares, the question that really needs to be answered is what costs would be escaped if there were no sales at all in the category concerned. The most difficult issue concerns the treatment of capacity costs. It can be argued that a disproportionately high share of capacity costs should be allocated to the first/business/full economy categories since, as illustrated before in the A320 versus B737 example, the airline needs to schedule high services at high frequencies in order to sell these fares. To a certain extent the higher frequency requirements of the first/business/full economy categories are reflected in higher space requirements and lower load-factors, but the frequency–space–load-factor inter-relationships are not all that close and may vary quite a lot between airlines, aircraft types and routes.

Where it proves difficult to arrive at an unequivocal allocation of costs between fare categories, it will be simpler to test if the revenue generated by all fare categories is greater or less than the variable costs incurred. In other words, is the average fare paid greater or less than AVC? If the average fare is less than AVC, then this might be considered by the competition authorities as prima facie evidence of predation taking place. But one problem with this is that it could induce an airline wishing to avoid being accused of predatory pricing, to discriminate still further against price inelastic passengers and to raise its more expensive fares beyond their otherwise most profitable levels, merely in order to disguise some predatory intent in a lowering of its cheaper fares.

Another problem arises in how the revenue is assessed, in particular that earned from fares sold to connecting passengers. Because of the taper in fares with the length of a passenger's journey, the through fare paid by the passenger is normally less than the sum of the separate fares for each flight sector involved. Hence the carrier on each sector has to accept something less than its local point-to-point fare. Where the passenger makes an inter-line connection, the IATA pro-rating method shares out the revenue in proportion to the distance of each sector, with shorter distances given greater weight to allow for higher operating costs per seat mile. But where the passenger makes an online connection, the value of the revenue earned by the shorter sector may be much greater than the weighted distance in the IATA method would suggest. If the route plays an important role in feeding (possibly high-yield) traffic to other (possibly long haul) routes in the airline's network, its effective contribution to the airline's total revenue can be much greater than the pro-rated division of through fares. The increasing emphasis on hub and spokes networks means that differences in this respect are becoming more and more important.

The problems of identifying the precise costs and revenues associated with particular fares mean that it is always going to be difficult to apply a criterion like the Areeda–Turner test, to determine whether an airline is engaging in predation by pricing below cost. This might partly explain why the US antitrust authorities, which have pursued cases of predation against firms in other industries, have yet to take a single airline to court on a charge of predation. The heavy burden of producing proof may also have deterred a number of civil suits, despite the possibility award of triple damages under US law. Proving anything is bound to be difficult, when an airline's short-run MC is close to zero, or when the airline can use its computerized yield management systems to cut fares selectively whilst ensuring that revenue still covers AVC for the service as a whole. But the burden of proof would become heavier still, if it were admitted that fares *above* costs can sometimes be predatory too.

Can a fare above cost be predatory?

As a number of academic economists have argued (Joskow and Klevorick, 1979; Vickers, 1985; and Tirole, 1988) pricing below cost is a sufficient condition for predation to be taking place, but not a necessary one. A price can still have predatory intent even when set above short-run MC or above AVC. In the formula for NPV (predation) given above, all that is necessary for predation to be rational is that the predator's sacrifice of current profits (the Λ_p losses) is less than the expected increase in future profits (the π_p gains). The Λ_p losses need not be accounting losses but only a reduction in profits from what they would have been, had the firm not sought to set a predatory price. Hence a more comprehensive definition of predatory pricing might omit any reference to cost, as in the one put forward by Joskow and Klevorick (1979):

> Predatory price behaviour involves a reduction of price in the short run so as to drive competing firms out of the market or to discourage entry of new firms in an effort to gain larger profits via higher prices in the long run than would have been earned if the price reduction had not occurred.

In other words an airline need not actually lose money on the service for its fares to be predatory: it only has to earn less profit on it, accepting a lower $(P - MC)/P$ margin than it earns on other services elsewhere.

A dominant airline that can make selective price cuts in a small segment of its market will aim to do so in such a way that they inflict maximum damage upon its competitor(s) at minimum cost to itself. The low fares may thus apply only over a limited number of seats (possibly some within each class) and not over the whole of the dominant airline's market share. Selective cuts in fares may also have an important 'demonstration effect' on potential entrants. Although the fares may never fall below short-run MC or AVC, the dominant airline may still be able to deter entrants by setting its fares at something less than profit-maximizing levels, as part of a policy of 'limit pricing'. Limit pricing means keeping fares low enough to ensure that entry by new airlines (or expansion by existing carriers) is not profitable. A new entrant airline may not have the same scope for selective pricing and therefore its low fares may have to apply across a large part of its market share. Hence it is possible for some low fares to be profitable for the dominant airline (albeit rather less profitable than before they were reduced) but unprofitable for the new entrant.

Thus predation can involve fares above or below costs. The signal conveyed to the prey about its future profitability matters as much as the predator's sacrifice of current profit (Milgrom and Roberts, 1982). If anything, predation with fares above costs is the more likely scenario.

6.7 Allegations of predatory pricing

It has been argued that predation is both a feasible and viable strategy for some airlines to adopt (Dodgson, Katsoulacos and Pryke, 1990). The

Organisation for Economic Co-operation and Development (1988) holds the same view, arguing that, when airlines operate in many different city pair markets, predatory pricing in one market can be financed through cross-subsidization out of revenues earned in other markets, especially if entry to the other markets is restricted in some way. A former chairman of the US Civil Aeronautics Board, considering predatory pricing to be a likely and rational response by incumbent airlines to the arrival of low cost new entrants, characterized as a 'lamentable failure of the administration' the fact that no action had been taken against a single case of predation (Kahn, 1988). So far there have not been that many formal inquiries into allegations of predatory pricing by airlines. In a survey of cases in OECD member countries, none of the investigations related to the airline industry (Organisation for Economic Co-operation and Development, 1989). And, apart from the Laker and Virgin Atlantic cases referred to earlier, competition authorities in the United States and in Europe have not so far pursued many allegations regarding predatory pricing.

One notable case in the United States concerned the reaction of Northwest to the arrival of People Express on the route between Newark and Minneapolis/St Paul in 1983. Before People Express came onto the route, Northwest offered an unrestricted one-way economy class fare of $263 and a number of restricted fares, the lowest of which was set at $149. People Express charged just two fares, initially set at $99 (on weekdays) and $79 (for evening and weekend travel). Northwest responded by introducing two new restricted fares, just below those of People Express, at $95 and $75, announcing them in full-page advertisements in the press. At the same time Northwest stepped up its service frequency, from ten to thirteen flights a day. And when People Express reduced its fares to $79 and $59, Northwest matched them. People Express then felt it necessary to cut frequency, from six to five daily flights; but Northwest maintained its number of flights at thirteen a day. In this case the new entrant offered the low fares on all seats, whereas the incumbent's low fares only applied to a limited number of seats. The competition authorities may have felt that Northwest's objective was to drive People Express off the route, but apparently feared that any intervention on their part would only make matters worse.

In a case that went before an antitrust court in 1993 the plaintiffs were Continental and Northwest and the defendant American. Continental and Northwest alleged that American was pursuing a predatory policy by introducing a 'Value Pricing' plan under which full coach fares were cut by 38 per cent and advance purchase excursions by 50 per cent. Continental and Northwest argued that American was trying to drive competitors from the market by pricing below cost with the intention of raising fares to supracompetitive levels to recoup losses once competitors had been eliminated. American responded by saying that its Value Pricing plan was merely an attempt to simplify consumer choice in a highly competitive market. The airline also made the point that, in such a competitive market, any attempt at predatory pricing was, in its view, doomed from the outset. In the event the court found in favour of American Airlines, the verdict accompanied by the opinion that the predatory scheme suggested by the plaintiffs would have been extraordinarily expensive and would have had no realistic chance of success. The court case proved to be rather expensive itself, something in the region of $20–30 million being spent on legal fees. The Chairman of American, Robert Crandall, complained that the large amount of resources which had to be devoted to a defence against the suit 'threatened the very existence of the company' (McKenna, 1993). And both the costs of the case and the ultimate verdict must have some effect on the readiness of airlines to bring such suits in the future. If the costs are forbidding for major carriers like Continental and Northwest, then they certainly must deter many of the low-cost airlines from taking legal action (Clouatre, 1995).

A number of low-cost airlines in the United States, feeling that they have been targeted for predatory action by the majors, formed themselves into a group, the Air Carrier Association of America (ACAA) to lobby for government support. The original members of the group included Air Tran Airways, Arrow Air, Carnival Air Lines, Frontier Airlines, Sun Jet, Spirit Airlines and ValuJet. Their main concern has been the majors' targeting of their low cost services from small cities into the major hubs. One extreme case frequently cited was that of the Atlanta–Mobile route, on which Delta raised its fares more than 500 per cent once ValueJet had withdrawn its service (Walker, 1997). Another case (US Department of Transportation, 1998) concerned Northwest's response to the entry (and subsequent exit) of Spirit Airlines to the Boston–Detroit route. In the first quarter of 1996, just before Spirit began offering service on the route, Northwest's average fare was $258.83. Following Spirit's entry with fares in the $69–159 range, Northwest's average fare fell to $106.05 in the second quarter of 1996 and $100.01 in the third quarter, a decline of 61 per cent. Spirit left the route at the end of the third quarter, claiming that it was driven out by Northwest's sharp cuts in fares. Northwest then raised its average fare to $189.52 in the fourth quarter and $267.54 in the first quarter of 1997. A very similar sequence of events apparently took place on the Denver–Billings route, on which Frontier Airlines challenged United and ended up being driven out after United had dropped its average fare by almost 50 per cent; and following Frontier's exit United's average fare rose to a level some 23 per cent above the level prevailing before Frontier entered. Cases like these, plus an increasing number of bankruptcies among low-cost airlines, including the failures of Air South WestPac and Pan Am, has produced greater Congressional pressure for something to be done about the reactions of majors to the entry of low cost competitors.

Similar issues have been raised by low-cost airlines in Europe. In 1994 the European Commission investigated complaints from Ryanair that Aer Lingus had responded to its entry to the Dublin–Birmingham route by cutting fares to below costs. The EC made what was referred to in the press as a 'dawn raid' upon the head office of Aer Lingus, presumably in an attempt to obtain documentary evidence of Aer Lingus's intent. In submitting its complaint Ryanair argued that Aer Lingus was only able to match its new low fares by financing price cuts out of the IR£175 million of state aid that the EC had approved some months earlier.

Two cases have been raised by EasyJet. One concerned the reaction of KLM to its entry to the Stansted–Amsterdam route. In a submission to the European Commission in 1997 EasyJet claimed that KLM was trying to price it out of the market and cited as evidence an internal KLM memorandum which spoke of the need 'to stop the growth and development of EasyJet and to make sure that this newcomer will not be able to secure a solid position in the Dutch market' (Skapinker, 1997). KLM did not deny the existence of the memo but said that it was not an official document. Nonetheless EasyJet argued that KLM had contravened Article 86 of the Treaty of Rome, which prohibits abuse of a dominant market position. More recently, in February 1998, EasyJet took British Airways to a UK High Court seeking an injunction to prevent BA operating its own low-cost subsidiary, Go. The ground on which EasyJet sought an injunction was that BA was preparing to cross-subsidize Go out of profits earned on its main network, thus enabling Go to compete in the low-cost market on an unfair basis. And later in the same year EasyJet applied to the EC asking for Go's lowest one-way fare on the Stansted–Edinburgh route, a fare of £15 (or £25 including airports Tax), to be barred.

Another airline to register a complaint with the EC was Air Liberté in France. Early in 1995 a fierce price war broke out on the Paris Orly–Toulouse route. This route used to be one of the most profitable routes in France, until the monopoly previously enjoyed by Air Inter was broken by liberalization of route licensing and the entry of two airlines, Air Liberté and Euralair. Air Inter responded to the new entry by launching a Fr540 'super leisure' return fare, at less than a third of its own standard fare and undercutting Air Liberté's inaugural promotional fare by Fr100. Air Liberté replied with a fare of Fr360, which was immediately met by Air Inter with a further cut in its super leisure return to Fr280. The complaint Air Liberté made to the EC demanded the immediate termination of the Fr20 billion of state aid to Air France, which now owns Air Inter, on the ground that the condition applying to the EC's approval of it, namely that French domestic routes should be opened up to competition, was still not in effect being realized. And Air Liberté also made a second formal complaint, this time to the French Government, demanding that Air Inter should be required to offer similar cuts in fares on its other domestic routes, where it did not face such competition. Air Inter rejected Air Liberté's viewpoint and argued that it should be left free to offer promotional fares where and when it wishes. In the event Air Liberté got into financial difficulties and its owners decided to put the airline up for sale. It was eventually bought by British Airways which merged it with its other French subsidiary TAT European Airlines. The fact that Air Liberté's slots, aircraft, route licences, etc., remained in use lends at least some support to the argument that, even if successful in causing the original airline to exit, predation does not remove capacity from the industry. So if indeed Air Inter's policy was to drive Air Liberté from the market, this may have only resulted ultimately in one competitor being replaced by another (more formidable) competitor in the shape of a BA subsidiary.

A case in Canada involved a charter airline seeking to break into the scheduled market. Nationair entered three domestic routes out of Toronto (to Montreal, Ottawa and Halifax) and competed against the two established carriers, Air Canada and Canadian Airlines International (CAIL). Its entry proved to be very short lived, however. Not long after commencing scheduled operations, Nationair was forced to seek bankruptcy protection in March 1993. At the same time it filed a complaint with Canada's Bureau of Competition Policy, alleging that the responses of Air Canada and CAIL to its deep discount fares on the three routes in question constituted predatory pricing.

Of the relatively rare cases where direct action has been taken to remedy a suspected instance of predatory pricing, one occurred in South Africa in 1993. The South African Competition Board found the domestic services of South African Airways (SAA) apparently being run at a substantial loss. The Competition Board suspected the airline was cross-subsidizing these losses out of net revenues earned on international services. After investigating, the Board concluded that SAA was pricing below cost on domestic trunk routes, forcing two rival airlines, Flitestar and Comair, to follow suit. The Board ordered SAA to restore fares to 1991 levels in real terms and to ensure that its discount fares were at the same (real) levels as those in place when one of the rivals, Comair, entered the routes.

Another case, this time concerning air freight services, was decided in Australia in 1994. Four years previously a small company, Discount Freight Express, complained to the Australian Trade Practices Commission that predatory pricing was widespread. There were also allegations of systematic price fixing, poaching of clients and various other anticompetitive practices. Two companies, Ansett Airlines and its parent TNT International Aviation Services were fined a total of A$5 million and were ordered to pay A$1.07 million in legal costs, equivalent to around twenty times the previous highest fines imposed for breaches of the Australian Trade Practices Act. Ansett and TNT had withdrawn their defence, without admitting liability, in order, as the TNT chairman explained, to limit the companies' legal expenses (which by the time an agreement was concluded had summed to A$11 million, but which were expected to reach A$17 million, if the case had gone the full distance in the courts).

In 1981 Laker Airways went into liquidation and then brought an antitrust suit alleging that a number of IATA airlines had conspired to force it out of business by predatory price cutting. The case never came to court. In 1984 an out-of-court settlement was reached, under which a total of $69 million was paid by a group of ten North Atlantic airlines. Just less than half, $33 million, was met by British Airways, with Pan American and TWA each contributing $9 million, with five European carriers (KLM, Lufthansa, Sabena, SAS and Swissair) each paying $2.8 million and with the remainder coming from British Caledonian ($3.9 million) and UTA ($0.1 million). All these payments were made with no admissions of liability. So far as British Airways was concerned there was a desire to reach a swift resolution of the dispute in the run-up to its privatization. The case was quite a complex one. The reasons why Laker Airways collapsed were many, most of them related to the airline's over-expansion. The airline's finances were highly geared, with an extremely high debt-to-equity ratio; and this made it vulnerable to hikes in interest rates. Much of the debt capital used to finance aircraft acquisitions was denominated in US dollars, whilst a high proportion of passenger revenues on the Skytrain North Atlantic services was earned in pounds sterling; and this exposed the airline to adverse movements in foreign exchange rates. When interest rates rose and sterling depreciated against the dollar, the airline got into some very serious financial difficulties. It would in all probability have gone bankrupt, whether it was involved in a fares war or not. At the time the fares war broke out, in the autumn of 1981, all the North Atlantic carriers were experiencing a downturn in traffic due to the economic recession of the time. One airline suffering from the effects of the recession as much as any other airline, if not more, was Pan American, and this airline matched Laker's Skytrain fares from the very beginning, obliging British Airways, TWA and the other transatlantic carriers to follow suit. So far as Pan American was concerned, matching Laker's fares was probably wholly defensive, a kind of 'knee-jerk' response to a fairly desperate situation. Ever since the Bermuda II agreement the North Atlantic has been an open market in which downward movements in any fare (except supersonic and perhaps also first class fares) tend to be matched more or less instantly. Hence, when Laker introduced a new 'Regency' class fare aimed at high-yield business travellers, it could have been fully expected that the other carriers would seek to match it. The main antitrust issue was whether the matching of fare cuts was concerted, something on which no final conclusion was reached since the matter never came to trial. But the matching did not need to be concerted to produce the same result: once Pan American matched, the others had to follow whether they wanted to or not.

Whatever the merits of the Laker Airways case, there was a further antitrust suit, this time brought by Virgin Atlantic. This alleged that British Airways used its monopoly power at London Heathrow to try to squeeze out competition from Virgin on transatlantic routes. The lawsuit was not so much concerned with predatory pricing as with other forms of predation involving things like 'switch selling', called 'bait and switch' in America, corporate discounts and travel agency commissions. Virgin sued for triple damages which, if awarded, could have amounted to an estimated $1 billion.

Generally speaking airlines have been somewhat reluctant to take legal action against alleged predators. A number of reasons have been identified for this (Dodgson, Katsoulacos and Pryke, 1990). One is all the time and expense involved. Another may be an unwillingness to offend large airlines on whose goodwill smaller airlines often rely for co-operation in aircraft maintenance, use of CRSs, through ticketing, etc. Also, it is possible that taking another airline to court could be bad for publicity: many of the victims of alleged predatory pricing may be new airlines whose owners or managers may have been amongst the most vocal in extolling the virtues of free competition and in calling for the abolition of regulation; and now it might appear as if, as plaintiffs, they are asking competition authorities to step in and raise fares. Then there is the attitude likely to be struck by the courts. In the United States courts have generally been rather unsympathetic to allegations of predatory pricing, partly because of the traditional view that predation can never be a rational strategy. Also airlines are rather unlikely to succeed in litigation, so long as the US Department of Justice uses the Areeda–Turner rules as the main yardstick for detecting predation.

6.8 Non-price forms of predation

Airlines can use a variety of weapons as predatory devices. One of the most common involves the scheduling of capacity. Incumbent airlines have sometimes been accused of responding to the entry of a competitor by starting 'frequency wars', flooding the route with such extra capacity that the new entrant finds it difficult to launch its new service and make it pay. This was the kind of complaint lodged by British Midland against British Airways' Shuttle service on the London–Glasgow route. Incumbent airlines may also try to undermine a competitor's service by following the practice of 'bracketing', scheduling departures to take off just before and just after the competitor's flights. Airline schedules are of course published, making data on frequencies, timings, size of aircraft used, etc. readily available. So it is relatively easy to observe what airlines are doing and to chart the sequence of events. But the central problem still remains: how to distinguish between predatory behaviour and competition on its merits. An incumbent airline is likely to argue that, since schedule frequencies and timings are powerful weapons in competition for market share, why should it be denied using them; whereas a new entrant is likely to claim that the incumbent does not intend the increase in capacity to be permanent, but to last only so long as it takes to drive the new entrant off the route.

The sort of dilemma that this presents to a regulatory authority can be seen in an application by Loganair (which, as it happened, was the incumbent airline with the greater market share in this case) to vary the air service licence held by British Airways on the Edinburgh–Manchester route (Civil Aviation Authority, 1992). Loganair used to operate the route with four daily frequencies as against one by BA. The route used to be profitable for Loganair, but that changed when BA decided to match Loganair's frequency. Loganair argued that, at eight flights a day, the frequency had become quite excessive in relation to demand and that, if it continued to incur losses, it would consider withdrawing from the route altogether. Loganair claimed that BA had predatory intent and sought to restrict its frequency back to just one a day. BA replied that in matching frequencies it was only acting in a normal competitive manner. As regulator, the Civil Aviation Authority did not wish to be seen to be curbing competition, but saw a real risk that Loganair would withdraw and accepted that, unless there was some reduction in capacity, the route was likely to end up as a monopoly for BA. So the CAA compromised and decided to restrict BA's frequency, not to just one a day but two.

Increased frequencies can be a form of pre-emptive action (Beesley, 1986). In regulated markets incumbents might use this weapon to forestall the entry of potential competitors. Abbott and Thompson (1989) have suggested that the increased frequencies incumbents operated on the London–Milan route at the time of some protracted negotiations to provide for the entry of British Caledonian as a new competitor on the route represent a good example of such pre-emptive action.

A quite extreme example of an attempt at non-price predation occurred in the United States. It involved Northwest's response to Reno Air's entry into the Reno–Minneapolis city pair market in 1993. Not only did Northwest institute service of its own on this route, a route which it had previously abandoned, it also opened a new mini hub in Reno that overlaid much of Reno Air's hub operation. It was only after the US Department of Transportation intervened that Northwest decided to abandon its overlay of Reno Air's network.

Another powerful weapon is advertising. In the debates on deregulation and contestable markets the significance of advertising for airline competition was rather underestimated. Expenditure on advertising, once made, is a sunk cost; and sunk costs act as entry barriers inhibiting contestability (Borenstein, 1992). Incumbent airlines usually have much deeper pockets out of which to finance a war in advertising expenditure.

Computer reservations systems (CRSs) and frequent flyer programmes (FFPs) are also weapons that can be used in a predatory or anticompetitive manner. Before intervention by regulatory authorities, CRSs could be used to bias the information on flights, in such a way that the services and/or fares of certain airlines were displayed less prominently than those of the carriers owning the system. Although this practice has now been largely eliminated, there is still some concern that small airlines are at a disadvantage, both in relation to CRS fees and in relation to the role of CRSs as an increasingly important source of market information. So far as the latter is concerned, whilst all participating airlines have equal access to the huge quantities of booking data which CRSs produce, only the large airlines have the resources to make full use of it. This was something given much publicity in the row between British Airways and Virgin Atlantic (Gregory, 1994).

Another aspect to CRSs is the facility they afford airlines to signal threats to their competitors, either to deter entry or to discourage cuts in fares. One way in which a threat like this might be played out is as follows: Carrier A, a small airline, attempts to boost its market share by cutting fares on routes served by Carrier B, a larger airline, in order to market its new fares. A enters them in the CRS used by B; B responds, not only by matching A's new fares but also by 'pre-announcing' lower fares in other markets served by A, signalling its intention (often by code) to subject the smaller airline to a form of 'discipline pricing'; and then Carrier A, receiving the message, withdraws its lower fares, before Carrier B agrees to cancel its threatened reductions. What Carrier B appears to be signalling to carrier A is that it should cease competing on the route in question or else face a damaging price war on a number of other routes as well. Two US airlines said to have been victims of this sort of predatory behaviour are Midway Airlines and America West.

Small airlines can also be at a disadvantage in relation to FFPs. There is some evidence that FFPs have become a significant barrier to entry, especially in the United States (Humphreys, 1991). Airlines can utilize their FFPs in a predatory or anticompetitive manner by calibrating the rewards so that mileage and other bonuses are temporarily increased on routes on which they face new competition. In the marketing of FFPs airlines tend to target first/business class passengers. Although these passengers typically represent only around 20 per cent of total traffic, their contribution to total revenue is often much higher, about 50 per cent or so. Hence the potential gains from predation can be rather large here, especially if the FFP succeeds in securing the loyalty of high-yield passengers, whose demand becomes even less cross-price elastic than it was before.

6.9 Policy questions

What, if anything, should government regulatory authorities – like for example the Civil Aviation Authority in London or the European Commission in Brussels – do about predatory behaviour? Their role in airline competition policy is one of identifying the point at which carriers cross the threshold between acceptable and desirable competitive action and destructive anticompetitive behaviour. In this, their position is analogous to that of a referee in a soccer match. The referee has to decide when a tackle is fair and when it is a foul, when to let a goal stand and when to disallow it for one reason or another. Much depends on the referee's discretion and judgement, but at least there are some basic rules. The regulatory authority's task is a little more difficult, in that the basic rules themselves are still a matter of some debate.

Any rule that condemns reductions in fares not only courts unpopularity with the travelling public, it may also have a chilling effect upon competition. A rule that makes it difficult to prove predation – like one requiring it to be shown that a fare is below an airline's cost – could make it more likely that predation is indeed attempted. Conversely, a rule under which it is relatively easy to claim predation could encourage a number of frivolous accusations from airlines seeking to frustrate the normal process of competition.

The crux of the matter is to find the dividing line between genuine revenue-enhancing yield-management techniques and practices aimed directly at undermining the economics of a competitor's operation. This is never going to be easy. It is not something that can be reduced to a simple criterion. A more pragmatic approach is required.

The UK Civil Aviation Authority (1993b) approaches the problem by tracking fare developments and trends over time on a selected number of routes, in order to focus on cases where unusually low, and therefore potentially predatory, fares are being offered. Ideally such monitoring should include accessing the CRSs through which the fares are distributed. It is important to note not just the levels of the fares, but also the numbers of seats being sold in each fare category. Further, because of the time it can take to investigate complaints of predatory behaviour, the authorities should if necessary have the power to suspend the practice subject to complaint whilst these investigations are being carried out.

The US Department of Transportation (1998) has proposed a set of rules for dealing with predation. These effectively put limits on how far incumbent airlines can go in reacting to the entry of new competitors. The rules go beyond the Areeda–Turner test in identifying as objectionable pricing and capacity additions by incumbents that have the result of producing 'lower local revenue than would a reasonable alternative response'. Under the DoT rules, predation would require not necessarily the acceptance of actual, out of pocket, losses but merely a sacrifice of profits that could have been achieved by some alternative policy, such as one involving lesser price reductions or the offer of fewer additional discount fares or a refraining from adding capacity (Kahn, 1999). The terms used are rather vague and imprecise, but what they mean is that the DoT would commence enforcement proceedings if it sees an incumbent carrier adding a very large number of seats at very low fares.

Many cases involving predatory behaviour arise on international routes and thus may fall partly outside the jurisdiction of national regulatory authorities like the CAA or the DoT. On routes within the EU responsibility for dealing with anticompetitive practices ultimately rests with the European Commission, under Articles 85 and 86 of the Treaty of Rome. The European Commission has been searching for meaningful criteria to adopt in identifying predation and seeking remedies for it. The Commission is considering a criterion based on short-run variable costs: fares assessed as 'likely to be predatory', if the revenue they yield is less than 90 per cent of the total (fully allocated) operating cost of the service concerned (Commission of the European Communities, 1992c). This is very much like the Areeda–Turner test. For reasons given earlier, a criterion based only on cost is likely to founder on the burden of proof and will not encompass cases of predation where revenue from fares does in fact cover costs. Experience with the Areeda–Turner test in the United States suggests that a *per se* policy of this kind might actually make it rather difficult to take any action against predatory behaviour in air transport.

However strongly it is suspected, it is always going to be difficult to *prove* predation. And cost-based rules like the Areeda–Turner test are not

really adequate to cope with those possibly more serious cases of predation that involve limit and/or discipline pricing together with other non-
price strategies designed to have similar effects.

There are some possible alternative policies in which direct recognition could be given to the dynamic and strategic nature of predatory behaviour. One of the more relevant in the present context is a
policy of leaving incumbent airlines entirely free to respond to new
entry by cutting fares, but, where predation is suspected, placing
restrictions on the subsequent raising of those fares in the event of the
new entrant airline exiting the route in question. This could reduce
incumbent airlines' incentives to engage in predatory pricing, by
reducing (if not eliminating altogether) the expected gains from it (the
π gains). A policy measure of this kind would have certain advantages
over other possible proposals insofar as it would place the emphasis
more on *ex ante* deterrence than on *ex post* prosecution. But the precise
modus operandi of any such policy would need to be very carefully
thought out. For exactly how long would any constraints on incumbent airlines' freedom to reverse cuts in fares need to be maintained?
(i.e. for many periods after period *t*?) And to which kinds of fares
should the controls apply – only those published in airline tariffs
manuals or those marketed through consolidators and bucket shops
as well? The latter would be difficult to police, but if they are not
covered by the policy, then the possibility would exist of incumbent
airlines channelling most (if not all) of their predatory fares through
'unofficial' travel agencies, rendering any constraints over published
fares that much less effective. Some discount fares sold through
unofficial travel agencies are advertised in the press (as shown in
Figure 6.8) but many are not. Also, there is the problem of deciding
what allowances should be made for general price inflation and for
changes in factors outside the airline's control, like increases in fuel
prices, increases in airport charges or an upsurge in market demand?
Clearly, there would be much to think about in implementing a policy
of this kind. But the main problem would still be in deciding when a
cut in fares has predatory intent. When a new competitor enters a
route, it attracts traffic away from the incumbent airline; and so the
residual demand left for the incumbent is less than before, something
that may call for lower fares independent of any predatory intent.
Conversely, if the incumbent does not respond to entry by lowering
fares, this may not necessarily mean that it has no predatory objective,
since it may (before entry) have been practising limit pricing and sees
no need to cut its fares further. It would be the task of the regulatory
authority's monitoring exercise to distinguish between cases like these,
possibly by close examination of the path that the incumbent airline's
fares take over time.

Figure 6.8 Advertisements of discount fares sold through unofficial travel agencies (*Source: The Sunday Times*)

Similar approaches might be adopted towards non-price forms of predation. For example, incumbent airlines could be required to maintain schedules following the withdrawal of a competitor, and rules could be devised to inhibit incumbents bracketing a new entrant's services. Codes of practice in the use of CRSs could perhaps be tightened up a little bit further, to discourage airlines using them to signal threats of discipline pricing. And temporary increases in FFP bonuses could be treated in the same manner as temporary cuts in fares: where predatory intent is suspected, airlines could be required to maintain the enhanced bonuses for a certain minimum period of time following the new entrant's withdrawal.

7 Mergers and alliances

7.1 Mergers and acquisitions within national boundaries

One of the most striking results of deregulation is the impetus it gave to the level of activity in airline mergers and acquisitions. The constraints imposed in inter-governmental air service agreements, and the restrictions placed on ownership, meant that most of this activity took place within national boundaries.

The highest level of activity had been in the United States where, as discussed in Chapter 3, deregulation led to some considerable restructuring of the industry. Deregulation first appeared to encourage a lot of new entry, but later a wave of mergers and acquisitions left the industry somewhat more concentrated than it was before.

The history of merger activity in the deregulated US industry is charted in Table 7.1. The flurry of activity in the early years of deregulation did cause some concern over increases in market power, but it was thought then that the impact was likely to be rather small. While responsibility for merger control remained with the Civil Aeronautics Board and the Department of Justice a fairly cautious approach was adopted; and in the late 1970s the competition authorities did in fact block a number of proposed mergers (such as that between Eastern and National and that between Continental and Western) because of the potential harm to competition. But then there was a substantial wave of mergers in the middle of the 1980s, leading to a sharp increase in industry concentration. In 1984 15 carriers accounted for 90 per cent of the total domestic air travel market; and by 1989 this share of the market was held by just eight carriers. Between 1984 and 1988 it was the Department of Transportation which had the ultimate say in merger references involving the airline industry; and the DoT had strong faith in contestable markets and so permitted to be consummated each and every merger submitted to it. The DoT has been heavily criticized for this (Kahn, 1988) although it should be recognized that the DoT's pro-merger stance probably saved the industry from even more bankruptcies than those that actually took place. What attracted the most criticism

Table 7.1 Mergers and acquisitions in the deregulated US airline industry

1979	July	Republic formed from merger of North Central and Southern
1980	January	National merged with Pan American
	October	Republic and Hughes Airwest merged
1982	June	Eastern purchased Braniff's South American routes
	October	Continental acquired by Texas International
1985	April	United purchased Pan American's Pacific Division
	July	Midway acquired Air Florida
	July	Southwest acquired Muse Air
	August	Continental acquired New York Air
	November	People Express acquired Frontier
1986	February	Piedmont acquired Empire
	February	People Express acquired Britt
	May	Continental acquired Rocky Mountain
	August	Northwest acquired Republic
	September	TWA acquired Ozark
	November	Eastern became a wholly owned subsidiary of Texas Air
	December	Delta acquired Western
	December	Texas Air acquired People Express
	December	Alaska acquired Horizon
1987	February	Continental became a wholly owned subsidiary of Texas Air
	April	Continental, People Express and New York Air merged
	May	USAir acquired Pacific Southwest
	August	American purchased Air California
	October	Alaska and Jet America merged
	November	USAir acquired Piedmont
1988	March	Delta acquired 20 per cent of Sky West
1989	June	Trump purchased Eastern's Shuttle services
	June	Midway purchased assets from Eastern
1990	August	American purchased Eastern's Latin American routes
	October	USAir purchased Midway's Philadelphia operations
	November	Northwest took 25 per cent stake in Hawaiian and purchased Hawaiian's Pacific routes
	November	United purchased Pan American's London routes
1991	January	American purchased Seattle–Tokyo route from Continental
	May	American purchased three of TWA's London routes
	August	Delta purchased Pan American's European routes and shuttle services
	December	USAir reached an agreement to operate Trump Shuttle services
1992	January	United acquired Air Wisconsin
1993	January	TWA ownership acquired by employees and creditors
	April	Continental acquired by an investor group including Air Canada
1994	July	Employees took 55 per cent in United
1998	October	Northwest acquired 14 per cent of share capital of Continental
	November	American purchased Reno Air
1999	March	American Eagle took over Business Express

was the approval of mergers between airlines based at the same airport (Bailey and Williams, 1988). The issues involved can be seen quite clearly in two mergers in 1986, that between Northwest and Republic and that between TWA and Ozark.

Before their merger Northwest focused on long and medium haul routes while Republic offered mainly short and medium haul services. In 1985 they had a combined share of 8 per cent of the total US domestic market. The carriers argued that a merger would produce efficiency gains, on the ground that their fleets and networks were complementary. However, many of the routes served were duopolies and both airlines used the airport at Minneapolis/St Paul as their main hub. Because of this the Department of Justice recommended that the merger be rejected, but the DoT, convinced of the efficiency advantages and of the underlying contestability of the markets, approved it. By 1993 the merged airline had built up a market share of 81 per cent at Minneapolis where Northwest's market share had been only 32 per cent in 1978 (Table 5.9). A similar criticism was levelled at the TWA–Ozark merger, which led to TWA dominating the St Louis hub (Hurdle *et al.*, 1989). Not long after the merger TWA increased fares on formerly competitive routes emanating from St Louis by between 13 and 18 per cent.

A lot has been made of the adverse effects of local monopolies on consumers, but sometimes with no acknowledgement of the beneficial effects from increased competition on through routes via hubs. Both Northwest at Minneapolis and TWA at St Louis have been in keen competition for connecting traffic, not just between themselves but also with United and American operating out of the Chicago O'Hare hub.

From time to time there are threats of further waves of mergers taking place in the US domestic industry. One such threat came in the latter part of 1998. Northwest attempted to secure a controlling 51 per cent stake in the share capital of Continental; American began making overtures to US Airways about a possible merger; and United and Delta planned a marketing alliance so comprehensive it was being described as a 'virtual' merger, a merger in everything but name. None of these proposals came to (full) fruition. Northwest did acquire a stake in Continental, but only one of 14 per cent; the talks between American and US Airways did lead to an alliance involving a tie-up between the two carriers' frequent flyer programmes, but stopped well short of a full merger; and the virtual merger between United and Delta was abandoned once it was clear it would meet with stiff opposition from both the DoT and the DoJ. But when the authorities discourage mergers between the majors, this does not necessarily mean that majors will not merge with smaller (regional) airlines. And indeed there has been a rash of small airline acquisitions and attempted takeovers by majors trying to strengthen key hub positions. American has taken over Reno Air, and its subsidiary, American Eagle, has taken over the commuter airline Business Express; United is seeking to acquire America West; and Delta is making a bid for Atlantic Southeast Airlines. Ensuring traffic feed ahead of the next economic downturn is a clear motive in all these moves, although the majors are also encountering some resistance from pilots' unions which suspect another motive to be the transfer of capacity to a cheaper form of service operation.

The trend towards mergers only emerged some time after deregulation in the United States. In Canada mergers had a somewhat longer tradition. Under the Canadian regulatory regime mergers were one means of solving the financial difficulties airlines got into when prevented by regulation from exiting loss-making routes. But when domestic deregulation effectively began in Canada, around 1983 or 1984, the nature of mergers changed and the major airlines took advantage of relaxation in government control to bring about a substantial reorganization of the industry. Under regulation domestic services were provided mainly by two transcontinental airlines, Air Canada and CP Air, and by five fairly large regional airlines (Eastern Provincial Airways, Nordair, Quebecair, Pacific Western Airlines and Transair). The chronological path that mergers and acquisitions took in the deregulated environment is set out in Table 7.2. Both CP Air and Air Canada began by acquiring sizeable stakes in the large regionals, until CP Air was taken over by Pacific Western (which, up to then, had been very much the smaller of the two airlines) to form Canadian Airlines International (CAIL) in 1987. One year earlier the former all-charter carrier Wardair was allowed to start scheduled services on domestic routes and this airline mounted something of a challenge to Air Canada and CAIL, but not for long. By 1988 it was losing substantial amounts of money and in January 1989 was sold to CAIL. The end result is that Canada has a duopoly in scheduled airline services, with just over 50 per cent going to Air Canada and correspondingly just less than 50 per cent to CAIL. In addition to sharing the trunk routes, the duopolists also control most of the feeder carriers in Canada, under their respective brandnames Air Canada Connector and Canadian Partner. In the early 1990s Air Canada and CAIL both incurred some heavy deficits (losing a combined total of more than US$1billion over the two years 1991 and 1992). Compared to the major US airlines, Air Canada and CAIL are still relatively small airlines and likely to remain so, given the size of Canada's population. In view of their poor financial performance serious consideration was given to them merging to form a single Canadian flag carrier; and this was almost agreed in September 1992. But an Air Canada/CAIL merger would have created a near-monopoly in Canadian domestic air transport and this would have generated some concerns about market power. So in the event the carriers have pursued partnerships with US airlines, Air

Table 7.2 Mergers and acquisitions in the deregulated Canadian airline industry

1983	Pacific Western acquired 42 per cent of Time Air
1984	CP Air acquired Eastern Provincial
1985	Air Canada and Pacific Western each acquired 24.5 per cent of Air Ontario
1986	CP Air acquired Nordair
	Air Canada acquired 49 per cent of Air Nova
1987	Pacific Western and CP Air merged to form Canadian Airlines International
	Air Canada acquired 75 per cent of both Air Ontario and Austin
	Air Canada acquired 87 per cent of Air BC
	Time Air acquired North Canada Air
	Pacific Western established Ontario Express with 49.5 per cent stake
	Merger of Quebecair, Nordair Metro and Quebec Aviation
	Pacific Western acquired 45 per cent stake in Calm Air
	Canadian Airlines International increased stake in Air Atlantic to 45 per cent
1988	Air Canada helped create Air Alliance with 75 per cent stake
	Air Canada acquired 90 per cent of Northwest Territorial
1989	Canadian Airlines International acquired Wardair
1991	Canadian Regional Airlines formed as the holding company for Time Air, Ontario Express (both 100 per cent), Inter-Canadian (70 per cent) and Calm Air (45 per cent) and as the name of the Canadian Airlines International (CAIL) regional network
1996	Time Air and Ontario Express completely amalgamated and began operating as Canadian Regional Airlines
1997	First Air took over Northwest Territorial

Canada taking a stake in Continental while American has invested in CAIL. There have been a few more mergers between smaller regional airlines, including that between Time Air and Ontario Express in 1996 and that between First Air and Northwest Territorial in 1997, but the Canadian majors are very much closer to their alliance partners than they are to each other.

For many years a duopoly had been the official government policy for domestic air transport in Australia. In the past, domestic interstate routes were served by the state owned Trans Australian Airlines, renamed Australian Airlines in 1986, and the privately owned Ansett Airlines. All international routes were reserved for the state owned flag carrier Qantas. This arrangement endured for over 30 years. The only other airlines operating scheduled passenger services were some fairly small regional airlines, most of which were acquired by Ansett, for example East West Airlines and Kendell Airlines. In 1987 the Australian government gave formal notice of its intention to terminate its 'two airline policy' for domestic routes; and domestic deregulation effectively took place in 1990.

A new entrant appeared in the shape of Compass Airlines. This independent carrier entered the most densely trafficked trunk routes, offering single class service in relatively large aircraft and charging relatively low fares. Compass achieved some early success in capturing market share but its existence was rather short lived: it was declared bankrupt in December 1991, after just over one year in business. In August 1992 a new airline under the name of Compass (but not directly related to its predecessor) was launched and once again concentrated on the dense routes with low fares. But this too suffered from some severe financial difficulties and ceased trading after only nine months. In the meantime Australian Airlines was privatized and then taken over by Qantas, which is now completely privatized. Qantas integrated its international service with Australian's domestic network, so that domestic routes are still mainly operated as duopolies, although the intensity of competition now, between Qantas and Ansett, is significantly greater than when Ansett operated alongside the former Trans Australian Airlines. In being able to feed traffic between international and domestic services Qantas became a considerable competitive threat to Ansett, which itself sought to expand into international markets and to forge links with foreign airlines.

Many other countries used to follow the practice of designating separate national airlines for domestic and international routes. As in Australia the trend towards mergers and takeovers has tended to bring them together. For example, in New Zealand domestic trunk routes used to be operated exclusively by the National Airways Corporation, while international routes were the preserve of Air New Zealand. The two were merged in 1978 when still in state ownership. In Thailand the domestic operator Thai Airways was merged with Thai International in 1987. For both these mergers a strong motive was network integration to ensure traffic feed. The same consideration might be an important factor in plans to merge the two large public corporations in India. At present Air-India is responsible mainly for long haul international routes, while Indian Airlines operates a vast domestic network as well as some short haul international routes to neighbouring countries. There could be some extensive economies of scope in merging them.

The model for airline industry organization in countries of the British Commonwealth was of course the distinction the UK drew between its two main national airlines, British European Airways (BEA) and British Overseas Airways Corporation (BOAC). BEA served the domestic and European markets and BOAC served the Middle East and long haul intercontinental routes. Their merger in 1974 resulted in British Airways

Table 7.3 Airline mergers and acquisitions in European countries

1974	BEA and BOAC fully merged to form British Airways
1975	Svensk Flygtjanst and Crownair merged to form Swedair
1985	Aeromediterranea incorporated into ATI (a subsidiary of Alitalia)
1986	Air UK created from merger of Air Anglia, Air Wales, Air West and British Island Airways
1987	British Airways took over British Caledonian
1988	Air Littoral merged with Compagnie Aerienne Languedoc KLM took over NLM which became KLM CityHopper
1990	Air France took over UTA and thereby acquired a controlling interest (75 per cent) in Air Inter
1991	Lufthansa took over Interflug KLM acquired a controlling interest (80 per cent) in Transavia KLM CityHopper took over Netherlines
1992	British Airways took over Dan-Air Air Outre-Mer merged with Minerve to form AOM French Airlines SAS acquired a controlling interest (57 per cent) in Linjeflyg British Airways formed Deutsche BA which took over Delta Air British Airways took a 49.5 stake in TAT European Lufthansa took over DLT and renamed it Lufthansa CityLine
1993	British Airways took over Brymon Airways Maersk Air took over Birmingham European Airlines
1996	TAT became wholly owned subsidiary of British Airways
1997	KLM took over Air UK (subsequently renamed KLM UK) Air Inter fully integrated into Air France British Airways acquired a controlling 67 per cent stake in Air Liberté Braathens took over Transwede SAS took 29 per cent in Wideroe's
1998	Aviaco became wholly owned subsidiary of Iberia KLM took a 50 per cent stake in Martinair SAS purchased Air Botnia KLM took 30 per cent stake in Braathens British Airways purchased CityFlyer Express

having the most comprehensive route network in the world, extending half a million miles with 200 destinations in 84 countries. The BEA/BOAC merger was the first example in Europe of national airlines with different spheres of influence being amalgamated; and it was some while before something similar occurred in other European countries (Table 7.3). Before Air France had taken over UTA and gained control of Air Inter in 1990, and before Lufthansa had absorbed Interflug in 1991, following the re-unification of Germany, British Airways had in 1987 bought the largest independent UK airline British Caledonian.

The acquisition of British Caledonian by BA raised concerns regarding its impact on competition. Over half BCAL's net revenue from scheduled services was earned on routes on which it was in competition with BA. There was also concern lest the takeover would leave BA in a position to dominate both of London's two main airports, Gatwick as well as Heathrow. The matter was referred to the UK Monopolies and Mergers Commission. It was clear that BCAL could not continue as it was and that its financial position was so serious as to preclude its survival as a slimmed down niche carrier. The only other alternatives were a takeover by a smaller UK airline or a merger of one kind or another with a foreign airline. The only other UK airline to express an interest in bidding for BCAL was Air Europe, a former charter airline with ambitions to enter the scheduled sector. But this airline had neither the financial resources, nor the synergy benefits, to rescue BCAL and went into liquidation itself some years later. There were several drawbacks in a merger with a foreign airline: if a stake large enough to support BCAL was taken by a foreign company, this might have been held to constitute the passing of control out of British hands, which might have led to BCAL's designation as a UK airline under bilateral air service agreements being challenged and its route licences possibly being revoked. Nonetheless, after BA had sharply reduced their offer price following the October 1987 stock market crash, BCAL actively considered a number of proposals from the Scandinavian airline SAS (Thomson, 1990). What can be described as an auction then took place, at the end of which BA finally purchased BCAL for the sum of £250 million. To assuage the MMC's fears over the effects of competition, BA gave a number of undertakings (Monopolies and Mergers Commission, 1987a). These included surrendering at least 5000 slots at Gatwick and returning quite a few of BCAL's route licences (all domestic, plus those to Paris, Brussels and Nice). The merger was then investigated by the European Commission, who imposed further conditions on BA: limiting it to no more than 25 per cent of total slots available at Gatwick; increasing the number of BCAL route licences it was required to give up; and requiring it to acquiesce in Air Europe being designated as the UK operator on the Gatwick–Rome route.

Thus the MMC and EC approved the BA/BCAL merger, but only on terms designed to encourage competition from other airlines. A similar view was taken by the EC in respect of the Air France/UTA/Air Inter merger three years later. The conditions under which the French merger was approved were: first, that eight domestic and 50 international route licences be transferred to other airlines; second, that Air France divest itself of the 35 per cent stake it had in TAT European Airlines, the next largest French airline; and third, that slots be made available at Paris Charles de Gaulle for independent operators to use on domestic routes.

At first sight the conditions applied to the BA/BCAL and Air France/UTA/Air Inter mergers seemed reasonable safeguards for the maintenance of competition. This has not, however, been altogether vindicated by subsequent experience: there has been little or no new entry and also a decline in the number of competitors on many point-to-point routes (Doganis, 1994; Dodgson, 1994). In the UK two of the independent airlines expected to provide competition for BA both failed financially, Air Europe in 1991 and Dan-Air in 1992. In France, many of the busiest domestic routes have remained virtual monopolies for the Air France Group, partly because of the stipulation that new entrants should fly from Paris Charles de Gaulle rather than from the congested Paris Orly (the more popular airport for domestic passengers). For example, the two main charter airlines in France, Minerve and Air Liberte, both bid for licences from Orly, where they might have reaped some economies of scope by combining their charter operations with some scheduled services; but the French government declared that, because of congestion, both carriers could only operate new scheduled services from Charles de Gaulle. And elsewhere in Europe national airlines have been able to consolidate their home markets, with the acquisitions of Transavia by KLM and Linjeflyg by SAS, and with the collapse of other independent airlines like Air Holland, Trans European Airways in Belgium and the German airline Wings. EC approval for KLM's acquisition of Transavia is difficult to justify on competitive terms, there being no other significant competitors in the Dutch home market. But the EC would have had some difficulty in applying a similar remedy to that in the BA and Air France cases, i.e. the release of slots at the airline's main airport, because there was space capacity and thus no great slot problem at Schiphol Airport in Amsterdam.

Mergers within national boundaries have always been a cause for concern, whenever the possibility exists of the merged airline attaining a position of unassailable dominance in home markets. For this reason, two mergers in 1998 have been referred to competition authorities, KLM's stake in Martinair (originally 50 per cent, but planned to increase to 100 per cent) and BA's takeover of CityFlyer Express. The KLM acquisition has been referred to the EC and the BA takeover to the Monopolies and Mergers Commission. In both cases the main concern is the increased presence that the mergers would give the acquirers at busy airports, KLM at Schiphol and BA at Gatwick. In the latter case, if the MMC rules against the takeover, there is another British airline willing to acquire CityFlyer Express and that is Virgin Atlantic. Virgin is willing to match BA's £75 million bid for CityFlyer, its Chairman, Richard Branson, stating that he regards the acquisition as the last chance to create a 'second force' airline in the UK that is capable of competing effectively against BA. The objective of encouraging a second force to compete against BA used to be part of official UK government policy (Committee of Inquiry into Civil Air Transport, 1969) and led to the formation and development of British Caledonian. But the question now is whether there is less reason for a specifically *British* second force, if airlines are permitted greater freedom to merge with carriers from other countries.

7.2 Cross-border acquisitions

As pointed out in Chapter 2 the idea of airlines making investments in foreign carriers is not a new one and can in fact be traced back quite a long time. There have also been some instances of fully fledged mergers creating multinational airlines. So far these have been limited to airlines from neighbouring countries agreeing to pool their resources and form consortia on regional bases: SAS in Scandinavia, Gulf Air in the Middle East, LIAT in the West Indies, Air Afrique in francophone West Africa plus some other consortia no longer in existence (Table 7.4). But neither these mergers nor the trade investments airlines used to make in the past are quite the same thing as the kind of acquisition airlines are most interested in making now. In the past, cross-border acquisitions were made by state owned airlines and were promoted by national governments; their success or failure depended almost entirely upon political considerations; and their overriding objective was to save operating costs, especially in the procurement and maintenance of aircraft. The main interest in cross-border acquisitions today is shown by privatized airlines seeking to break free from inter-governmental air service agreements and extend their marketable networks by taking equity stakes in carriers operating complementary services, not just in neighbouring countries but, increasingly, in regions at the other ends of long haul routes.

In the airline context the ability to acquire shares in foreign companies is heavily constrained by governments, which so far still largely adhere to the principle that air carriers should be 'substantially owned and effectively controlled' by nationals of the state in which the carrier is registered. For example, when British Airways was privatized in 1987, its prospectus declared that not more than 22 per cent of its share capital would be allocated to investors outside the UK, although it was accepted that foreign holdings might subsequently rise to almost double that figure. In its initial flotation some 17 per cent of BA shares were purchased by foreign nationals, but six years later the proportion had grown to somewhere between 35 and 45 per cent. BA has around 230 000 shareholders, amongst whom the nationality spread covers more than 100 countries worldwide, although the majority of foreign shareholders reside in the United States (British Airways, 1998). A year after the BA privatization, when SAS attempted to acquire British Caledonian,

Table 7.4 Multinational state owned airline consortia[a]

Name	Year established	Participating countries	Share held[b]
Air Afrique[c]	1961	Benin	7.3
		Burkina Faso	7.3
		Central African Republic	7.3
		Chad	7.3
		Congo	7.3
		Ivory Coast	7.3
		Mali	7.3
		Mauritania	7.3
		Niger	7.3
		Senegal	7.3
Alliance Air	1995	South Africa	40
		Tanzania	30
		Uganda	30
East African Airways Corporation (EAAC)	1946 (ceased 1977)	Kenya	68
		Uganda	23
		Tanzania	9
Gulf Air	1971	Bahrain	25
		Oman	25
		Qatar	25
		United Arab Emirates	25
Leeward Islands Air Transport Services (LIAT)[d]	1956	Barbados	10
		Trinidad and Tobago	10
		Antigua	5
		Grenada	5
		St Lucia	5
		Dominica	2
		Guyana	2
		Jamaica	2
		Montserrat	2
		St Kitts	2
		Nevis	2
Malaysia-Singapore Airlines	1966 (ceased 1972)	Malaysia	–
		Singapore	–
Scandinavian Airlines System (SAS)	1946	Sweden	42.8
		Denmark	28.6
		Norway	28.6

[a] In addition to those named here there has for many years been a planned consortium between several North African countries (Algeria, Libya, Morocco and Tunisia) to form a multinational airline to be known as Air Maghreb. But so far this consortium has not come to fruition.

[b] The percentage shares do not always sum to 100, because other organizations sometimes hold shares as well.

[c] Two of the original member countries dropped their participation, Cameroun in 1971 and Gabon in 1977.

[d] The company was subsequently reorganized and became known as LIAT (1974). In 1995 the airline BWIA (of Trinidad and Tobago) took a 29% stake in LIAT.

– Not available.

the UK government made it clear that a foreign airline would not be allowed to achieve overall control of a British airline. In the United States there is a statutory limit on foreign ownership of airline stock: foreign airlines can hold only up to 25 per cent of voting shares, and the president and two-thirds of the board of directors must be US citizens. The Chinese government has placed a ceiling of 35 per cent on foreign investments in domestic airlines. And similar, if not more restrictive, limitations used to apply in Europe, until the EU implemented its Third Liberalization Package on 1 January 1993, since when ownership of any EU airline has (at least in principle) been opened up to nationals of any member state. However, there are still the restrictions implied by the ownership clauses in inter-governmental air service agreements (e.g. if BA were to buy, say, 40 per cent of Olympic Airways, the Greek national carrier, some non-EU countries might no longer accept Olympic as the designated Greek carrier on international routes to/from Greece).

There are signs that governments are now beginning to relax restrictions on foreign ownership. Some airlines have been able to build up some sizeable stakes in foreign carriers (Table 7.5). SAS has been able to increase its stake in Airlines of Britain, the parent company of British Midland, from 25 per cent in 1988 to 35 per cent in 1992 and then to 40 per cent in 1994; and KLM has been permitted to increase its stake in Air UK, now known as KLM UK, from the original 14.9 per cent stake taken out in 1997 to full 100 per cent ownership in 1997. As one of the more profitable airlines in recent years, British Airways has taken something of a lead in this. In addition to its investments listed in Table 7.5, BA had also invested in USAir but sold its 24.6 per cent share in that airline when it joined American in proposing a new transatlantic alliance in 1996; and it has also recently been announced that BA and American are to purchase equity stakes in Iberia when the Spanish airline is privatized, BA signing up for 9 per cent of the shares and American 1 per cent. Most other airlines have been unable to acquire equity stakes on anything like this scale, either because of their financial position or because of their status as wholly or partly nationalized industries. Air France appears in Table 7.5 with the longest list of shareholdings in foreign airlines but more than half these are in relatively small carriers from countries with which France has historical or colonial links. Its major foreign shareholding had been in Sabena, but in the autumn of 1994 Sabena began questioning the future of the 37.5 per cent stake that Air France (in conjunction with a consortium of Belgian investors) took in 1992, as part of a rescue plan for Sabena. The two airlines had rationalized their maintenance operations and set up a joint shuttle service between Paris and Brussels, but plans for further co-operation failed to materialize after Air France was forced to implement a rescue plan for itself. Other European airlines then made overtures about replacing Air

Table 7.5 Equity stakes in foreign airlines, December 1998. *Sources:* Compiled from data published in *Airline Business* and in various press reports

Held by	Held in	Percentage of share capital	Year first acquired
Aer Lingus	Futura International	85.0	1989
Air France	Air Afrique	10.0	1992
	Air Caledonie	2.7	1968
	Air Gabon	11.2	1955
	Air Madagascar	3.5	1963
	Air Mauritius	12.8	1967
	Austrian	1.5	1989
	Cameroun Airlines	3.6	1971
	Middle East Airlines	0.9	1949
	Tunisair	5.6	1948
Air Malta	Azzura Air	49.0	1996
Air New Zealand	Air Pacific	2.0	1988
	Ansett Australia	50.0	1997
Air-India	Air Mauritius	8.8	1975
All Nippon	Austrian	9.0	1989
American	Aerolineas Argentinas	10.0	1997
	CAIL[a]	33.0	1994
	Iberia	1.8	1998
Austrian	Ukraine International[b]	14.3	1996
Braathens	Transwede	100.0	1997
	Malmo Aviation	100.0	1998
British Airways	Air Liberte	70.0	1996
	Air Mauritius	12.8	–
	Deutsche BA	100.0[c]	1992
	Qantas	25.0	1993
	TAT European[d]	100.0[e]	1992
Delta	AeroPeru	30.0	1998
	SIA	2.7	1991
	Swissair	4.5	1989
EasyJet	TEA Switzerland	40.0	1998
Emirates	Air Lanka	40.0	1998
Iberia	Aerolineas Argentinas	10.0[f]	1990
	Royal Air Maroc	1.3	–
Japan Air System	Air Philippines	10.0	1996
Japan Airlines	DHL International	25.0	–
KLM	ALM Antillean	40.0	1991
	Braathens	30.0	1997
	Kenya Airways	26.0	1996
	KLM UK	100.0	1987[g]
Lufthansa	DHL International	25.0	–
	Lauda Air	20.0[h]	1993
	Luxair	13.0	1992

Maersk	Estonian	49.0	1996
Malaysian	Royal Air Cambodge	40.0	1995
Martinair	Tampa Airlines	40.0	1996
Olympic Airways	Macedonian Airlines	100.0	1992
Qantas	Air Pacific	17.5	1987
Royal Brunei A.	Malaysian	10.0	–
SAS	Air Botnia	100.0	1998
	British Midland	40.0	1988[i]
	SpanAir	49.0	1986
SIA	CAIL	5.0	1998
	Delta	3.0	1991
	Swissair	2.7	1991
Swissair	Austrian	10.0	1989
	Cargolux	33.7	1997
	Delta	3.0	1989
	Sabena	49.5	1995
	SIA	0.6	1991
	Ukraine International[b]	4.1	1996
Taca	Aviateca	30.0	1989
	Lacsa	10.0	1992
	Nica	49.0	1992
Varig	Pluna	49.0	1996
	Ecuatoriana	50.1	1996
	LAB	49.0	1996
	TAM	3.3	–

[a] Parent company of American (AMR Corp.) holds 25% voting rights.
[b] Held via a holding company 77.78% owned by Austrian and 22.22% owned by Swissair. (The holding company owns 18.37% of Ukraine International.)
[c] Increased from 49% in 1998.
[d] Now absorbed into Air Liberté.
[e] Increased from 49.9% in 1997.
[f] Reduced from 83% in 1997.
[g] The original 1987 holding in what was then known as Air UK was 14.9%, the full takeover occurring in 1997.
[h] Reduced from 39.7% in 1997 (when 19.7% was sold to Austrian).
[i] Originally 25% in 1988 and increased to 35% in 1992 and increased again to 40% in 1994.
– Not available.

France, and eventually it was Swissair which took a stake of 49.5 per cent in 1995. This was not the first time that Air France experienced a partner demanding the relinquishment of share capital: in January 1994 Czechoslovak Airlines (CSA) declared that it wanted Air France to sell back its 19.1 per cent stake in CSA equity, to which, somewhat reluctantly, Air France agreed.

What are the advantages and disadvantages of holding shares in another airline? One possible advantage is that the act of purchasing shares demonstrates commitment, and this assures the other airline of a serious interest in long-term collaboration. Alliances struck without either partner purchasing shares might be relatively short lived or rather ineffectual. The BA/United marketing agreement, for instance, did not survive the failure of BA's bid to participate in the buyout of United; and the co-operation agreement between Air France and Lufthansa, which involved no exchange of shares, did not materialize into a closer relationship. Where alliances are accompanied by share purchases they tend to be durable. For example, Swissair and Delta each have a small stake in each other and this alliance was one reason why the proposed 'Alcazar' grouping, which would have united KLM, SAS and Austrian and created the largest airline group in Europe was not consummated. The collapse of this project was precipitated by disagreement over the choice of a US partner: Swissair naturally preferred this to be Delta, whereas KLM clearly wanted it to be its own partner, Northwest.

Taking an equity stake can often give the investing airline 'first mover' advantages over other airlines seeking stakes at a later date. This much has been evident in the case of SAS's increasing investment in British Midland. Having built up a substantial holding in take-off and landing slots at Heathrow where slots are in scarce supply, British Midland became something of a target for marketing deals and ownership offers. In September 1994 Lufthansa approached British Midland with the offer of an equity stake – either to replace SAS as the airline's main partner or to form a three-way alliance – but it was rebuffed. British Midland has also been asked about the possibility of buying shares by both Virgin Atlantic and United; and these two airlines were also told that British Midland had no interest in an equity arrangement with any airline other than SAS. Sir Michael Bishop, the Chairman of British Midland, was reported in the press as saying that other airlines had 'missed their opportunity'. It is clear that much of the urgency that airline managements have been showing in this matter has been due to fears of being pre-empted by deals struck with other airlines. As the number of alliances formed increases, the difficulty of finding suitable partners becomes that much greater.

An equity stake is not a riskless investment, of course. If the partner airline gets into financial difficulties this will obviously reduce the market value of the stake and, in the extreme circumstances of the partner entering bankruptcy and ceasing operations, the investment may have to be written off altogether. The experience of three European airlines investing in US domestic carriers – SAS in Continental, KLM in Northwest and BA's past stake in USAir – is testimony to the nature of the risks involved. SAS has perhaps lost the most in this respect, because when Continental entered Chapter 11 bankruptcy, it had to write off an investment of $100 million. Both KLM and BA have seen the value of their shares fall, but of course any losses sustained in share values have to be set against the value of the additional traffic that the alliance generates.

7.3 Alliance patterns

Many alliances struck between airlines involve no investments in equity at all. Many are limited to marketing agreements and technical co-operation. Over the past five years there has been a frenzy of activity in alliance formation. Annual surveys by *Airline Business* magazine show the growth in alliances (Table 7.6). The number of alliances has increased from 280 in 1994 to 502 in 1998, while the number of airlines involved has risen from 136 to 196. Airline executives have felt a growing sense of urgency to get their consortia together before the best partners were spoken for, so to speak. But it is interesting to note that the number of alliances entailing equity stakes has remained more or less constant over this period.

Most alliances tend to be between just one airline and another, but several major groupings, or global alliances, have begun to emerge. Some details of the three largest groupings – Oneworld, Star and Wings – are given in Table 7.7. In addition there is the group forming around Delta, Swissair, Sabena, Austrian, THY Turkish and TAP Air Portugal, which is referred to as the 'Atlantic Excellence' alliance (or, in relation to just the European airlines, the 'Qualiflyer' alliance). The situation is still quite fluid and there could be many changes in the future. Perhaps the biggest uncertainty surrounds the position of Air France and the

Table 7.6 Growth in airline alliances, 1994–98. *Source: Airline Business*

	1994	*1995*	*1996*	*1997*	*1998*	*Percentage change 1994–98*
Number of alliances	280	324	390	363	502	79.3
Number of airlines involved	136	153	159	177	196	44.1
Alliances entailing equity stakes	58	58	62	54	56	–3.4

question of the grouping to which it might ultimately become aligned. Air France is the largest carrier currently not a member of any of the four main alliance groupings. It has no main US partner in the same way that BA is partnered with American, Lufthansa with United, KLM with Northwest and Swissair with Delta. It is true that since April 1997 it has been in alliances with both Delta and Continental, but these alliances have been rather limited and Air France's prospects of signing up to a full transatlantic alliance have been inhibited by the need to retain a protective Franco–US bilateral while the airline was being restructured in preparation for privatization. But now there is a strong motive for Air France to join a global alliance so as not to lose out on the extra revenues that membership of a global alliance can bring. At the same time the Wings alliance might well be interested in welcoming Air France as an additional member, since it must be anxious to accelerate the development of its grouping in order to counter the challenge of the Oneworld and Star alliances. And if Air France were to join Wings, this would leave the Atlantic Excellence (Qualiflyer) alliance, which in any case is a much looser grouping, as very much the smallest of the four. The race to become the largest grouping, with the most extensive global reach, is increasingly reflected in some intense courting of non-aligned carriers. Witness the 'bidding war' taking place for equity stakes in the soon-to-be-privatized South African Airways.

The *Airline Business* surveys contain details of the diverse areas covered by alliances. They include: joint sales and marketing; joint purchasing and insurance; joint passenger and cargo flights; codesharing; block spacing; links between frequent flyer programmes; management contracts; and joint ventures in catering, ground handling and aircraft maintenance. To some extent the proliferation of bilateral deals within groups of airlines is a partial substitute for multilateral collaboration through the International Air Transport Association on interlining and revenue proration. Interlining and proration agreements continue but are becoming less significant for traffic transferring between alliance partners.

The interest in alliances shown by airlines mirrors the interest that firms in some other industries have been displaying. The growth in alliances between otherwise separate enterprises is a prominent feature of contemporary business across the world. One analysis of this development, in referring to the explosion of alliances worldwide, talks of the 'revolution amongst us' (Lynch, 1993, p. 1). It is difficult to be precise on the quantitative extent of alliances, for the relevant statistics are deficient in various ways. Nevertheless, the evidence overall certainly supports the contention that the last two decades have witnessed a mushrooming growth in alliances in a great many different industries, ranging from electronics to retailing. One estimate (Krubasik and Lautenschlager,

Table 7.7 International passengers carried by members of global alliances, 1997. *Source: Airline Business*

Oneworld	*International passengers (millions)*	Star	*International passengers (millions)*	Wings[a]	*International passengers (millions)*
Existing members		Existing members		Existing members	
British Airways	27.8	Lufthansa	22.5	KLM	14.4
American	16.9	United	12.2	Alitalia	10.8
Cathay Pacific	10.0	SAS	12.0	Northwest	9.5
Qantas	6.4	Thai International	8.5	Continental	5.0
CAIL	3.4	Air Canada	7.6	Kenya Airways	0.5
		Varig	2.8	Braathens	0.4
Total	64.5	Total	65.6	Total	40.6
World share	15%	World share	15%	World share	9%
Other associated airlines[b]		Other associated airlines[b]			
Japan Airlines	11.3	SIA	12.1		
Iberia	7.5	Air N. Zealand	3.3		
Finnair	3.6	All Nippon	3.0		
Aerolineas Argentinas	2.0	Ansett Australia	0.8		
LOT Polish	1.7				
Lan-Chile	1.5				
Potential total	92.1	Potential total	84.8		
Potential world share	21%	Potential world share	20%		

[a] At the time of writing the name 'Wings' had not been confirmed.
[b] Those which have signed partnerships with one or more members of the alliance grouping concerned.

1993) is that the annual growth rate in alliances in hi-tech industries, such as electronics, computers, aerospace, pharmaceuticals and telecommunications, has risen about fourfold.

Not only have alliances boomed in number over the past few years, they have also proliferated in type. Joint ventures and licensing arrangements have long been a feature of international business, and they are now a fairly common phenomenon in domestic commerce as well. Other alliances take on a wide variety of forms; such as co-operation in research and development, management servicing, training agreements, agreements on franchising, contact assembly, supply chains, etc. Sometimes these alliances are backed by minority equity holdings and sometimes they are not.

How does the pattern of alliances developing in the airline industry compare with those observed in other industries? To explore this question it is useful to categorize alliances accordingly to three main criteria:

- Whether they are horizontal, vertical or external alliances.
- Whether they are motivated more by technological factors than by market forces.
- Whether the mode of interfirm governance is of a relatively strong or relatively weak kind.

Horizontal, vertical and external alliances

Horizontal alliances are those between firms selling in the same product or service market. Vertical alliances are those with suppliers, distributors or buyers. External alliances are drawn up with potential entrants or with the producers of substitutes or complements in other industries.

Recent examples of horizontal alliances can be found in the pharmaceutical and telecommunications industries. In July 1993 the giant triad in the pharmaceutical industry, Glaxo, Wellcome and Warner-Lambert, announced that they were forming an alliance to develop and market over-the-counter (non-prescription) drugs across the world. There has also been a considerable flurry of activity in the telecommunication industry, with a number of major transatlantic alliances being struck. Three large rival alliances are emerging; Worldsource, Concert and Atlas. Each of these groups is seeking to compete in the market for one-stop international telecommunications contracts. It seems likely that competition for the lucrative business of multinational companies will replace the traditional cartel-like arrangements that have governed international telecommunications for many years. Something similar may well be occurring in international air transport. In many ways the links in telecommunications resemble the European and transatlantic links formed in air transport.

In the airline industry there have been horizontal agreements of one kind or another for a great many years. Before liberalization, and before government authorities took steps to eliminate them, international airlines often had pooling agreements with each other. Under these arrangements the revenue earned by different carriers operating a particular route was shared between them in accordance with a specific formula. In some cases revenues were divided up in proportion to the capacity offered by each carrier. In others, airlines pooled revenues only up to a certain percentage of seats sold, or by some other more complex revenue allocation scheme. Pooling agreements also often provided for co-operative scheduling and joint marketing, two things that are important aspects of the alliances airlines are currently entering into. But there is an essential difference: the old pooling agreements were between carriers co-operating the *same* route, whereas the current alliances are mostly between airlines operating *different* routes. Two of the most important strategic objectives behind the current alliances are traffic feed and access to new markets. Airlines are now tending to ally themselves with partners that have complementary networks rather than services against which they are in head-to-head competition. Major airlines operating trunk routes seek alliances with small regional carriers flying short haul routes; international airlines with no cabotage rights seek to be associated with airlines serving large domestic networks in foreign countries; and airlines with a large presence in one part of the world often wish to team up with others in areas where they are not all that well represented. Thus the alliances of today are not so horizontal in nature as inter-airline pooling agreements used to be in the past; and, to the extent that the partners supply each other with traffic and other kinds of business the alliances do have something of a vertical nature about them. This is also what appears to be happening in the telecommunications industry. And it is also, to a certain extent, a feature of alliances in the motor industry. The alliance between General Motors and Toyota for example, while mainly horizontal in that it involves some joint manufacturing and joint marketing, does have some vertical attributes as well, to the extent that one company supplies components to the other, parts manufactured by Toyota being fitted to GM cars (and vice versa).

In the motor industry – and also in electronics – a major focus over the past decade has been to develop vertical alliances in order to match the perceived benefits of good relations with suppliers, such as those enjoyed by the Japanese Keiretsu. In the computer industry the development of vertical alliances has had the effect of intensifying competition in the product market, there being little in the way of horizontal collaboration between the main manufacturers of computers.

The clearest example of vertical alliances in the airline industry are the collaborative arrangements that exist between carriers and hotels, car hire firms, travel agents and other companies involved in travel and tourism. For a while some airlines diversified into these travel-related businesses, in attempts to offer total travel products and thereby secure for themselves higher proportions of consumers' total expenditure on travel. But generally speaking these ventures were unsuccessful, because of the strain they put on airlines' capital and managerial resources; and in times of financial stringency these kinds of investment are often among the first to be curtailed. For example, in 1980, Pan American sold its chain of Intercontinental Hotels to Grand Metropolitan, in order to meet a high deficit on its airline operations. For similar reasons TWA transferred its interests in Hilton International to its holding company,

Trans World Corporation (which subsequently sold it to Ladbroke). And more recently Air France sold its Meridien hotel chain to Forté, and Aer Lingus divested itself of its Copthorne Hotel group. Airlines now prefer alliances instead, leaving other travel and tourism business to specialist managements with long experience in these industries. British Airways, for instance, is in partnership with a number of hotel chains including Marriot, Hilton Mandarin Oriental, the Ritz-Carlton Group, the Savoy Group, Radisson Edwardian, the Taj Group in India, and the Southern Sun Group in South Africa. Apart from hotels, BA is also in partnership with Hertz for car hire and with Diners Club for charge cards.

Few airlines have been able to integrate vertically with airport authorities, usually because airports are almost always in public ownership and because governments usually prohibit airlines from taking equity stakes in them. One exception is Alitalia, one of whose subsidiaries is responsible for the management of Aeroporti di Roma, Italy's main airport. Another is Cathay Pacific with its investment in Xiamen airport in China, about 500 miles south west of Shanghai.

These few cases apart, the only instances in which there is a significant degree of vertical integration between airlines and airports is where airlines own their own airport terminals. This is not unusual in the United States and also applies in the case of domestic terminals in Australia. Governments also intend to constrain airlines' equity holdings in undertakings running air traffic control facilities if and when these are transferred to the private sector. The UK government for example has said that there would be limitations on the maximum number of shares that airlines could hold in the National Air Traffic Services (NATS) company when this is privatized.

External alliances – or, as they are sometimes known, 'diversification' alliances – are seen only relatively infrequently. Over the past decade the chemical industry has shown a lot of interest in developing external collaboration, especially with small biotechnology firms in search of new products. So far as airlines are concerned, external alliances have traditionally been limited largely to joint ventures in marketing promotions, e.g. special offers on fares, frequent flyer bonuses, package holidays, insurance, etc. But there are now some indications of airlines hiving off other specialized activities to external alliances. The 50/50 joint venture between Delta Airlines and AT&T, under which AT&T handles much of Delta's internal computing requirements – although not its reservations system – is a good case in point.

In short, the main kind of alliance in the airline industry is that formed amongst carriers themselves, although this has perhaps become less horizontal and more vertical in nature as markets have become more and more liberalized. This reflects similar developments in other industries like telecommunications.

Technological and market motives

What fundamentally accounts for the proliferation of alliances, both generally in business and in airlines in particular? This is an interesting question in its own right. It is also central to the formulation of business strategy. This is so because the potential for sustainable advantage to be achieved via interfirm collaboration will depend on the nature and strength of the underlying forces motivating alliances, and these may vary from industry to industry and from case to case.

Some accounts of the growth in strategic alliances visualize it as the result of a large number of different forces at work (Lynch, 1993). It is helpful, however, to refer to a prominent analysis that sees the main explanation in terms of a small set of forces of a pervasive nature. This is the globalization thesis of the Japanese business guru, Kenichi Ohmae.

According to Ohmae it is the sheer scale of contemporary global industries and global markets that requires interfirm collaboration, as opposed to the establishment of large global enterprises. In Ohmae's words:

> globalization mandates alliances, makes them absolutely essential to strategy. Uncomfortable perhaps – but that's the way it is. Like it or not, the simultaneous developments that go under the name of globalization make alliances – [business] entente – necessary
>
> (Ohmae, 1993)

The simultaneous developments Ohmae identifies are:

- The convergence of consumer preferences across the world.
- The fact that modern products require access to, and control of, so many critical-edge technologies that many companies (however large) cannot maintain a leading competence in all of them at the same time.
- The need with global products to incur immense fixed costs, e.g. in research and development, in information technology, in building transnational brand loyalty and in setting up worldwide sales and distribution networks.

Ohmae emphasizes the last factor so far as alliances are concerned:

> the need to bolster contribution points in a single, clear direction: towards the forging of alliances to share fixed costs. This is a fundamental change from the competitive world of 15, or even 10, years ago. . . . This new logic forces managers to amortize their fixed costs over a much larger market base . . . this logic mandates alliances that both enable and facilitate global, contribution-based, strategies
>
> (Ohmae, 1993)

The fundamental question here concerns the significance of fixed costs. Most of the costs incurred in airline operation are escapable and therefore variable; and it is generally accepted that the airline industry is one in which the ratio of fixed to variable costs is relatively low. As argued in Chapter 3 it is not fixed costs in general but more specifically sunk costs that represent the critical dimension to be considered in this regard. The relevant point is that, if sunk costs are zero, what would be the underlying motive for alliances? Where sunk costs are zero – as the model of 'perfect' contestability has it – firms could make go-it-alone hit-and-run entries to, and exits from, given industries to earn a stream of net returns, without needing to go through all the costs and difficulties of forming complex alliances with other firms. In other words, Ohmae's point may be more appropriate, especially in the airline context, if it is recast in terms of sunk costs.

In a major empirical study of some 10 000 co-operation agreements between firms in various industries (but not including airlines) over the period 1980–89, Hagedoorn (1993) identified the existence of two broad sets of reasons why firms join alliances: motives associated with technology, such as that required for basic or applied research; and motives concerned with market access and/or with influencing the structure of the market. Hagedoorn's study concentrated specifically on alliances in which there were at least some technology motives, but even within this constrained data set, it was found upon detailed examination that market motives often predominated over technology ones. This was particularly the case in mature industries such as automobiles, food and drink, chemicals and consumer electronics; and, more surprisingly, it was also the case in hi-tech growth industries like telecommunications, computers and microelectronics. But it would not ordinarily be expected that essentially service-based industries – even some of those that make extensive use of hi-tech equipment – would find much reason to form alliances based on the technology motive. Almost by definition the scope for technological collaboration is smaller in a service industry than it is in manufacturing.

There are however some instances in the airline industry in which technological factors are strong motives for alliances. Back in the 1960s two groups of European airlines formed international consortia with the objective of economizing on aircraft maintenance. With the introduction of large aircraft like B747 and DC-10, airlines realized that a fleet size of at least 20 would be needed by each carrier to justify the necessary investments in hangars, equipment and simulators. So, KLM, SAS, Swissair and the former UTA got together to form KSSU in 1968, this organization becoming known as KSS following the merger of UTA with Air France. Air France itself, together with Alitalia, Lufthansa and Sabena, set up Atlas, Iberia joining in 1972.

The purpose of these alliances was to permit airlines to specialize in certain aspects of maintenance, whether airframes, engines, avionics or landing gear, or to concentrate on particular aircraft types, so that for example, Air France specializes on 747 airframes and landing gear plus GE CF6 engines; Lufthansa on A300 airframes and landing gear plus JT9D engines; Sabena on A310 engines; and Alitalia on DC-10 airframes. In this way savings in aircraft maintenance of the order of some 10 to 20 per cent could be achieved. The KSSU and Atlas consortia have evolved to encompass other aspects of technical co-operation and co-ordination. In 1989 three of the Atlas members – Lufthansa, Air France and Iberia – signed a more comprehensive agreement covering, among other things, harmonization of aircraft purchasing policies, establishment of a joint catering company, joint training of pilots and increased collaboration in the development of computer reservations systems. The Atlas consortium is now formally disbanded, but some co-operation continues on a bilateral subcontracting basis. The KSS consortium remains more or less in being, with KLM maintaining 747 airframes and CF6 engines; Swissair maintaining the MD-11s, DC-10s and A310s; SAS maintaining JT9D engines; and Air France maintaining landing gear (a task originally assigned to the former airline UTA). But a number of developments are limiting the usefulness of these two European consortia. The fleet sizes of the airline partners have now reached levels sufficient to justify each carrier investing in its own maintenance facilities. At the same time membership of the maintenance consortia does not correspond to membership of the global alliances, the three members of Atlas being likely to end up in three separate global alliances (Lufthansa in Star, Air France in Wings (?) and Iberia in Oneworld). Indeed there is now often closer co-operation across the Atlas/KSS divide than there is within Atlas or KSS. Lufthansa and SAS, for example, both members of the Star global alliance but one originally in Atlas and the other in KSS, have entered a maintenance joint venture with each other. And it seems likely that future co-operation on maintenance is going to be more with partners in the global alliances than in the traditional maintenance consortia. One disadvantage with maintenance consortia is the time taken up transporting parts and spares from one centre to another; and a further development is the growing trend for some major airlines to set up and run specialist maintenance subsidiaries (e.g. Lufthansa Technik and Swissair's SR Technics) which undertake third party maintenance for other carriers, including some against which they are in competition for passengers (e.g. Lufthansa Technik maintaining the fleets of some Lufthansa rivals like Eurowings and Deutsche BA).

Besides Atlas and KSS there have been other technical consortia with similar objectives. The decision of Cathay Pacific, SIA, Garuda and Thai Airways International to establish SEAMA (the South East Asian

Maintenance Alliance) formed the first multi-airline collaborative venture of its kind in Asia. This was intended to reduce costs by eliminating duplication of equipment, training and spares inventories. There are now many examples of technical collaboration between established airlines in Western countries and carriers in developing countries. Western airlines often have comparative advantages in technological expertise while developing countries' airlines have much lower labour costs. The recent opening up of the aviation sector in the People's Republic of China seems likely to presage a lot of joint ventures between international airlines and Chinese regional carriers. Among international airlines seeking to collaborate in China are Lufthansa, Qantas, SIA, Cathay Pacific and Japan Airlines. The last three, along with Air China and the Boeing aircraft company, have all invested in a joint maintenance facility in Xiamen, to service the fleets operated by Xiamen Airlines. Lufthansa Technik also has a joint venture with Air China, Aircraft Maintenance and Engineering (AMECO) based in Beijing, to carry out D checks on Boeing aircraft. And Qantas has been in discussions about setting up something similar with airlines in Shenzhen, Shanghai and Yunan. The indications are that these initiatives are merely the start of more extensive links between Chinese and foreign airlines, especially given the explosive growth of air travel in China.

Alliances to achieve savings in cost are important but so far they have been far less common than market motivated alliances. In a survey of some 200 alliances the Boston Consulting Group found the most common objectives to be traffic feed, access to new markets, defence of current markets and economies in marketing generally (Flanagan and Marcus, 1993). The emphasis in many marketing alliances on code-sharing, block space agreements, franchising, links between frequent flyer programmes, etc. comes from airlines seeking to reap economies of scope by extending route networks, as discussed in Chapter 4. The motive behind many marketing agreements stems from the belief that the airlines that will be in the best position to compete in the future will be those that can offer the most extensive global networks. Co-operating with other airlines is a means of tapping into worldwide traffic flows and enhancing the 'global reach' of a carrier's network, which might otherwise be limited by the traffic rights which its national government had been able to negotiate.

One of the most important marketing objectives of alliances is to encourage interline hubbing by facilitating co-operation between domestic and international services where restrictions on cabotage prevent the international carrier from serving domestic routes and where, under existing bilateral air service agreements, the domestic carrier had no traffic rights on the relevant international routes. They also encourage closer links between the services of two international carriers. It is possible through forming alliances to make good fits between the networks of the partners and to provide swift connections at the hub airports each partner serves.

Before leaving the question of technological and market motives, there is one area in which both sets of motives come into play. This is in the development of sophisticated computer reservations systems. Sophisticated CRSs require huge investments in hardware, software and technological expertise. Few airlines would be able to muster the resources to develop one on their own. Billions of dollars are needed to develop state-of-the-art CRSs and their associated communications networks. This is why for example nine airlines in the Asia–Pacific region grouped together to form the CRS known as Abacus (see Figure 3.7 in Chapter 3). There are many marketing and technical links between the various CRSs. But there are important differences between the way airlines line up in CRS agreements and the way they have been developing other alliances. The CRS groupings are on a regional basis only, whereas alliances formed for the purpose of traffic feed tend to be between airlines based in different regions. So partners in the following alliances find themselves in different CRS consortia: BA/Qantas, KLM/Northwest, United/Lufthansa and Swissair/Delta. Because of this it is likely that links between the CRSs will multiply still further. And another factor promoting greater interrelationship, and possibly some further consolidation in the CRS industry, is the trend towards mergers in the travel trade, more especially in the marketing of business travel. Shortly after the US travel agency Carlson combined its business travel business with that of Wagonlits, American Express acquired the international business arm of Thomas Cook.

Interfirm governance

Modes of governance in alliances vary greatly from case to case. There are some 'strong' forms of governance, where the directors of one company sit on the board of the other. But some alliances merely involve informal understandings with no exchange of managerial control. Hagedoorn (1993) suggests that strong modes of interfirm governance tend to be associated with a more long-term strategic dimension to the collaborative relationship; and that 'weaker' forms of interfirm governance reflect more limited objectives. Strong modes of governance are often backed up by the partners taking stakes in each other's equity capital.

Some commentators (e.g. Flannagan and Marcos, 1993) suggest that if one partner has control of an alliance, then it is more likely to succeed. Given that much of a company's stock is widely distributed among institutional and private investors, a holding of around 25 per cent of voting shares normally implies control. But governments often constrain the control exercised by foreign investors, whether they hold a 25 per cent voting share or not. Over the past five years the number of airline alliances involving equity stakes has been declining, both relatively and absolutely (Table 7.6). But this does not necessarily mean that their overall significance is declining, because since 1992 the heavier stakes – those of 20 per cent or more – have tended to predominate. On the other hand the growth in employee shareholdings is tending to dilute the stakes held by alliance partners. In the United States, the industry's cost cutting drive, in which airlines exchanged shares for labour concessions, has led to employees owning 26 per cent of Northwest, 45 per cent of TWA and 55 per cent of United. And the trend is now spreading to airlines in other countries (e.g. Air France). Where employee representatives secure overall control of voting shares, a powerful brake may thus be applied to outsourcing and the move of airline jobs from high- to low-wage economies.

7.4 Experience of alliances

A number of studies have investigated the effects of alliances, with a view to estimating their impacts on both airlines and passengers. Gellman Research Associates (1994) conducted a counterfactual scenario analysis – comparing outcomes with what might have been expected to have happened had the alliances not been struck – and drew the conclusions summarized in Table 7.8 in relation to the British Airways/USAir and KLM/Northwest alliances. The findings on the BA/USAir case indicated that both partners gained in terms of net profit, although BA gained much more (almost five times more) than USAir; and that most of the extra profits came at the expense of other carriers, especially other US carriers. In total US airlines lost as a result of the alliance while non-US airlines (mainly BA) gained. Passenger benefits were estimated in terms of reduced fares and improved services and both US and non-US passengers gained, so that in overall terms the change in social benefits (change in airlines' net profits plus change in passenger benefits) was positive. Similar findings were made in respect of the KLM/Northwest alliance, except that the gain to Northwest more or less cancelled out the loss to other US carriers, so that US airlines as a whole broke even on the alliance, unlike in the BA/USAir case where they lost heavily.

A later study by the US General Accounting Office (1995) was not an econometric analysis, being based mainly on interviews with airline representatives and government officials. In addition to the BA/USAir and KLM/Northwest alliances, the General Accounting Office also

Table 7.8 Estimated effects of the British Airways/USAir and KLM/Northwest alliances (first quarter, 1994). *Source:* Gellman Research Associates (1994)

Airline	Change in net profit ($ million)	Change in passenger benefits ($ million)	Change in social benefits ($ million)
BA/USAir alliance			
British Airways	27.2		
USAir	5.6		
Other US carriers	–26.7		
Other non-US carriers	–0.8		
US total	–21.1	4.9	–16.2
Non-US total	26.4	5.4	31.8
Grand total	5.3	10.3	15.0
KLM/Northwest alliance			
KLM	10.6		
Northwest	16.1		
Other US carriers	–15.7		
Other non-US carriers	–8.6		
US total	0.4	13.0	13.4
Non-US total	2.0	14.1	16.1
Grand total	2.4	27.1	29.5

looked at three alliances involving United, those with Lufthansa, Ansett and British Midland. Its conclusions were similar: all airlines in these alliances benefited in terms of net profits, albeit to varying degrees; and a lot of the gains came from carriers outside the alliances. For example, some representatives of Continental told the GAO that their airlines had lost an estimated $1 million in 1994 because some traffic it would normally have carried between the United States and Europe had transferred to the KLM/Northwest alliance. Some estimates were produced of increased passenger numbers travelling on alliance partners, for example United gaining 600 passengers a day from its alliance with Lufthansa, 120 passengers a day from its alliance with Ansett and 30 000 passengers a year from its alliance with British Midland.

There is little doubt that some airlines have experienced some significant revenue enhancement from alliances. And some more recent estimates are given in Table 7.9. What is more open to doubt is the effect of alliances on airline fares. An extensive investigation aimed at casting some light on this was conducted by Park (1997) who estimated a number of econometric models on annual panel data for North Atlantic

Table 7.9 Estimated revenue enhancements from alliances, 1997[a]. *Source: Aviation Strategy*

Airline	Route group	Revenue (millions)	Enhancement (millions)	Enhancement as percentage of revenue
Delta	Atlantic	US$ 2223	US$ 138	6.2
KLM	Atlantic	DFL 2011	DFL 400	19.9
Lufthansa	Atlantic	DM 3000	DM 300	10.0
Northwest	Atlantic	US$ 644	US$ 65	10.1
Qantas	Kangaroo[b]	A$ 723	A$ 35	4.8
United	Atlantic	US$ 1745	US$ 120	6.9

[a] The estimates refer to claims made by the airlines.
[b] Australia/Europe routes.

routes for the 1990–94 period. In this study a distinction was drawn between 'complementary' and 'parallel' alliances, the former being one where the main purpose is to link up two partners' complementary, or non-overlapping, networks and the latter one where the networks do overlap. Most alliances involve a mix of overlapping markets (e.g. the inter-continental routes) and non-overlapping markets (e.g routes in two different continents). There was some evidence in the Park study that complementary alliances (e.g. KLM/Northwest) led to lower fares while predominantly parallel alliances (e.g. Delta/Swissair/Sabena) had something of an opposite effect in increasing them; but, overall, Park's findings suggest that passengers in North Atlantic markets are generally better off as a result of alliances and that most alliance partners experience greater traffic increases on their alliance routes than they do on their non-alliance routes.

7.5 Pro- and anti-competitive effects

It is widely expected that the growing number of alliances, possibly followed by some outright mergers, will result in the airline industry continuing to become more and more highly concentrated. Forecasts may vary on exactly how many airlines will survive or on how far the industry will be dominated by just a few large carriers, or consortia of carriers bound together in some form of global alliance. But what is generally agreed is that the number of major airlines operating as entirely separate entities will fall quite sharply. This once again raises the question of what will happen to inter-airline competition.

Increased concentration is often associated with a higher risk of collusion or with firms being able to set wider price–cost margins, whether because of enhanced market power exerted by individual firms or because of the umbrella effect under which market power carries over to other firms in the industry as well. Where airlines are lining up in alliance groupings there is also the possibility of certain groupings dominating certain market areas. Much may depend on how far the alliances are complementary, linking airline networks in different areas, and how far they are parallel, with airlines operating head to head on the same routes. Emphasizing that his airline needs partners with complementary rather than overlapping networks, the Vice President of International Relations at Lufthansa claimed that, of 3000 services covered by the alliance with United, only two had been operated by both airlines before the alliance (Schulte-Strathaus, 1994). In cases like this alliances are likely to increase market power only on routes between the market areas. But here they could increase it quite a lot, creating virtual monopolies on routes between the hubs of alliance partners, permitting the exercise of considerable market power in hub-to-hub markets. In the international context entry to such routes is inhibited not just by airport capacity constraints but often by government regulation as well; and, in addition to the monopolization effect, alliances may inhibit competition in hub-to-hub markets that might otherwise have come from airlines seeking to expand their networks through internal expansion.

In a study of the market power effect of alliances, Youssef and Hansen (1994) examined the former alliance between Swissair and SAS, an alliance which, on account of the specially close relationship between the airlines, had been dubbed an 'alliance within an alliance', both airlines being members of what was then the broader European Quality Alliance. What Youssef and Hansen found was that in hub-to-hub markets (between Copenhagen, Stockholm and Oslo in Scandinavia and Geneva and Zurich in Switzerland) competition was virtually eliminated; and that on non-stop hub-to-hub routes fares increased much more than fares on other non-alliance non-stop routes in the same region over the same period. The conclusion drawn was that the airlines had taken advantage of the increased concentration in hub-to-hub markets to earn higher profits on these routes. The alliance between Swissair and SAS now no longer exists, the two airlines having gone their separate ways and joined different alliance groupings, Swissair continuing with membership of the Atlantic Excellence alliance and SAS becoming a member of the Star alliance. As a member of Star, SAS now has a close relationship with Lufthansa, which is possibly reflected in some relatively high fares on hub-to-hub routes between Germany and Scandinavia.

A statistical analysis undertaken by the author sought to identify routes on which fares charged are unusually high. The samples were limited to routes within the European Union and the focus of attention was on the levels of fully flexible fares charged by major EU airlines (in July 1997). Fare levels taper with route distance in a manner indicated in a study by the Civil Aviation Authority (see Figure 6.1 in Chapter 6). An appropriate way of representing this is to regress fare level upon route distance by estimating the equation:

$$\hat{Y}_i = \hat{a} + \hat{b}X_i$$

where Y denotes fare level (expressed here in ECUs), X denotes route distance (in kilometres), a is an intercept term, b the slope of the relationship, $i = 1, 2, ..., n$ are sample observations across routes, and where the hat ($\wedge$) indicates estimates. The coefficients were derived by first estimating the slope as:

$$\hat{b} = \frac{n\Sigma X_i Y_i - \Sigma X_i \Sigma Y_i}{n\Sigma X_i^2 - (\Sigma X_i)^2}$$

which was then substituted into the following equation to find the intercept:

$$\hat{a} = \frac{\Sigma Y_i - \hat{b}\Sigma X_i}{n} = \bar{Y} - \hat{b}\bar{X}$$

The degree of statistical explanation was assessed by the coefficient of determination r^2, calculated as:

$$r^2 = \frac{\Sigma(\hat{Y}_i - \bar{Y})^2}{\Sigma(Y_i - \bar{Y})^2}$$

where $\bar{Y}$ is the sample mean. The level of statistical explanation was considered satisfactory if $r^2 > 0.7$, implying that over 70 per cent of the variation in the dependent fare variable is explained statistically by variation in the independent distance variable. In testing for observed fares that are unusually high or unusually low, the standard error of estimate, S, was used, where:

$$S = \sqrt{\frac{\Sigma Y_i^2 - \hat{a}\,\Sigma Y - \hat{b}\,\Sigma X_i Y_i}{n}}$$

On the assumption that the errors, the differences between the observed fare levels and the levels predicted by the equation $(Y_i - \hat{Y}_i)$ are normally distributed, 68 per cent of the sample of observed levels should lie between plus and minus S either side of the estimated regression line. Hence any observed level outside this range can be considered either unusually high or unusually low. An unusually high fare level would be where $(Y_i - \hat{Y}_i) > S$.

Separate regressions were run for each airline studied; and the results for Lufthansa (LH) and SAS (SK) were as follows:

LH: $\hat{Y}_i = 125.42 + 0.32824X_i$ $\quad r^2 = 0.856$
$$S = 56.90$$
$$n = 204$$

SK: $\hat{Y}_i = 113.60 + 0.24690X_i$ $\quad r^2 = 0.724$
$$S = 86.90$$
$$n = 137$$

These equations imply that fares on the following hub-to-hub routes were unusually high:

	X_i	Y_i	$\hat{Y}_i$	$(Y_i - \hat{Y}_i)$ as % of $\hat{Y}_i$
LH: Frankfurt–Copenhagen	678	404	348	16
LH: Frankfurt–Stockholm	1221	601	526	14
LH: Munich–Stockholm	1316	680	557	22
SK: Copenhagen–Frankfurt	678	329	281	17
SK: Copenhagen–Munich	809	401	313	28
SK: Stockholm–Frankfurt	1221	502	415	21

The comparisons here are affected by fluctuations in currency conversion factors, but nonetheless it is clear that fares between the two largest hubs in Germany and the two largest hubs in Scandinavia are well above the estimated regression lines. Apart from a very few flights by other operators, all six routes were effective LH/SK duopolies and so the hub airlines were in a position to exert some market power.

When two airlines serving the same route enter into an alliance it is only to be expected that they will take steps to co-ordinate their marketing of that route. The alliance usually includes reciprocal arrangements for the carriers to act as sales agents for one another at each end of the route. In these circumstances there is a natural suspicion that the airlines will not compete against each other head-to-head and will prefer to fix mutually acceptable fares, to schedule services at mutually convenient times and, where code-sharing agreements apply, to arrange joint listings in CRSs. There is then some fear that competition will be curtailed in some important travel markets. There are for instance some hub-to-hub markets in which the majority of passengers flying the route have both origins and destinations in the hub cities concerned. Where entry is restricted, by the terms of the relevant bilateral air service agreement for example, and where alternative routeings are of much greater circuitry and consequently involve much longer journey times, the alliance partners could indeed be left with considerable market power on the route in question.

Market power is often a major concern for government competition authorities; and concerns of this nature have caused governments to intervene in two of the alliances struck by British Airways. The Australian Trade Practices Commission blocked a proposal by the BA/Qantas alliance for the joint fixing of passenger fares and freight rates on Europe–Australia services. And the original BA/USAir deal was only approved by the US government after USAir was divested of its UK–US route authorities, these being passed to other US carriers. The policy of the UK government has for many years been to foster and promote the entry of third carriers on routes that would otherwise remain as duopolies (Civil Aviation Authority, 1993). This may be an eminently suitable policy for some heavily trafficked hub-to-hub routes, but the question is whether it should be applied generally. Where partner airlines seek to fix fares and co-ordinate capacity in a hub-to-hub market, this threatens a return to the old horizontal pooling agreements of the past. Competition authorities are always likely to oppose moves in this direction, but then it is hard to see any (eventual) outcome other than the withdrawal of one or other of the partners from the route in question. The maintenance of competition on the route will then depend heavily on the entry of airlines outside the alliance. But this may be seriously inhibited by capacity constraints at either or both the hubs involved.

Alliances, in effect, enable each airline to extend its marketable network to cities served by its partner. If this results in each member of the alliance being able to attract more traffic without increasing the number of routes operated, then each member's marginal cost may fall through economies of density. And this cost reduction may be achieved very soon after the forming of the alliance, thus reducing the significance of the timing qualification to Williamson's trade-off analysis in this instance. For there is no reason to expect the density economies to take all that long to come through. However, if competition authorities foster new entry on some of the routes within an alliance's hub and spokes system, this may benefit passengers flying the routes in question, but at the same time it may cause some loss of density economies for the alliance partners, resulting in an increase in marginal cost. Competitive pressure may counteract the higher marginal cost on routes on which new entry has occurred, but not of course on those on which there has been no increase in competition. In this sense the entry of new competition on an individual spoke may generate negative externalities across the network as a whole.

Across the network as a whole competition may be increasing anyway. As argued above (in Chapters 3 and 5) any reductions in competition in hub-to-hub markets may be offset, or more than offset, by increased competition in through markets via hubs. Alliances are clearly stimulating competition in through markets by, among other things, encouraging 'double hubbing'. An illustrative example of this is given in Figure 7.1. Around the world there are a great many city pairs not served by direct flights. One such city pair in the North Atlantic market is Kansas City–Gothenburg, but passengers wishing to travel between these two cities have a fairly wide choice of indirect services: all four transatlantic

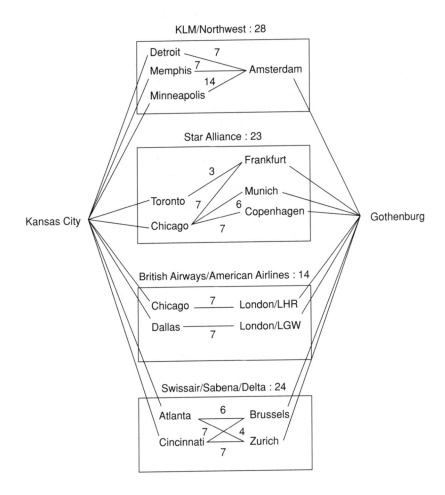

This chart shows the number of weekly frequencies which offer connecting times of 2 hours or less through the hubs

Figure 7.1 Competition between hubs: an example of double hubbing on routes between Gothenburg and Kansas City, Autumn 1997 (*Source: Airline Business*)

alliances provide multiple connection options, making up a grand total of 89 services a week (albeit services that entail two connections to be made, one at a hub in the United States and one at a European hub). And this is not an isolated example of where all four alliances compete. In Autumn 1997 Stuttgart in Germany had no less than 22 transatlantic city pairs in which all four alliances competed (ter Kuile, 1997).

Where mergers and alliances increase market power on routes to and from hubs, but at the same time induce greater competition in through markets via hubs, there is a further trade-off to consider. Passengers in hub-to-hub markets may lose while passengers in through markets gain. As argued in Chapter 5 (section 5.7) the balance between these two effects will depend on: the relative widths of price–cost margins on short and long haul routes; own- and cross-price elasticities of demand in through markets as compared with those in hub-to-hub markets; and the distribution of passenger gains and losses by income or journey purpose. Ideally all these factors should be taken into account in determining the balance between pro- and anti-competitive effects. While mergers and alliances may often appear anti-competitive, in practice some of their effects will be pro-competitive. Competition authorities then face the following dilemma: how to curb the market power wielded on routes to and from congested hubs without at the same time impairing the ability of merged airlines or alliances partners to compete for through traffic via these hubs.

8 Transnational airlines

8.1 Are airlines losing their nationalities?

The so-called 'flag carrier' concept is now outdated, mainly because it is incompatible with the need to make the European airline industry competitive on a global scale

(Comité des Sages, 1994)

It is possible that alliances are, in certain cases, simply precursors to outright mergers. The signs are there. With the same logo, joint advertising and close co-ordination of service schedules, KLM and Northwest have already gone quite some way in the direction of merger. In other cases the fact that alliances have adopted common aircraft liveries, or common uniforms for cabin staff, is possibly a portent of some more fully consummated relationships to come. Also there are some instances in which equity purchases have earned investing airlines options to acquire further shares in the future. The scope for cross-border shareholders seems certain to increase as state ownership declines and as privatized airlines seek greater access to foreign capital in a deregulated or liberalized environment. But there are still some formidable impediments to cross-border mergers.

It is true that some national governments are beginning to relax restrictions on foreign ownership, but if foreign ownership goes beyond a certain point, this raises serious questions regarding traffic rights on international routes. Ownership clauses in bilateral air service treaties restrict the grant of the relevant freedoms of the air to airlines owned and controlled by nationals of the state concerned. As things stand, if an airline of one state takes over the airline of another state, then this could invalidate the third, fourth and fifth freedoms held by the airline being taken over, on the ground that it no longer qualifies as a national airline of the state concerned. In terms of Figure 4.4, if the airline of State B took over the airline of State A, this could mean the loss of third and fourth freedoms between State A and States X and Y.

It is possible for one airline to buy up another. A US airline could in principle buy shares in any publicly quoted European airline and might, for a time, acquire a controlling interest. But would such control be worth anything? The ownership and control provisions in air service agreements mean that the acquired company would cease to be a 'national' airline. It would then risk losing international rights negotiated under air service agreements with states outside the European Union; and, incidentally, it would also lose its right to an operating licence for routes within the EU (since the EU's definition of a 'community carrier' excludes majority ownership by non-EU citizens). Thus the new owner of the airline 'would have acquired an impressive but costly static aircraft display' (Staniland, 1998).

A consideration of this kind became a central issue in the bid SAS made for British Caledonian in 1987. If the SAS bid had succeeded, and SAS had acquired a majority stake and effective control of BCAL, other countries might not have accepted the merged airline as a UK designated airline on international routes. Other countries have separate agreements on traffic rights with Scandinavia and they might not have been prepared to grant SAS rights on former BCAL routes out of London, which in this context they might have interpreted as seventh freedoms. Similar concerns were felt by the Dutch and German governments when KLM and Lufthansa were being privatized. Both adopted procedures designed to protect the airlines' status as national carriers. The Dutch government insisted on having the option to buy back KLM shares if there was any danger of non-nationals acquiring a controlling position. And in Germany the shares of all publicly listed German airlines (not just Lufthansa) must be registered shares whose transfer is subject to the consent of the company, which enables the company to force the sale of foreign owned stock if in aggregate it approached 50 per cent of the total. Doubts about what might happen to traffic rights could be a serious deterrent to full cross-border mergers. For often the main objective of such mergers is to achieve economies of scope by extending marketable networks, enhancing access to through markets by combining rights held separately by the airlines involved. If there is some risk of either or both parties to the merger losing some of these rights, then the perceived advantages in merging are going to be that much less. This partly explains the current preference for alliances over mergers. There is much less risk of losing traffic rights as a result of an alliance.

However, one aspect of alliances that can have important implications for traffic rights is code-sharing. There has been some debate over whether or not code-sharing should require specific authorization, in the same way that third, fourth and fifth freedom traffic rights do. The vast majority of inter-governmental bilateral agreements were drawn up and signed long before code-sharing became commonplace on international routes; and in many of these agreements, like for example the Bermuda II agreement between the United Kingdom and the United States, there is no reference at all to code-sharing. Some countries have argued that code-sharing should be regulated, on the ground that airlines are in fact holding out services to the public as if they had the traffic rights concerned. This has been the view of the United States, which has been worrying that code-sharing might give the appearance of foreign airlines possessing cabotage rights on internal US domestic routes. US policy on code-sharing has been evolving through several stages (de Groot, 1994). When code-sharing first became a matter of international aeropolitical concern, the United States sought to restrict it to routes on which the foreign carrier held the appropriate rights, effectively limiting its use to routes to/from gateway airports specified in the applicable bilateral agreement. In 1988 the United States adopted the position that code-sharing has to be covered by an express statement of authorization; the next step was to introduce traffic rights for the sole purpose of code-sharing. Code-sharing with carriers operating US domestic routes then became part of the 'Open Skies' concept: the United States was prepared to be fairly liberal in granting permission for code-sharing in exchange for foreign countries agreeing to liberal bilaterals on traffic rights and the associated issues of market access, frequencies and pricing freedom. For example, the US–Netherlands Open Skies bilateral led to extensive code-sharing possibilities for the Northwest/KLM alliance. But bringing code-sharing into bilateral negotiations has turned it into another bargaining chip which some countries have used to demand reciprocity. Some countries whose airlines see relatively few opportunities for code-sharing have tended to argue that code-sharing infringes traffic rights, especially restrictions on fifth freedom. Germany, Greece, Israel and Saudi Arabia, for example, have all complained of the disadvantage at which they perceive their airlines to be in competition with code-shared services of the Northwest/KLM alliance via Amsterdam. The governments of these countries have argued that through traffic carried on routes east of Amsterdam should be regarded as beyond-point fifth freedom traffic and therefore should not exceed a certain proportion (e.g. 15 or 20 per cent) of third and fourth freedom traffic on the route concerned. At one time Germany considered applying frequency limitations on such connecting services. But the main response has been to demand aeropolitical concessions in exchange for permitting code-sharing. For example, Finland granted Northwest code-sharing authority only after it obtained traffic rights to San Francisco.

Complex negotiations over code-sharing hark back to the old disputes over sixth freedom traffic and point up once more the tensions between airlines pursuing commercial interests and governments pursuing national interests. If the trends towards liberalization, privatization, foreign ownership and ultimately cross-border mergers continue, the long-term future of present bilateral system must be in some doubt.

Nationalism in civil aviation may die hard, but die it probably will – eventually. This is certainly the view (or hope?) of a number of airline executives. The Managing Director of British Airways has expressed it as follows:

National interest is no longer the same as producer interest. The producer is less an arm of state and more of a normal international business that happens to be based in the country. If the choice boils down to what is good for the consumer against what is good for the indigenous airlines, how is a nation to decide? And if a country wishes to maintain a multi-airline policy, but its market is too small to support more than one airline efficiently, should airline competitiveness or national policy be sacrificed? . . . the nationality principle is weaker today than it has ever been.

(Ayling, 1993)

On one view, if any industry should be leading the drive towards globalization, it should be civil aviation (Skapinker, 1998). After all, airlines are in the business every day of transporting millions of people across international boundaries, dealing with dozens of different currencies and languages. Airlines are under some considerable pressure to become global firms, given that their most important customers, international business travellers, want to be able to fly anywhere in the world without having to check in their luggage at every stopover or to switch terminals at every airport where they change flights. On any given flight there could be a broad cosmopolitan mix of passengers by nationality, as illustrated in Figure 5.5. It was largely in recognition of this that British Airways decided to remove the Union Jack flag design from its tailfins in favour of ethnic designs from around the world. As the Chairman of BA's alliance partner American Airlines has put it, there are no flag companies in the oil, pharmaceutical, chemical, motor, tobacco, or hotel industries, nor even in telecommunications. So why should there be flag carriers in air transport?

It may be some time yet before governments retreat from pursuing mercantilist policies 'in the national interest'. Although the role of airlines as a form of military reserve is not so important these days, many countries still see their flag carriers as part of their national identity, as a means of promoting trade and developing tourism, and as an earner of foreign currency. For benefits of this kind many countries are prepared to protect their airlines from the full force of international competition, supporting them with state aids and adopting restrictive stances over traffic rights. But the costs of this are rising, both in terms of the magnitude of subsidies required and in terms of lost opportunities, as more and more airlines elsewhere are privatized and follow purely commercial objectives. Public opinion is increasingly against the idea of airlines being subsidized and there is mounting pressure for the bilateral system of traffic rights to be reformed so as to remove many of the restrictions on where airlines may fly.

The latter is the key to whether – or when – transnational airlines will emerge in any true sense. One might foresee the bilateral system gradually falling away for the very reason that it may soon become rather difficult to say exactly which nationality an airline actually has, that of the country in which it is (or was originally) based or that of the country of the carrier owning a controlling share of its equity. For we are now beginning to see foreign airlines taking majority control of carriers based in other countries. One suggestion is that the present system under which bilateral negotiations are conducted between individual countries will be replaced, at least in part, by one in which negotiations take place between groups of countries or regional blocs. It is possible to envisage bilaterals being negotiated between the European Economic Area (which includes EFTA countries) and the North American Free Trade Area (United States, Canada and Mexico). And other possible blocs for this purpose might include the ASEAN countries in South East Asia, the Andean Pact countries in Latin America, the Australian and New Zealand Single Market and, conceivably, various associations of African, Middle East countries, etc. There are bound to be some fundamental problems with regional negotiations. For instance, how would any traffic rights successfully negotiated by the bloc be allocated among carriers from different countries within the region? In the absence of political union, the regional bloc may have no sovereignty over this and therefore no mandate to trade off the interests of airlines in one member state against those of airlines in others.

More importantly, the cross-border alliances and investments airlines are now making are not limited geographically to the particular region in which they are based. Indeed, in their search for partners with complementary networks, airlines are more interested in alliances and investments *outside* their region rather than within it. It is true that many of the alliances and cross-border investments airlines have made so far have in fact been with airlines of the same region: the shareholdings in Sabena taken, first by Air France, and then by Swissair; the British Airways investments in Air Liberté, TAT European and Deutsche BA; the increased stake in British Midland taken by SAS; the stake in Lauda Air purchased by Lufthansa; the investment Air New Zealand has made in Ansett Australia; and so on. Increasingly however, there are close relationships between airlines in *different* regions: the pairings in the four transatlantic alliances, Northwest/KLM, United/Lufthansa, Delta/Swissair and American/BA; the stake that Delta has taken in AeroPeru; the 10 per cent shareholding in Aerolineas Argentinas now held by both Iberia and American; the 25 per cent stake in Qantas that BA has held since 1993; and the interest shown by a number of US and European airlines in taking a stake in South African Airways which is soon to be privatized.

Airlines' global ambitions will make any attempt to substitute regional aviation agreements for bilaterals signed by individual countries a rather difficult matter. More and more airlines will want to be released from the constraints that their nationalities impose on what they want to do. Nothing is likely to happen suddenly in the near future. But in the longer term it would not be altogether surprising to find that firm's nationality is of no more importance in the airline industry than it is in many other transnational industries.

8.2 Regulating competition in a transnational industry

Predicting the future is always a hazardous business, especially so in respect of an industry in the process of some profound change. It is always difficult to forecast exactly which airlines will fail, which airlines will survive and which will merge. One in three marriages end in divorce and a similar fate might well befall a large number of the inter-airline links that are being forged in the current wave of alliance formation. The alliance groupings may undergo a lot of changes in the months and years to come. But what is more certain is that the building of alliances will fairly swiftly result in the emergence of some truly global airlines. What is much harder to see is how the current system of traffic rights, presently negotiated under the Chicago Convention in terms of freedoms of the air, will change, or at least evolve, to accommodate transnational airlines operating under the flags of several different nations at one and the same time.

To mark the Silver Jubilee of the Chicago Convention the International Civil Aviation Organisation convened a special world conference in Montreal from 23 November to 6 December 1994, almost exactly 50 years to the day from the signing of the original agreement. This, the most important meeting on international aviation for half a century, was attended by over 800 delegates from 137 ICAO contracting states. The object of the conference was to consider whether, in the light of changing attitudes towards various forms of regulation, some new internationally established regulatory arrangements are necessary, or whether indeed they are even possible. No radical decisions were reached. There was, for instance, no consensus on the question of whether the rule that a country's airlines must be owned and effectively controlled by interests based in that country should be changed to allow increased foreign investment. But on one matter there was a consensus, the meeting agreeing that global 'open skies' is not at the present time a feasible option.

The most controversial issue discussed concerned the possibilities of some kind of multilateral system replacing, at least in part, the present bilateral regime.

Under a bilateral regime one individual country negotiates with another; under a multilateral system the negotiations would take place between groups of countries (Kaspar, 1988). The ICAO conference, while recognizing that there is for the foreseeable future no prospect of a global multilateral agreement in the exchange of traffic rights, accepted that the two kinds of system could co-exist. The United States, which because of the vast size of its air travel market could constitute a 'group' on its own in this context, clearly wants to see multilateral open skies agreements being developed, believing that its airlines would fare better under such a regime. Some countries in Europe also want a multilateral system, as does the Transport Directorate of the European Commission. But other European countries do not. Nor is the concept of multilateralism especially appealing to countries in Africa, the Middle East or the Asia–Pacific region. Many of these countries still prefer to retain sovereignty in their negotiations of air transport agreements, and it seems likely that the concept of multilateralism will take longer to develop than the United States and some other countries might wish. Given that many countries still jealously guard their own national interests in international air transport, it is difficult to see how a body representing a group of separate countries could be given a mandate to trade the interests of one against the other. For example, if the European Commission is to negotiate traffic rights on intercontinental routes to and from the European union, it could frequently find itself in the position of having to trade concessions for one country in order to get traffic rights for another. That could become very difficult. Would, for instance, the Italians be willing to sacrifice some market opportunities for Alitalia so that the Greeks could gain some additional rights for Olympic? Or would the Spanish government accept certain limitations on Iberia in order that the EC could secure more openings for TAP Air Portugal? Negotiations of such a kind would clearly involve a lot of hard bargaining, not just between the different groups of countries but among individual countries within the groups as well. EU countries might well find themselves in a stronger bargaining position *vis-à-vis* the United States and other groups of countries if they negotiated as a bloc. But even if bloc negotiations could be conducted successfully at government level, there is still the problem that they could conflict with strategies being pursued at airline level.

As explained earlier, airlines are seeking to reap economies of scope by extending their marketable networks. This they seek to achieve through franchising, block spacing and code-sharing, and by taking equity stakes in, and forming alliances with, airlines operating complementary networks in other parts of the world. As most people envisage them, multilateral negotiations are most likely to take place on an inter-regional basis, where the countries represented in each group are either contiguous or at least neighbouring states in close proximity. But inter-airline marketing agreements and alliances are now less likely to be drawn up between airlines within a particular regional bloc. For airlines are seeking to maximize their 'global reach', in the belief that those that will be in the best position to compete in the future will be those that can offer the most global service.

The most important air travel markets, and their forecast rates of growth, are shown in Figure 8.1. To be a truly global airline a carrier needs to have a substantial presence in as many of these markets as possible. This is clearly the central objective of the global alliance group-ings now forming, Oneworld, Star, Wings and Atlantic Excellence. Airlines' ambitions to become global firms may well in the end lead to the complete removal of controls over international route entry, if not across the entire world, then at least among groups of like-minded states (with group membership not limited to states within particular regional blocs). This concept has been termed 'pluralateralism' and it seems to have more potential as a step in the direction of open skies than either bilateralism or multilateralism (when that is seen as negotiations between regional blocs).

A more freely competitive regime in international air transport is likely to lead to increased market concentration, but that in itself will not neces-

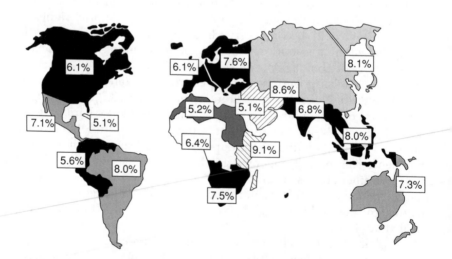

Figure 8.1   Forecast growth in passenger traffic by region, 1997–2001 (*Source:* International Air Transport Association)

sarily reduce the intensity of competition. There will be places where competition intensity might be expected to increase, despite greater concentration. Where it is likely to increase the most is on those long haul through routes on which airlines' price–cost margins have been at their widest. As such this would be a most beneficial effect, but it may often come only at the expense of increases in monopoly power on shorter routes to and from hubs. Hence there may often be trade-offs to consider.

8.3 A global competition authority?

Who should assess these trade-offs? When controls over entry and pricing are relaxed, it would seem very important that greater attention should be paid to competition policy issues of this kind, especially when the scope for predatory behaviour is as great as it appears to be in air transport. The extra-territorial application of national competition laws is not always appropriate when dealing with international competition taking place at the level of the network. The problems were highlighted when British Airways and American announced their intention to form an alliance in June 1996.

As originally announced the BA/American alliance would involve:

1   The co-ordination of passenger and cargo services between the US and Europe, with revenue pooled according to the profitability of individual routes.
2   Code-sharing across both airlines' global network of about 36 000 city pairs.
3   The establishment of a fully reciprocal, worldwide frequent flyer programme.

There was to be no exchange of equity or any other form of cross-share-holding; and the arrangement was to last for at least six years in the first instance. With such an alliance there would be a particularly comple-mentary fit of the two airlines' networks. One is strong where the other is weak, BA being strong in Europe and the East, American being strong in the United States and in Latin/South America. But in order to imple-ment the alliance fully, BA and American needed regulatory approval from three separate competition authorities, the UK Office of Fair Trading in London, the European Commission in Brussels and the US Department of Transportation in Washington, DC. The UK Office of Fair Trading would grant its approval if the alliance were to surrender 168 weekly slots in London, but the European Commission's requirement was for the surrender of 267 weekly slots (a reduction of 86 from its original recommendation of 353). The surrender of 267 slots would permit other airlines (Delta, TWA, British Midland, Virgin Atlantic, Continental or US Airways) to operate an additional 19 flights a day. BA and American considered this too great a sacrifice and offered to release 196 slots a week (sufficient for 14 new daily flights). But a further bone of contention arose over the disposal of the slots: should BA (or American) be able to sell them? The OFT recommended that selling them should be permitted, but this was opposed by the EC. The US Department of Transportation also requires greater access to slots at Heathrow as a condition for approving the alliance but in addition it wants the UK government to agree an 'open skies' air service agreement with the United States as a kind of *quid pro quo* for granting antitrust immunity. Under this condition the US has already granted antitrust immunity to the other three transatlantic alliances, Lufthansa/United, Northwest/KLM and Delta/Sabena/Swissair/Austrian. The EC, which wants to negotiate an EU–US open skies agreement, is taking to the European Court those member states which have negotiated their own bilateral agreements with the United States, on the basis that, by unilaterally granting US carriers traffic rights within the EU, they are distorting competition. Nonetheless the other three alliances are already operating and offering network benefits that the BA/American alliance is still prevented from offering. Naturally enough, BA and American have questioned this, BA pointing out that, increasingly, competition is between airline networks rather than individual airlines, and claiming that the delay in gaining regulatory approval for the alliance is causing it to lose corporate business travel contracts to airlines whose alliances are already fully operational (House of Commons Environment, Transport and Regional Affairs Committee, 1999). It is, however, understandable why the BA/American alliance has worried competition authorities more. The UK–US market with more than 12.5 million passengers a year is more than twice as big as the next largest North Atlantic market, that between Germany and the United States. It is thus a very important market *per se*. Also, the combination of BA and American would give the alliance a high market share, 60 per cent of UK–US scheduled passenger traffic, and this, together with the importance of Heathrow as a hub airport, may be sufficient for the authorities to regard the BA/American alliance as especially challenging to competition.

However, it is, at the time of writing, almost three years since the airlines announced their alliance and the matter is still not resolved, one way or the other. So far as the industry is concerned, the regulatory regime, or regimes, might be seen as something of a mess in this context. A dog's breakfast! There must be a case for some institutional change in the interests of speedier decision making and in order to prevent airlines having to make multiple applications for regulatory approval from several different competition authorities. If airlines are going to become global entities, then (ideally) the competition authority should be global too. This might suggest an additional role for ICAO (the International Civil Aviation Organisation) or perhaps for the recently formed World Trade Organization, if that body is to assume responsibility for competition issues in international trade generally.

Whichever body ultimately becomes responsible for administering them, competition laws are likely to be applied more rigorously. In many international markets airlines still co-ordinate tariffs through the machinery of the International Air Transport Association. The IATA system still survives in some parts of the world, because governments, especially those that still own airlines, find it a convenience and because it facilitates the setting of joint fares for interline passengers. Fares agreements at IATA Traffic conferences are subject to government approval and are presently granted block exemption from the competition rules of the Treaty of Rome and also immunity from US antitrust legislation. But in an increasingly deregulated and liberalized environment there is pressure to remove these concessions. Antitrust authorities in the United States are becoming increasingly reluctant to grant immunity to IATA airlines and would like to see the laws governing international air transport to be much like those they apply domestically. In Europe, the Comité des Sages considered the borderline between consultations on tariffs and a price cartel to be a sensitive issue requiring careful handling by competition authorities. During difficult times of weak demand consultations on fares can do much to prevent revenue yields falling to such low levels as to prejudice the financial stability of the whole industry. But at the same time colluding on price offers airlines opportunities to limit the spread of competition. This has been a particular concern of the UK Civil Aviation Authority (1994) especially in relation to routes on which there is intrinsically less scope for competition from smaller airlines that do not participate in IATA Traffic Conferences. The CAA feels that 'a watchful eye' needs to be kept on airlines' use of loyalty marketing schemes especially when the rebates and discounts incorporated in them are structured in such a way as to disadvantage smaller airlines. There is clearly much to concern competition authorities here, but in general terms the danger of widespread price collusion is much less than it was in the past. The justification for IATA fares co-ordination in terms of interlining benefits is going to decline. Experience on international routes is going to mirror that on US domestic routes, with more and more interline connections being substituted for by online ones, or at least by intra-alliance ones, through the increasing use of code-sharing, franchising and block spacing. And governmental interests in tariffs co-ordination is also going to decline as the number of airlines being transferred from state to private ownership increases.

Recommendations for further reading

The airline industry

A very good text amplifying many of the points highlighted in Chapter 2 is that by Doganis (1991). This book is now in its second edition, the original version having appeared as long ago as 1985. Many recent developments are not included, but its discussion of factors affecting demand, costs, fares, financial performance, etc. remain highly relevant to problems facing airlines today. Another good text which covers much ground on the basic economics of airline operation is that by Holloway (1997).

Competition issues

There is now quite an extensive literature on the effects of deregulation, much of which is concisely summarized in Williams (1993). Accounts of experience with deregulation in the United States, Canada and Australia and some discussion of prospects for liberalization in Europe are given in a book edited by Button (1991). For a critique of deregulation, see Dempsey and Goetz (1992) who challenge the view that US deregulation has been a success, in a book that contains much interesting material on the fortunes of particular airlines. Three reports from the Civil Aviation Authority (1993b, 1994 and 1998) provide valuable commentaries on the prospects for competition both on short routes within Europe and on long haul routes to/from Europe. Finally, a book by Morrison and Winston (1995) deals with the economics of airline competition in some depth, drawing upon the results of some detailed econometric analyses.

Networks/hubbing

Some clear explanations of freedoms of the air and how they are traded in bilateral air service agreements are given in the books by Graham

(1995) and Dobson (1995). The paper by Sealy (1992) contains interesting material on the development of international routes. And the contributions of Doganis and Dennis (1989) and Dennis (1994) provide good treatments of the principles involved in scheduling through hubs.

Pricing and predatory behaviour

A good explanation of the concepts and techniques airlines use in yield management is given in a short volume produced by the Institut du Transport Aerien (Daudel and Vialle, 1994). The Organisation for Economic Co-operation and Development (1998) has produced an excellent discussion of the economics of predatory pricing; and another very good discussion of predatory behaviour, this time specifically related to civil aviation, is presented in a report prepared for the European Commission by Dodgson, Katsoulacos and Pryke (1990).

Mergers and alliances

Quite a number of papers in academic journals investigate the consequences of mergers for market concentration, competition intensity, fare levels and so on, including those by Shepherd (1988), Hurdle, Johnson et al. (1989), Borenstein (1991) and Morrison and Winston (1990). In addition there are important reports from two departments of the US Government, the General Accounting Office (1990) and the Department of Transportation (1990). Much less has been written on the subject of alliances, on which a definitive study has yet to be published. However, a recent book by Button, Haynes and Stough (1998) considers alliances from the viewpoint of air transport policy in the European Union.

General

On both sides of the Atlantic official commissions have issued their findings on the state of competition in the airline industry. The Clinton Commission (1993) and the Comité des Sages (1994) reviewed performance in, respectively, the US and European industries and came up with a number of important recommendations. Two other useful references on possible future developments are those published by the Organisation for Economic Co-operation and Development (1993) and the World Tourism Organization (1994). The OECD volume contains some profound, well-written contributions presented to a conference of airline chief executives and other high-ranking officials in Paris in 1992, papers that examine the problems faced by international air transport and assess the prospects for a change from the current regime of bilateral air service agreements to a more multilateral system. The book from the World Tourism Organization, which was written by Stephen Wheatcroft, considers the impact that different policies on air transport can have on the nature and growth of international tourism, illustrating this with a number of interesting case studies.

In addition there are a few books on specialist aspects of air transport which contain much useful material: two on air law, one by Balfour (1995) and the other by Goh (1997); one on airline finance by Morrell (1997); and one on tourism forecasting by Frechtling (1996).

References

Abbott, K. and Thompson, D.J. (1989) 'Deregulating European aviation: impact of bilateral liberalisation', Centre for Business Strategy Working Paper, London Business School

Airbus Industrie (1993) *Market Perspectives for Civil Jet Aircraft*, Report No A1/CM-P312.0111/93, Blagnac, France

Airline Users Committee (1976) *European Air Fares*, London: Civil Aviation Authority

Air Transport Association (1993) *Annual Report of the US Scheduled Airline Industry*, Washington DC

Alperovich, G. and Machnes, Y. (1994) 'The role of wealth in the demand for international air travel', *Journal of Transport Economics and Policy*, **28**(2) (May) 163–73

Areeda, P. and Turner, D. (1975) 'Predatory prices and related practices under Section 2 of the Sherman Act', *Harvard Law Review*, **88**(4), 697–783

Association of European Airlines (1992) *Yearbook*, Brussels

Ayling, R. (1993) 'National protectionism and worldwide competition', paper delivered to a conference on the Future Regulation of Air Transport, London: 5–6 October

Bailey, E.E., Graham, D.R. and Kaplan, D.P. (1985) *Deregulating the Airlines*, Cambridge, Mass.: MIT Press

Bailey, E.E., Graham, D.R. and Baumol, W.T. (1984) 'Deregulation and the theory of contestable markets', *Yale Journal on Regulation*, **1**, 111–28

Bailey, E.E. and Williams, J.R. (1988) 'Sources of economic rent in the deregulated airline industry', *Journal of Law and Economics*, **31**, (April) 173–202

Balfour, J. (1995) *European Community Air Law*, London: Butterworths

Banister, D. and Button, K. eds (1991) *Transport in a Free Market Economy*, London: Macmillan

Barnett, A., Curtis, T. Goranson, J. and Patrick, A. (1992) 'Better than ever: nonstop jet service in an era of hubs and spokes', *Sloan Management Review*, **33**(2), (Winter) 49–54

Baumol, W.J. (1982) 'Contestable markets: an uprising in the theory of industry structure', *American Economic Review*, **72**(1) (March) 1–15

Baumol, W.J., Panzar, J.C. and Willig, R.D. (1982) *Contestable Markets and the Theory of Industry Structure*, New York: Harcourt Brace Jovanovich

Beesley, M. E. (1986) 'Commitment, sunk costs and entry to the airline industry', *Journal of Transport Economics and Policy*, **20**, 173–90

Belobaba, P.P. and Van Acker, J. (1994) 'Airline market concentration: an analysis of US origin–destination markets', *Journal of Air Transport Management*, **1**(1), (March) 5–14

Berry, S.T. (1990) 'Airport presence as product differentiation', *American Economic Review*, **80**(2), (May) 394–99

Betts, P. (1993) 'Why is it cheaper to fly to New York than Rome?' *Financial Times*, 4 January

Boeing Commercial Airplane Company (1986) 'Overview of US Passengers' Connect Patterns under Deregulation', unpublished, Seattle

Boeing Commercial Airplane Company (1993) *Current Market Outlook: World Market Demand and Airplane Supply Requirements*, Seattle

Borenstein, S. (1989) 'Hubs and high fares: airport dominance and market power in the U.S. airline industry', *RAND Journal of Economics*, **20**(3), (Autumn) 344–65

Borenstein, S. (1991) 'The dominant-firm advantage in multi-product industries: evidence from the U.S. airlines', *Quarterly Journal of Economics*, **106**(4), (November) 1237–66

Borenstein, S. (1992) 'The evolution of U.S. airline competition', *Journal of Economic Perspectives*, **6**(2), (Spring) 45–73

Braden, K.A. (1990) 'Frequent flyer coupon brokering: a valid trade?' *Journal of Air Law and Commerce*, **55**, 727–62

Brenner, M.A., Leet, J.O. and Scholt, E. (1985) *Airline Deregulation*, Westport, Conn: Eno Foundation for Transportation

British Aerospace (1991) 'The role of regional aviation in a single market economy: a British Aerospace View', unpublished, Hatfield

British Airports Authority (1994) *Heathrow Terminal 5: Statement of Case*, London

British Airways (1977) 'A Reply to the Airline Users Committee on European Air Fares', unpublished, London

British Airways (1992) *Annual Report and Accounts 1991–92*, London

British Airways (1993) *British Airways Fact Book*, London

British Airways (1998) *British Airways Fact Book 1997*, London

British Midland (1991) *A Fair Deal? Business Air Travel in Europe – the Facts*, Castle Donnington

Brueckner, J.K., Dyer, N.J. and Spiller, P.T. (1992) 'Fare determination in airline hub-and-spokes networks', *RAND Journal of Economics*, **23**(3), (Autumn) 309–33

Butler, R.V. and Huston, J.H. (1990) 'Airline services to non-hub communities ten years after deregulation', *Logistics and Transportation Review*, **26**(1), (March) 3–15

Button, K.J. (1989) 'Liberalizing the Canadian scheduled aviation market', *Fiscal Studies*, **10**, 19–52

Button, K.J. (ed.) (1991) *Airline Deregulation: International Experiences*, London: David Fulton

Button, K.J. (1996) 'Liberalising European Aviation: is there an empty core problem?', *Journal of Transport Economics and Policy*, **30**(3), (September) 275–91

Button, K.J., Haynes, K. and Stough, R. (1998) *Flying into the Future: Air Transport Policy in the European Union*, Cheltenham: Edward Elgar

Cairns, R.D. and Galbraith, J.W. (1990) 'Artificial compatibility, barriers to entry and frequent flyer programs', *Canadian Journal of Economics*, **23**(4) (November) 807–16

Caves, D.W., Christensen, L.R. and Tretheway, M.W. (1984) 'Economies of density versus economies of scale: why trunk and local service airline costs differ', *RAND Journal of Economics*, **15**(4), 471–89

Caves, R.E. (1962) *Air Transport and its Regulators: an Industry Study*, Cambridge, Mass: Harvard University Press

Chambers, A. (1993) 'European regional airlines: cross-border alliances and feed consolidation', *Avmark Aviation Economist*, **10**(8) (October) 12–17

Chartered Institute of Transport (1994) *A New Solution for Heathrow*, London

Cherington, P.W. (1958) *Airline Price Policy: a Study of Domestic Airline Fares*, Cambridge, Mass.: Harvard University Press

Civil Aeronautics Board (1973) *Domestic Passenger Fare Investigation Phase 5: Discount Fares*, Docket 21866–5, Washington DC

Civil Aeronautics Board (1982) *Competition and the Airlines: an Evaluation of Deregulation*, Washington DC: Office of Economic Analysis, CAB

Civil Aviation Authority (1977) *European Air Fares – a Discussion Document*, London

Civil Aviation Authority (1988) *Business Air Fares: a UK Survey*, CAA Paper 88015, London, July

Civil Aviation Authority (1992) 'Decision on Application 1A/10/34 by Loganair', unpublished report PH 1/92, April

Civil Aviation Authority (1993a) *Passengers at London Airports in 1991*, CAP 610, London, January

Civil Aviation Authority (1993b) *Airline Competition in the Single European Market*, CAP 623, London, November

Civil Aviation Authority (1994) *Airline Competition on European Long Haul Routes*, CAP 639, London, November

Civil Aviation Authority (1995) *Slot Allocation: a Proposal for Europe's Airports*, CAP 644, London, February

Civil Aviation Authority (1997) *Passengers at Birmingham, Gatwick, Heathrow, London City, Luton, Manchester and Stansted Airports in 1996*, CAP 677, London

Civil Aviation Authority (1998) *The Single European Aviation Market: The First Five Years*, CAP 685, London, June

Clinton Commission (1993) *Change, Challenge and Competition; a Report to the President and Congress*, The National Commission to Ensure a Strong Competitive Airline Industry, Washington DC: Government Printing Office, August

Clouatre, M.T. (1995) 'The legacy of Continental Airlines v. American Airlines: a re-evaluation of predatory pricing theory in the airline industry', *Journal of Air Law and Commerce*, **60**, 869–915

Comité des Sages (1994) *Expanding Horizons, Civil Aviation in Europe: an Action Programme for the Future*, Brussels: European Commission, January

Commission of the European Communities (1991) 'Merger Procedure Article 6(1) B Decision: Case No. IV/M. 130 – Delta Airlines/Pan Am', Brussels, 13 September

Commission of the European Communities (1992a) 'Merger Procedure Article 6(1) Decision: Affaire No. IV/M. 157 – Air France/Sabena', Brussels, 5 October

Commission of the European Communities (1992b) 'Merger Procedure Article 6(1) B Decision: Case No. IV/M.259 – British Airways/TAT', Brussels, 27 November

Commission of the European Communities (1992c) 'Predatory pricing in air transport', draft discussion paper, unpublished, Brussels

Commission of the European Communities (1993a) 'Council regulation on slot allocation at community airports', *Official Journal of the European Communities,* Regulation 95/93, Brussels, 22 January

Commission of the European Communities (1993b) 'Frequent flyer programmes in the internal aviation market', consultation document, Brussels, March

Crane, J.B. (1944) 'The economics of air transportation', *Harvard Business Review* **22**, (Summer) 495–509

Crossair (1991) *Annual Report 1990*, Basel, Switzerland

de Groot, J.E.C. (1994) 'Code-sharing; United States' policies and the lessons for Europe', *Air and Space Law,* **19**(2) 62–75

Daudel, S. and Vialle, G. (1994) *Yield Management: Applications to Air Transport and Other Service Industries*, Paris: Institut du Transport Aerien

Dempsey, P.S. (1990) 'Airline deregulation and laissez-faire mythology', *Journal of Air Law and Commerce,* **56**(4), (Winter) 305–412

Dempsey, P.S. and Goetz, A.R. (1992) *Airline Deregulation and Laissez-faire Mythology*, Westport, Conn: Quorum Books

Dennis, N.P.S. (1993) 'Introduction to hubbing', University of Westminster Conference on Hubbing, London: 10–12 June

Dennis, N.P.S. (1994) 'Scheduling strategies for airline operation', *Journal of Air Transport Management,* **1**(3), (September) 131–44

Department of Transport (1993) *Runway Capacity to Serve the South East. A Report by the (RUCATSE) Working Group*, London, July

Dobson, A.P. (1995) *Flying in the Face of Competition*, Aldershot: Ashgate

Doganis, R.S. (1991) *Flying off Course: The Economics of International Airlines*, 2nd edn, London: HarperCollins

Doganis, R.S. (1992) *The Airport Business*, London: Routledge

Doganis, R.S. (1994) 'Impact of liberalisation on European airlines', *Journal of Air Transport Management,* **1**(1), (March) 15–25

Doganis, R.S. and Dennis, N.P.S (1989) 'Lessons in hubbing', *Airline Business,* (March) 42–5

Dodgson, J.S. (1994) 'Competition policy and the liberalisation of European aviation', *Transportation,* **21**, 355–70

Dodgson, J.S., Katsoulacos, Y. and Pryke, R.W.S. (1990) *Predatory Behaviour in Aviation*, Brussels: Commission of the European Communities

Douglas, G.W. and Miller, J.C. (1974) *Economic Regulation of Domestic Air Transport*, Washington DC: The Brookings Institution

Economist, The (1992) 'A survey of the airline industry', 12 June

European Regional Airlines Association (1991a) *Yearbook 1991/92*, Burnham: The Shephard Press

European Regional Airlines Association (1991b) *The Vital Link; Regional Operations into Major Hubs*, Fairoaks Airport: ERA, February

Federal Aviation Administration (1992) *FAA Aviation Forecasts 1992–2003*, Washington DC: US Government Printing Office, February

Flanagan, A. and Marcus, M. (1993) 'Airline alliances: secrets of a successful liaison', *Avmark Aviation Economist,* **10**(1) (January/February) 20–23

Flint, P. (1990) 'Hubbing revisited', *Air Transport World,* (September) 129–32

Frechtling, D.C. (1996) *Practical Tourism Forecasting*, Oxford: Butterworth-Heinemann

Gallacher, J. and Odell, M. (1994) 'Airline alliances: tagging along', *Airline Business*, (July) 25–42

Gellman Research Associates (1994) *A Study of International Airline Code Sharing*, Office of Aviation and International Economics, US Department of Transportation, Washington, DC

Gialloreto, L. (1988) *Strategic Airline Management: The Global War Begins*, London: Pitman

Gidwitz, B. (1980) *The Politics of International Air Transport*, Lexington, Mass: D.C. Heath

Gill, T. (1998) 'Ryanair passes go in Europe', *Airline Business*, (April) 30-32

Gillen, D.W., Oum, T.H. and Tretheway, M.W. (1988) 'Entry barriers and anti-competitive behaviour in a deregulated airline market: the case of Canada', *International Journal of Transport Economics*, 15(1), (February) 29–41

Goh, J. (1997) *European Air Transport Law and Competition*, Chichester: Wiley

Gordon, R.J. (1965) 'Airline costs and managerial efficiency' in National Bureau of Economic Research, *Transportation Economics*, New York: Columbia University Press

Graham, B. (1995) *Geography and Air Transport*, Chichester: Wiley

Gregory, M. (1994) *Dirty Tricks: British Airways' Secret War against Virgin Atlantic*, London: Little, Brown and Company

Hagedoorn, J. (1993) 'Understanding the rationale of strategic technology partnering: interorganizational modes of co-operation and sectoral differences', *Strategic Management Journal*, 14, 371–85

Hamilton, M.M. (1988) 'Airline pricing: highly complex, hotly competitive', *Washington Post*, 20 November, H1 and H16

Hanlon, J.P. (1973) 'The demand for air travel: an econometric study of business travel over international routes', PhD Thesis. University of Birmingham

Hanlon, J.P. (1981) 'Air fares and exchange rates', *International Journal of Tourism Management*, 2(1), (March) 4–17

Hanlon, J.P. (1984) 'Sixth freedom operations in international air transport', *Tourism Management*, 5(3), (September) 177–91

Hanlon, J.P. (1986) 'Indian air transport: factors affecting airline costs and revenues', *Tourism Management*, 7(40), (December) 259–78

Hannegan, T.F. and Mulvey, F.P. (1995) 'An analysis of codesharing's impact on airlines and consumers', *Journal of Air Transport Management*, 2(2), (June) 131–37

Hansen M. and Kanafani, A. (1989) 'Hubbing and airline costs', *Journal of Transportation Engineering*, 115(6), (November) 581–96

Holloway, S. (1997) *Straight and Level: Practical Airline Economics*, Aldershot: Ashgate

House of Commons Environment, Transport and Regional Affairs Committee (1998) *Regional Air Services*, Eighth Report Session 1997–98, HC Paper 589-1, London: HMSO

House of Commons Environment, Transport and Regional Affairs Committee (1999) *Meeting with European Commission Officials to Discuss Air Transport*, Seventh Report 1998–99 Session, HC Paper 272, London: HMSO

House of Commons Transport Committee (1988) *Airline Competition: Computer Reservations Systems*, Third Report Session 1987–88, London: HMSO

House of Commons Transport Committee (1991) *Developments in European Community Air Transport Policy*, First Report Session 1991–92, London: HMSO

House of Lords European Communities Committee (1988) *Inter-regional Air Services*, First Report Session 1988–89, HL Paper 10, London: HMSO

House of Lords European Communities Committee (1990) *Civil Aviation: a Free Market by 1992?* Sixteenth Report Session 1988–89, HL Paper 63, London: HMSO

Humphreys, B.K. (1991) 'Are FFPs anticompetitive?' *Avmark Aviation Economist*, (July/August) 12–15

Humphreys, B.K. (1994) *New Developments in CRSs*, Paris: Institut du Transport Aerien

Hurdle, G.J., Johnson, R.L., Joskow, A.S., Werden, G.J. and Williams, M.A. (1989) 'Concentration, potential entry, and performance in the airline industry', *Journal of Industrial Economics*, **38**(2), (December) 119–39

International Air Transport Association (1993) *World Air Transport Statistics 1992*, Geneva: IATA

International Civil Aviation Organisation (1980) *Convention on International Civil Aviation*. 6th edn, ICAO Doc. 7300/6, Montreal

International Civil Aviation Organisation (1986) *Third Air Transport Conference (22 October–7 November 1985)*, ICAO Doc 9470, Montreal

International Civil Aviation Organisation (1991) 'Fleet-personnel: commercial air carriers', *Digest of Statistics*, No. 396, Montreal

International Civil Aviation Organisation (1993a) 'Annual report: the year in review', *ICAO Journal*, **48**(5), (July/August) 7–34

International Civil Aviation Organisation (1993b) *Survey of International Air Transport Fares and Rates*, Circular 239-AT/29, Montreal

International Civil Aviation Organisation (1994) 'The evolution of the air transport industry' *ICAO Journal*, **49**(7), (September) 46–58

International Civil Aviation Organisation (1996) *Survey of International Air Transport Fares and Rates*, Circular 255-AT/105, Montreal

International Civil Aviation Organisation (1997a) *Implications of Airline Codesharing*, Circular 269-AT/110, Montreal

International Civil Aviation Organisation (1997b) *Outlook for Air Transport to the Year 2005*, Circular 270-AT/111, Montreal

Jensen, R.B. (1990) 'US hubbing: the myth of the fortress-hub', *Avmark Aviation Economist*, (October) 6–9

Joskow, P.L. and Klevorick, A.K. (1979) 'A framework for analyzing predatory pricing policy', *Yale Law Journal* **89**(2), 213–270

Jones, I., Viehoff, I. and Marks, P. (1993) 'The economics of airport slots', *Fiscal Studies*, **14**(4), (November) 37–57

Kahn, A.E. (1970) *The Economics of Regulation: Principles and Institutions* (two volumes), New York: Wiley

Kahn, A.E. (1988) 'Surprises of airline deregulation', *American Ecomonic Review*, **78**(2), (May) 316–22

Kahn, A.E. (1993) 'The competitive consequences of hub dominance: a case study', *Review of Industrial Organisation*, **8**(4), 381–405

Kahn, A.E. (1999) 'Comments on exclusionary airline pricing', *Journal of Air Transport Management*, **5**(21), (January) 1–12

Kasper, D.M. (1988) *Globalisation and Deregulation: Liberalising Trade in Air Services*, Cambridge, Mass.: Ballinger

Keeler, T.E. (1972) 'Airline regulation and market performance', *Bell Journal of Economics*, **3**, (Autumn) 399–424

Keeler, T.E. (1991) 'Airline deregulation and market performance: the economic basis for regulatory reform and lessons from the US experience' in *Transport in a Free Market Economy*, (D. Banister and K.J. Button, eds), London: Macmillan, pages 121–70

Kleit, A. and Kobayashi (1996) 'Market failure or maket efficiency? Evidence on airport slot usage', in *Research in Transportation Economics* (B. McMullen ed.), Connecticut: JAI Press

Koontz, H.D. (1951) 'Economic and managerial factors underlying subsidy needs of domestic trunk line air carriers', *Journal of Air Law and Commerce*, **18**(1), (Spring) 127–5

Koontz, H.D. (1952) 'Domestic airline self-sufficiency: a problem of route structure', *American Economic Review*, **42**(1), (March) 103–25

Krubasik, E. and Lautenschlager, H. (1993) 'Forming successful strategic alliances in high-tech businesses' in *Collaborating to Compete*, (J. Bleeke and D. Ernst, eds), New York: The Free Press, pages 55–65

Levine, M.E. (1965) 'Is regulation necessary? California Air Transportation and National Regulatory Policy', *Yale Law Journal*, **74**(8), (July) 1416–47

Levine, M.E. (1987) 'Airline competition in deregulated markets; theory, firm strategy and public policy', *Yale Journal on Regulation*, **4** (Spring) 393–494

Lissitzyn, O.E. (1964) 'Bilateral agreements on air transport', *Journal of Air Law and Commerce*, **30**(3), (Summer) 248–63

Lodge, D. (1984) *Small World. An Academic Romance*, Harmondsworth: Penguin Books

Loy, F.E. (1968) 'Bilateral air transport agreements: some problems of finding a fair route exchange' in *The Freedom of the Air*, (E. McWhinney and M.A. Bradley, eds), Doble Ferry, New York: Ocean Publications, pages 174–89

Lyle, C. (1988) 'Computer-age vulnerability in the international airline industry', *Journal of Air Law and Commerce*, **54**(1), (Fall) 161–78

Lynch, R.P. (1993) *Business Alliances Guide: the Hidden Competitive Weapon*, New York: Wiley

McDonnell Douglas Aircraft Company (1993) *1992–2011 Outlook for Commercial Aircraft*, Long Beach, January

McGowan, F. and Seabright, P. (1989) 'Deregulating European Airlines', *Economic Policy*, (October) 283–344

McKenna, J.T. (1993) 'American cleared of unfair pricing', *Aviation Week and Space Technology*, 16 August, 34

McShane, S. and Windle, R.J. (1989) 'The implications of hub-and-spoke routeing for airline costs and competitiveness', *Logistics and Transportation Review*, **25**(3), (September) 209–30

Milgrom, P. and Roberts, J. (1982) 'Predation, reputation and entry deterrence', *Journal of Economic Theory*, **27**, (August) 280–312

Miroux, A. (1991) *Tourisme et Transport Aerien de l'Essor a la Maturite*, Paris: Institut du Transport Aerien

Molloy, J.F. Jr. (1985) *The US Commuter Airline Industry*, Lexington, Mass.: D.C. Heath

Monk, D.G. (1992) 'The lessons of airline regulation and deregulation: will we make the same mistakes in space?', *Journal of Air Law and Commerce*, **57**(3), (Spring) 715–53

Monopolies and Mergers Commission (1987) *British Airways Plc and British Caledonian Group Plc: a Report on the Proposed Merger*, Cm 247, London: HMSO

Monopolies and Mergers Commission (1990) *British Airways Plc and Sabena S.A.*, Cm 1155, London: HMSO

Moore, T.G. (1986) 'US airline deregulation: its effects on passengers, capital and labour', *Journal of Law and Economics*, **29**(1), (April) 1–28

Morrell, P.S. (1997) *Airline Finance*, Aldershot: Ashgate

Morrison, S.A. and Winston, C. (1986) *The Economic Effects of Airline Deregulation*, Washington DC: Brookings Institution

Morrison, S.A. and Winston, C. (1987) 'Empirical implications and tests of the contestability hypothesis', *Journal of Law and Economics*, **30**, (April) 53–66

Morrison, S.A. and Winston, C. (1990) 'The dynamics of airline pricing and competition', *American Economic Review*, **80**(2), (May) 389–93

Morrison, S.A. and Winston, C. (1995) *The Evolution of the Airline Industry*, Washington, DC: The Brookings Institution

Muirhead, G. (1993) 'Airport initiatives: the interline hub' unpublished, Manchester Airport

Naylor, M. (1991) 'Regional carriers: an endangered species?' unpublished paper delivered to the Avmark International Conference, London, 27 September

Nuutinen, Heini (1994) 'ValuJet: no tickets but amazing profits', *Avmark Aviation Economist*, (November) 16–21

Ohmae, K. (1993) 'The global logic of strategic alliances' in *Collaborating to Compete*, (J. Bleeke and D. Ernst, eds), New York: The Free Press, 35–54

O'Leary, M. (1994) 'The challenge of replicating Southwest Airlines in Europe', *Institute of Economic Affairs Second International Aviation Conference*, London: 14–15 November

Organisation for Economic Co-operation and Development (1988) *Deregulation and Airline Competition*, Paris: OECD

Organisation for Economic Co-operation and Development (1989) *Predatory Pricing*, Paris: OECD

Organisation for Economic Co-operation and Development (1993) *International Air Transport: the Challenges Ahead*, Paris: OECD

Oster, C.V. and Pickrell, D.H. (1988) 'Code sharing, joint fares and competition in the regional airline industry', *Transportation Research*, **22A**(6), 405–17

Oum, T. H., Park, J.-H., and Zhang, A. (1996) 'The effects of airline code-sharing agreements on firm conduct and international air fares', *Journal of Transport Economics and Policy*, **30**(2), (May) 187-202.

Park, J. H. (1997) 'Strategic airline alliance: modelling and empirical analysis', PhD Dissertation, University of British Columbia

Peterson, R. (1993) *The Official Frequent Flyer Guidebook*, 2nd edn, Colorado Springs, Co.: AirPress

Pickrell, D. (1991) 'The regulation and deregulation of US airlines' in *Airline Deregulation: International Experiences*, (K.J. Button, ed.) London: David Fulton, 5–47

Poole, C.P. (1989) 'US airline deregulation: the lessons for the European

Community', Government Economic Service Working Paper No 109, London: Department of Transport

Proctor, J.W. and Duncan, J.S. (1954) 'A regression analysis of airline costs', *Journal of Air Law and Commerce*, **21**(2), (Summer) 282–92

Pryke, R. (1987) *Competition among International Airlines*, Thames Essay No. 46, London: Trade Policy Research Centre

Pryke, R. (1991) 'American deregulation and European liberalisation' in *Transport in a Free Market Economy*, (D. Banister and K. Button, eds), London: Macmillan, 220–41

Regional Airline Association (1993) *Annual Report 1993*, Washington DC: RAA

Reichheld, F.F. (1996) *The Loyalty Effect: the Hidden Force behind Growth, Profits and Lasting Value*, Boston, Mass: Harvard University Press

Richmond, S.B. (1962) *Regulation and Competition in Air Transportation*, New York: Columbia University Press

Rose, N.L. (1992) 'Fear of flying? economic analyses of airline safety', *Journal of Economic Perspectives*, **6**(2), (Spring) 75–94

Sawers, D. (1987) *Competition in the Air*, Research Monograph No. 41, London: Institute of Economic Affairs

Schulte-Strathaus, U. (1994) 'Strategies for success and survival of airlines in the European market', paper presented to the Institute of Economic Affairs Second International Aviation Conference, London, 14–15 November

Sealy, K. (1992) 'International air transport' in *Modern Transport Geography*, (B.S. Hoyle and R.D. Knowles, eds), London: Belhaven, 233–56

Shenton, H. (1993) 'Frequent flyer programmes: what next in Europe? *Avmark Aviation Economist*, (November) 20–22

Shepherd, W.G. (1984) 'Contestability vs. competition', *American Economic Review*, **74**(4), (September) 572–87

Shepherd, W.G. (1988). 'Competition, contestability, and transport mergers', *International Journal of Transport Economics*, **15**(2), (June) 113–28

Simons, P. (1994) 'From hard values to outside-in marketing', *Avmark Aviation Economist*, **11**(2) (March) 8–9

Skapinker, M. (1997) 'easyJet withdraws KLM complaint', *The Financial Times*, 22/23 November, 2

Skapinker, M. (1999) 'National flags keep flying', *The Financial Times*, Special Survey on Global Business Outlook, 29 January, III

Small, N.O. (1993) 'Hub airports: the regional economic implications', *University of Westminster Conference on Hubbing*, London: June 10–12

Snow, J. (1990) 'The future for regional airlines in a liberalised environment' unpublished paper presented to the 'Montreaux Event', a conference on Regional, Commuter and Business Aviation, Montreaux, Switzerland, 21–21 June

Stanford Research Institute (SRI) International (1990) *A European Planning Strategy for Air Traffic to the Year 2010*, Report prepared for the International Air Transport Association: Volume 1 Analysis and Recommendations; Volume 2 Supporting Data, Menlo Park, Ca.: SRI

Staniland, M. (1998) 'The vanishing national airline?' *European Business*, **10**(2), 72–77

Starkie, D. (1994) 'The US market in airport slots', *Journal of Transport Economics and Policy*, **28**(3), (September) 325–29

Starkie, D. (1998) 'Allocating airport slots: a role for the market?' *Journal of Air Transport Management* **4**(2), (April) 111–16

Straszheim, M.R. (1969) *The International Airline Industry*, Washington DC: The Brookings Institute

Taylor, L. (1988) *Air Travel: How Safe is it?* Oxford: BSP Professional Books

Telser, L.G. (1978) *Economic Theory and the Core*, University of Chicago Press

ter Kuile, A. (1997) 'Hub fever', *Airline Business*, (December) 66–71

Thomson, A. (1990) *High Risk: the Politics of the Air*, London: Sidgwick and Jackson

Times, The (1989) 'The eagle and the ugly duckling', 1 December

Tirole, J. (1988) *The Theory of Industrial Organisation*, Cambridge, Mass.: MIT Press

Tretheway, M.W. (1989) 'Frequent flyer programs: marketing bonanza or anti-competitive tool?', *Proceedings of 24th Annual Meeting of the Canadian Transportation Research Forum*, Halifax, Nova Scotia

Truitt, L.J, Teye, V.B. and Farris, M.T. (1991) 'The role of computer reservations systems: international comparisons', *Tourism Management*, **11**(1), (March) 21–36

US General Accounting Office (1990) 'Airline competition: higher fares and reduced competition at concentrated airports', Washington DC

US General Accounting Office (1995) *International Aviation: Airline Alliances Produce Benefits but Effect on Competition is Uncertain*, GAO/RCED-95-99, Washington, DC

US General Accounting Office (1996) *Airline Deregulation: Barriers to Entry Continue to Limit Competition in Several Key Domestic Markets*, Report to US Senate, Washington, DC

US Department of Transportation (1988) *A Study of Airline Computer Reservations Systems*, Washington, DC: Government Printing Office

US Department of Transportation (1990) *Secretary's Task Force on Competition in the U.S. Domestic Airline Industry*, Washington, DC.: Government Printing Office

US Department of Transportation (1998) *Statement of Enforcement Policy Regarding Unfair Exclusionary Conduct*, Office of the Secretary, Docket No. OST-98-3713, 6 April

Vickers, J. (1985) 'The economics of predatory practices', *Fiscal Studies*, **6**(3), 24–36

Walker, K. (1997) 'When the wolf's at your door', *Airline Business*, (May) 62–67

Wassengbergh, H. (1993) *Principles and Practice in Air Transport Regulation*, Paris: Institut du Transport Aerien

Wheatcroft, S.F. (1964) *Air Transport Policy*, London: Michael Joseph

Wheatcroft, S.F. and Lipman, G. (1986) *Air Transport in a Competitive Market European Market*, London: Economist Intelligence Unit

Wheatcroft, S.F. and Lipman, G. (1990) *European Liberalisation and World Air Transport*, London: Economist Intelligence Unit

White, L.J. (1979) 'Economies of scale and the question of natural monopoly in the airline industry', *Journal of Air Law and Commerce*, **44**(3), (Spring) 545–73

Windle, R.J. (1991) 'The world's airlines: a cost and productivity comparison', *Journal of Transport Economics and Policy*, **25**(1), (January) 31–49

Williams, G. (1993) *The Airline Industry and the Impact of Deregulation*, Aldershot: Ashgate

Williamson, O.E. (1968) 'Economies as an antitrust defense', *American Economic Review*, **58**(1), (March) 18–36

World Tourism Organization (1994) *Aviation and Tourism Policies: Balancing the Benefits*, London: Routledge

Youssef, W. and Hansen, M. (1994) 'Consequences of strategic alliances between international airlines: the case of Swissair and SAS', *Transportation Research*, **28A**(5), 415–31

Index